MCSE JumpStart™:
Computer and Network Basics

Lisa Donald

SYBEX®

San Francisco ◆ Paris ◆ Düsseldorf ◆ Soest

Associate Publisher: Guy Hart-Davis
Contracts and Licensing Manager: Kristine O'Callaghan
Acquisitions Editor: Bonnie Bills
Developmental Editors: Bonnie Bills, Brenda Frink
Editor: Deborah J. English
Project Editor: Brianne Hope Agatep
Technical Editor: James Tower
Book Designer: Maureen Forys, Happenstance Type-O-Rama
Design Illustrations: Chris Gillespie
Graphic Illustrator: Tony Jonick
Electronic Publishing Specialist: Maureen Forys, Happenstance Type-O-Rama
Production Coordinator: Shannon Murphy
Indexer: Nancy Guenther
Cover Designer: Archer Design
Cover Illustrator/Photographer: Archer Design

Screen reproductions produced with Collage Complete.

Collage Complete is a trademark of Inner Media Inc.

Library of Congress Card Number: 98-83172
ISBN: 0-7821-2462-3

Manufactured in the United States of America

10 9 8 7 6 5 4 3 2 1

This book is for the woman who taught me self-confidence. If I could do this, so can all of you! Thanks, Mom. That's Terry Whinery to all of the people she corners in the bookstores.

Acknowledgments

As always, a book is not the work of an individual but rather a team.

This book was first inspired by all of the people I have met who are interested in the MCSE program but don't know where to begin. I took this idea to Bonnie Bills at Sybex, who encouraged me to write this book. Bonnie acted as the acquisitions editor and the developmental editor for the design, feel, and content of the book. She has since left Sybex, and I know I will miss her very much.

Maureen Forys acted as the designer for the book and served as the electronic publishing specialist. She was the creative force behind this book and did an excellent job with the design.

As for my editors, Brianne Agatep served as the project editor and worked very hard at keeping us all on track, which was not always easy. She did so with encouragement and support, which was always appreciated. Debby English was the editor. Debby made sure that we explained everything properly and that the form and content of each chapter were correct. Her thoroughness was a wonderful asset to the book. She is one of the best editors I have had the pleasure to work with, and I'm hoping to repeat the experience again.

James Tower served as the technical editor. He also contributed Chapter 1 on microprocessors, Chapter 3 on input/output devices, and Chapter 4 on hardware configuration. These chapters turned out great. Thanks, James!

The nature of this book required a great deal of artwork. Tony Jonick acted as the illustrator and did an excellent job of creating artwork that was appropriate for the book. They say a picture is worth a thousand words, and his art is an essential part of this book.

Shannon Murphy acted as the production coordinator and caught any errors that the rest of the team missed. And when the team needed a special graphic, Jeff Wilson stepped in to save the day. The indexer, Nancy Guenther, did a great job.

Finally, I want to thank my family for all of their support. And last but not least, I want to thank Kate Socha, who acts as my right arm at home. Without her, I would never be able to get anything done.

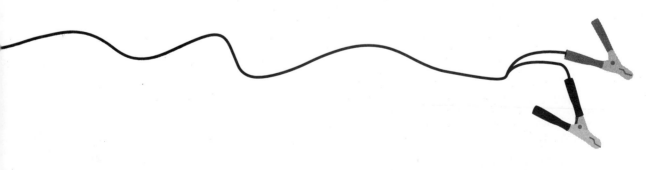

Contents at a Glance

Contents at a Glance

Introduction

One of the greatest challenges facing corporate America today is finding people who are qualified to manage corporate computer networks. Many companies have Microsoft networks that run Windows 95, Windows NT, and other Microsoft BackOffice products (such as Microsoft SQL Server and Systems Management Server).

Microsoft developed its Microsoft certification program to certify those people who have the skills to work with Microsoft products and networks. The most highly coveted certification is the MCSE, or Microsoft Certified Systems Engineer.

Why become an MCSE? The main benefits are that you will have much greater earnings potential and that an MCSE carries high industry recognition. Certification can be your key to a new job or a higher salary—or both.

So what's stopping you? If it's because you don't know where to begin, this book is for you. The first step in Microsoft certification is a good understanding of the prerequisite information. Microsoft defines the prerequisites, but assumes you will acquire this information on your own.

This book takes all of the prerequisites and puts them in a single book that is specifically targeted toward MCSE candidates. This book is designed for the novice user who wants to become Microsoft certified but doesn't know where to start. When you are done with this book, you will have the foundation you need to study for the MCSE exams.

The next step in the certification quest will be preparation for each Microsoft exam. This can be accomplished by taking Microsoft approved training classes or by purchasing the Sybex MCSE books that will prepare you for each exam.

What This Book Covers

Before you begin the MCSE or any Microsoft certification, Microsoft recommends that you have this prerequisite information:

◇ A working knowledge of an operating system such as DOS, Unix, Windows 3.x, Windows 95, Windows 98, or Windows NT

◇ Proficiency with the Windows interface and a working knowledge of Windows Explorer

◇ An understanding of networking concepts such as networks, servers, clients, network adapter cards and hardware, protocols, network operating systems, and drivers

◇ An understanding of computer hardware, including processors, memory, hard disks, communication ports, and peripheral devices

Introduction

This book covers the MCSE prerequisites in easy-to-understand language with graphics to illustrate the concepts. Information is presented in small chunks so that it won't be overwhelming.

Based on the knowledge you need to start MCSE study, this book is organized as follows:

Chapters 1–4 These chapters deal with computer hardware. They cover computer processors, data storage, input/output devices, and hardware configuration issues.

Chapters 5–8 These chapters cover software. In these chapters, you will learn about the different local operating systems, get a good overview of DOS, learn the basics of the Windows 95 interface, and have an overview of popular applications used on personal computers.

Chapters 9–13 The Networking Basics chapters cover common networking concepts such as the OSI model, network architectures, networking hardware, network protocols, and common network operating systems.

Chapters 14–17 These chapters focus on NT, covering the history of NT, the NT platforms, NT user and group management, and file and print resource management.

Understanding Microsoft Certification

Microsoft offers several levels of certification for anyone who has or is pursuing a career as a network professional working with Microsoft products. These certifications are

- ◆ Microsoft Certified Professional (MCP)
- ◆ Microsoft Certified Systems Engineer (MCSE)
- ◆ Microsoft Certified Professional + Internet
- ◆ Microsoft Certified Systems Engineer + Internet
- ◆ Microsoft Certified Trainer (MCT)

The one you choose depends on your area of expertise and your career goals.

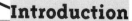

Microsoft Certified Professional (MCP)

This certification is for individuals with expertise in one specific area. MCP certification is often a stepping stone to MCSE certification and allows you some benefits of Microsoft certification after just one exam.

By passing one core exam (meaning an operating system exam), you become an MCP.

Microsoft Certified Systems Engineer (MCSE)

For network professionals, the MCSE certification requires commitment. You need to complete all of the steps required for certification. Passing the exams shows that you meet the high standards that Microsoft has set for MCSEs.

NOTE

The following list applies to the NT 4 track. Microsoft still supports a track for NT 3.51, but NT 4 certification is more desirable, because it is the current operating system.

To become an MCSE, you must pass a series of six exams:

1. Networking Essentials (waived for Novell CNEs)
2. Implementing and Supporting Microsoft Windows NT Workstation 4.0 (or Windows 95 or Windows 98)
3. Implementing and Supporting Microsoft Windows NT Server 4.0
4. Implementing and Supporting Microsoft Windows NT Server 4.0 in the Enterprise
5. Elective
6. Elective

Some of the electives include

◆ Internetworking with Microsoft TCP/IP on Microsoft Windows NT 4.0

◆ Implementing and Supporting Microsoft Internet Information Server 4.0

◆ Implementing and Supporting Microsoft Exchange Server 5.5

◆ Implementing and Supporting Microsoft SNA Server 4.0

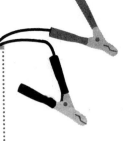

- Implementing and Supporting Microsoft Systems Management Server 1.2
- Implementing a Database Design on Microsoft SQL Server 6.5
- System Administration for Microsoft SQL Server 6.5

Microsoft Certified Professional (MCP) + Internet

This certification is for individuals who will specialize in Internet technologies. In order to qualify as an MCP + Internet, you must pass three exams:

1. Internetworking with Microsoft TCP/IP on Windows NT 4.0
2. Implementing and Supporting Microsoft Windows NT Server 4.0
3. Implementing and Supporting Microsoft Internet Information Server 4.0 (Or you could substitute Implementing and Supporting Microsoft Internet Information Server 3.0 and Microsoft Index Server 1.1.)

Microsoft Certified Systems Engineer (MCSE) + Internet

One of the newest certification designations is MCSE + Internet. This certification allows you to show that you have completed additional exams that qualify you as an Internet specialist. The requirements for MCSE + Internet are described below.

You must pass seven required exams:

1. Networking Essentials (waived for Novell CNEs)
2. Internetworking with Microsoft TCP/IP on Windows NT 4.0
3. Implementing and Supporting Microsoft Windows NT Workstation 4.0 (or Implementing and Supporting Windows 95, or Implementing and Supporting Window 98)
4. Implementing and Supporting Microsoft Windows NT Server 4.0
5. Implementing and Supporting Microsoft Windows NT Server 4.0 in the Enterprise
6. Implementing and Supporting Microsoft Internet Information Server 4.0
7. Implementing and Supporting Microsoft Internet Explorer 4.0 by Using the Internet Explorer Administration Kit

You must also pass two elective exams. You can choose from

- System Administration for Microsoft SQL Server 6.5
- Implementing a Database Design on Microsoft SQL Server 6.5
- Implementing and Supporting Web Sites Using Microsoft Site Server 3.0
- Implementing and Supporting Microsoft Exchange Server 5.5 (can also use version 5 exam)
- Implementing and Supporting Microsoft Proxy Server 2.0 (can also use version 1 exam)
- Implementing and Supporting Microsoft SNA Server 4.0

Microsoft Certified Trainer (MCT)

As an MCT, you can deliver Microsoft certified courseware through official Microsoft channels.

The MCT certification is more costly, because in addition to passing the exams, you must sit through the official Microsoft courses. You also need to submit an application that Microsoft must approve. The number of exams you need to pass depends on the number of courses you want to teach.

TIP

For the most up-to-date certification information, visit Microsoft's Web site at www.microsoft.com/train_cert.

Preparing for the MCSE Exams

To prepare for the MCSE certification exams, you should try to work with the products as much as possible. In addition, there are a variety of resources from which you can learn about the products and exams.

- You can take instructor-led courses.
- Online training is an alternative to instructor-led courses. This is a useful option for people who cannot find any courses in their area or who do not have the time to attend classes.
- If you prefer to use a book to help you prepare for the MCSE tests, you can choose from a wide variety of publications. These range from complete study guides (such as the Network Press *MCSE Study Guide* series, which covers the core MCSE exams and key electives) through test-preparedness books.

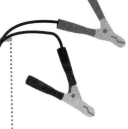

After you have completed your courses, training, or study guides, you'll find the *MCSE Test Success* books an excellent resource for making sure that you are prepared for the test. You will discover whether you've got it covered or you still need to fill in some holes.

> **NOTE**
>
> For more MCSE information, point your browser to the Sybex Web site, where you'll find information about the MCP program, job links, and descriptions of other titles in the Network Press line of MCSE-related books. Go to http://www.sybex.com and click the MCSE logo.

Scheduling and Taking an Exam

Once you think you are ready to take an exam, call Prometric Testing Centers at (800) 755-EXAM (755-3926). They'll tell you where to find the closest testing center. Before you call, get out your credit card, because each exam costs $100.

You can schedule the exam for a time that is convenient for you. The exams are downloaded from Prometric to the testing center, and you show up at your scheduled time and take the exam on a computer.

Once you complete the exam, you will know right away whether you have passed or not. At the end of the exam, you will receive a score report. It will list the six areas that you were tested on and how you performed. If you pass the exam, you don't need to do anything else—Prometric uploads the test results to Microsoft. If you don't pass, it's another $100 to schedule the exam again. But at least you will know from the score report where you did poorly, so you can study that particular information more carefully.

Test-Taking Hints

If you know what to expect, your chances of passing the exam will be much greater. Here are some tips that can help you achieve success.

Get There Early and Be Prepared

This is your last chance to review. Bring your books and review any areas you feel unsure of. If you need a quick drink of water or a visit to the restroom, take

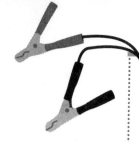

the time to do so before the exam. Once your exam starts, it will not be paused for these needs.

When you arrive for your exam, you will be asked to present two forms of ID. You will also be asked to sign a piece of paper verifying that you understand the testing rules (for example, the rule that says you will not cheat on the exam).

Before you start the exam, you will have an opportunity to take a practice exam. It is not related to the exam topic and is simply offered so that you will have a feel for the exam-taking process.

What You Can and Can't Take in with You

These are closed-book exams. The only thing that you can take in is scratch paper provided by the testing center. Use this paper as much as possible to diagram the questions. Many times, diagramming questions can help make the answer clear. You will have to give this paper back to the test administrator at the end of the exam.

Many testing centers are very strict about what you can take into the testing room. Some centers will not even allow you to bring in items like a zipped-up purse. If you feel tempted to take in any outside material, be aware that many testing centers use monitoring devices such as video and audio equipment (so don't swear, even if you are alone in the room!).

Prometric Testing Centers take the test-taking process and the test validation very seriously.

Test Approach

As you take the test, if you know the answer to a question, fill it in and move on. If you're not sure of the answer, mark your best guess, then "mark" the question.

At the end of the exam, you can review the questions. Depending on the amount of time remaining, you can then view all of the questions again, or you can view only the questions that you were unsure of. It's a good idea to double-check all of your answers, just in case you misread any of the questions on the first pass. (Sometimes half of the battle is in trying to figure out exactly what the question is asking you.) Also, sometimes a related question may provide a clue for a question that you are unsure of.

Be sure to answer all questions. Unanswered questions are scored as incorrect and will count against you. Also, make sure that you keep an eye on the remaining time so that you can pace yourself accordingly.

If you do not pass the exam, note everything that you can remember while the exam is still fresh in your mind. This will help you prepare for your next try. Although the next exam will not be exactly the same, the questions will be similar, and you don't want to make the same mistakes.

After You Become Certified

Once you become an MCSE, Microsoft kicks in some goodies, including

- ✦ A one-year subscription to Microsoft TechNet, a valuable CD collection that contains Microsoft support information.

- ✦ A one-year subscription to the Microsoft Beta Evaluation program, which is a great way to get your hands on new software. Be the first kid on the block to play with new and upcoming software.

- ✦ Access to a secure area of the Microsoft Web site that provides technical support and product information. This certification benefit is also available for MCP certification.

- ✦ Permission to use the Microsoft Certified Professional logos (each certification has its own logo), which look great on letterhead and business cards.

- ✦ An MCP certificate (you will get a certificate for each level of certification you reach), suitable for framing or sending copies to Mom.

- ✦ A one-year subscription to *Microsoft Certified Professional Magazine*, which provides information on professional and career development.

Chapter

1

The Computer's Brain: Processors and Memory

Every computer consists of a microprocessor and memory. Without the two, the computer would not function. The microprocessor, commonly referred to as the Central Processing Unit (CPU), is the brain of the computer. The CPU also acts like the boss of the computer, managing the timing of each operation and carrying out the instructions or commands from an application or operating system.

The CPU uses memory as a place to store or retrieve information. Memory comes in several forms, such as Random Access Memory (RAM) and Read-Only Memory (ROM). Memory provides a temporary location for storing information and contains more permanent system configuration information. Performance has continued to improve over the years, allowing CPUs to execute millions of instructions every second.

This chapter will provide an overview of these microprocessors and memory concepts:

 Processor types

 The Intel lineup

 The clones

 Multiprocessor computers

 Memory

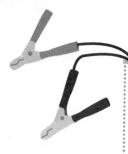

Considering Processor Types

There are so many types of processors on the market today that it can be quite confusing to wade through them all. All chips are not created equal, and each chip has its own characteristics that make it unique among similar chips. For instance, a chip of the same generation may operate at double or triple the speed of others. Fierce competition between the various chipmakers lays the groundwork for new technological innovations and constant improvements.

The most noticeable difference between processors is in the overall physical appearance of the chips, meaning that many processors are noticeably different in size and shape. When Intel released its first processor, it was packaged in a small chip that contained two rows of 20 pins each. As processor technology improved, the shape and packaging scheme of the processor also changed. Modern processors, like the Intel Pentium II, use an advanced packaging scheme in which the processor is encased in a **single-edge cartridge (SEC)** module that plugs into a 242-pin slot on the system board, much as an expansion card plugs into the system board.

The second noticeable difference among processors is the type of instruction set they use. The types of instruction sets that are most common to processors are either **Complex Instruction Set Computing (CISC)** or **Reduced Instruction Set Computing (RISC)**. CISC is the most common type and uses a full, or complete, instruction set. RISC uses a smaller, or limited, instruction set, allowing it to operate at higher speeds. The theory is that the greater the number of instructions the processor instruction set type contains, the more complex the circuitry to accommodate that condition. Therefore, it works at a slower rate.

Last, different manufacturers design processors to varying specifications. You should be sure that the processor type and model you choose are compatible with the operating system that runs on the computer. If the processor is not 100 percent compatible with the installed operating system, the computer will not operate at its best or may not work at all.

NOTE

The terms *CPU*, which stands for Central Processing Unit, and *processor* are used interchangeably. Intel is the largest manufacturer of CPUs. Other manufacturers include IBM, Cyrix, Advanced Micro Devices (AMD), and Motorola.

Single-Edge Cartridge (SEC)

An advanced packaging scheme that the Intel Pentium II uses. The processor is encased in a cartridge module with a single edge that plugs into a 242-pin slot on the system board, much as an expansion card plugs into the system board.

Complex Instruction Set Computing (CISC)

The most common type of processor produced. It is composed of a full complement of instructions used by the processor. Intel processors are currently based on this standard.

Reduced Instruction Set Computing (RISC)

A reduced set of instructions used by a processor. PowerPC and Alpha processors are manufactured using this standard. The reduced instruction set allows a microprocessor to operate at higher speeds.

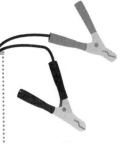

Understanding Processor Terminology

For most computer novices, terms like *microcode efficiency* and *internal cache RAM* can sound like a foreign language. To help you keep things straight, here are some common terms and their definitions.

CPU speed is the number of operations that are processed in one second.

Clock cycles is the internal speed of a computer or processor expressed in MHz. The faster the clock speed, the faster the computer performs a specific operation.

Word size is the largest number in bits that can be processed during one operation.

Numeric coprocessor is a secondary processor that speeds operations by taking over some of the main processor's work. It typically performs mathematical calculations, freeing the processor to tend to other tasks.

Internal cache RAM shows how much internal high-speed memory the chip includes.

Data path represents the largest number of instructions that can be transported into the processor chip during one operation.

Central Processing Unit (CPU)

The microprocessor, or brain of the computer. It uses logic to perform mathematical operations that are used in the manipulation of data.

NOTE

All of the computer's components, including the processor, are installed on a fiberglass sheet called a motherboard. The motherboard is designed for a specific **CPU** type. This means that if you want to upgrade an Intel 486 processor to a Pentium Pro, you will have to change the motherboard.

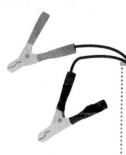

Considering the Intel Lineup

Several generations of Intel processors are available in today's market. Since the arrival of the first Intel chip in the IBM PC, Intel has dominated the market. It seems that every time you turn around, a new chip promises greater performance and processing capabilities than the previous one.

What makes Intel the market leader is the ability to bring the newest innovations in chip technology to the public, usually before its competitors, which are not far behind. Competition is fierce, and each manufacturer attempts to improve on the designs of the others, releasing similar chips that promise better performance. You should read the specifications and reviews of each processor to understand its capabilities and reliability.

Over time, Intel has introduced several generations of microprocessors. Each processor type is referred to as a generation; each is based on the new technological enhancements of the day. With each product release come new software and hardware products to take advantage of the new technology.

This table shows the specifications for the various Intel processors issued to date.

Model	Year Introduced	Maximum Internal Clock Frequency (MHz)	Data Bus Width (in Bits)
8086	1978	8	16
8088	1979	8	8
80286	1982	20	16
80386	1985	40	32
80486	1989	100	32
Pentium	1993	200	32
Pentium MMX	1997	233	32
Pentium Pro	1995	200	32
Pentium II	1997	450	32
PII Celeron	1998	333	32

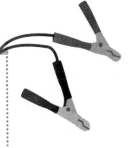

History of Intel Chips

Intel released the world's first microprocessor, the Intel 4004, in 1971. It was a 4-bit microprocessor containing a programmable controller chip that could process 45 different instructions. The 4 bits meant that the chip had four lines for data to travel on, much like a four-lane freeway. Because of its limitations, it was implemented only in a few early video games and some other devices. Later the same year, Intel released the 8008, an 8-bit microprocessor with enhanced memory storage and the ability to process 48 instructions.

Intel began to research and develop faster, more capable processors. From the research emerged the 8080, which could process instructions 10 times faster than its predecessors. Although the speed had dramatically improved, it was still limited by the number of instructions it could process. Finally, in 1978, Intel broke many barriers by releasing the first of many computer-ready microprocessors, the 8086. This new processor was immediately followed a year later by the 8088.

Intel continued to break new ground as the release of each new generation of processor offered improved functions and processing capabilities. The most dramatic improvement was the number of instructions, based on a scale of millions, that the processor could process in one second. This rate, referred to as MIPS (Millions of Instructions Per Second), ranges from 0.75 MIPS for the 8088 to over 200 MIPS for Pentium II processors.

The second most dramatic improvement was the speed of the internal clock, measured in **megahertz (MHz)**. All processors are driven by an internal clock mechanism that keeps the rhythm of the chip, much like the rhythm of a heartbeat. The faster the speed of the internal clock, the faster the processor can process instructions. Intel continued to increase the speed of the internal clock from 4.77MHz for the 8088 to over 400MHz for the newest generation of Intel microprocessors.

Constant improvements in design and commitment to excellence allow the chipmaker to continue to reign as the world market leader in PC-based processor technology. What the future holds in terms of faster, smaller, high-performance processors is a closely guarded secret that only the designers and engineers know until they are ready to roll out the next generation of processors.

Megahertz (MHz)
One million cycles per second. The internal clock speed of a microprocessor is expressed in MHz.

8088 and 8086

The first major processor release from Intel was the 8086 microprocessor. The processor debuted as the first evolutionary step in a multitude of processors, each improving on the design of the original 8086. The lineage is referred to as the *x86* family of microprocessors. Although this first release was crude compared with today's standards, it paved the way for the others to follow.

The 8088 was released a short time after the 8086 but was not as powerful as its predecessor. The 8086, a true 16-bit processor, contained 16-bit registers and a 16-bit data path. Motherboard technology had not quite reached the 16-bit level and was still costly in 1981. IBM decided to use a version of the 8088 chip, with the same design but with an 8-bit data path to accommodate the widely used 8-bit technology of the time.

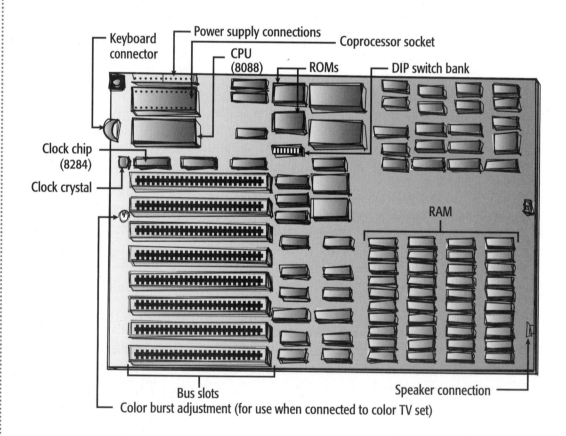

80286

Intel forged a new milestone in PC processor technology with the release of the 80286, more commonly called the 286. The 286 offered a significant performance increase over the 8086 and 8088 while still operating at the same internal clock frequency. One unique feature that proved itself very useful was the ability to operate in a protected mode. The protected mode provided the ability for the processor to multitask and still included its normal, or real, mode of operation.

Real mode allowed memory to be accessed in a linear format, meaning one line or range of memory locations at a time. Memory could not be divided into sections and allocated to programs. Information was written to memory by filling it from the start of the address range, with no compromise. With this limitation, instructions were usually processed one at a time. Multitasking, or the ability to run more than one program instruction at a time, was not easy.

Protected mode was introduced in this 286 generation of Intel processors. This new operating mode allowed multitasking to occur by allocating a specific range of memory for each task. Memory access time was improved to take advantage of this feature. Today all major operating systems use protected mode, including Microsoft Windows, which was first to take advantage of this feature.

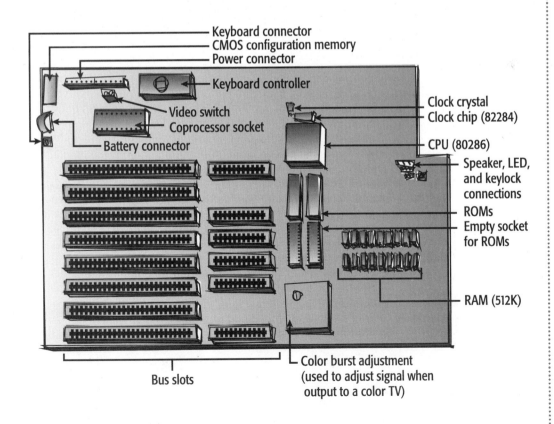

Keyboard connector
CMOS configuration memory
Power connector
Keyboard controller
Clock crystal
Clock chip (82284)
Video switch
Coprocessor socket
CPU (80286)
Battery connector
Speaker, LED, and keylock connections
ROMs
Empty socket for ROMs
RAM (512K)
Bus slots
Color burst adjustment (used to adjust signal when output to a color TV)

80386

Intel's introduction of the 80386 processor reached yet a new milestone, condensing over 250,000 transistors onto a single 32-bit processor chip. This new generation of processors incorporated true, fully functioning multitasking capabilities. Protected mode was now commonly referred to as the 386 Enhanced Mode, because the 80386 was able to overcome the multitasking limitations of the 80286.

The 80386 included a new operating mode called Virtual Real Mode. This new mode allowed DOS programs to run within the Windows operating system. Each DOS program was allowed to run in a virtual mode that resembled real mode but was within a virtual window. Virtual Real Mode, or Virtual DOS Mode, as it is commonly called, is still used for running DOS-based games and applications within Windows 95.

Several types of 80386 chips were issued, each with a unique combination of features. When the 80386 was released, Intel stopped its previous practice of licensing its chip technology to other manufacturers.

With the 80386 line, Intel offered two different options: the 80386DX and the 80386SX CPUs. Both were 32-bit processors, but the 80386DX processor used a 32-bit data path, and the 80386SX CPU used a 16-bit data path. The advantage of the SX chip was that it was more competitively priced.

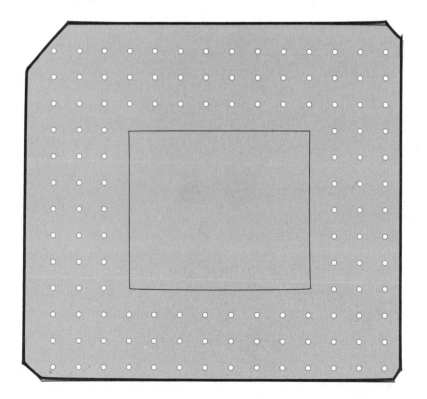

80486

The 80486DX was released a few years after the 80386. Interesting research led to the development of a new processor that included the 385 cache controller and 387 numeric processor on a single chip made up of over 1.25 million transistors. The new family of processors included a 32-bit internal and external data path and an original internal clock frequency of 33MHz.

A dramatic improvement was engineered into later deployments of the processor. A mechanism called a clock doubler allowed the internal system clock to run at twice the normal bus speed. Soon the 486DX-33 became the 486DX2-66, with the "2" signifying the clock-doubling technology. Eventually the idea of increasing the clock speed led to the tripled clock.

The 80486 chip was so versatile that it was modified through the release of several model types. The SX version was released with the numeric processor disabled and the internal clock speed slowed to 20MHz to offer a lower-cost processor to the consumer. Later this became a limitation with the emergence of more powerful software applications. A numeric processor was issued to complement the SX, turning it into a fully functioning DX.

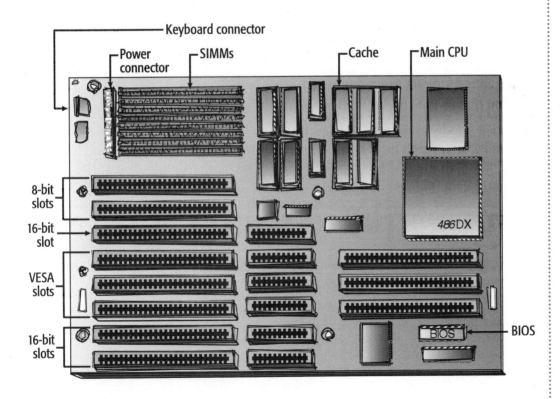

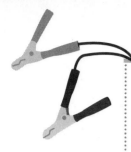

Pentium Family

**MultiMedia
Extension (MMX)**

A processor technology that dramatically improves the response time of games and multimedia-based applications. The technology was introduced through the MMX-equipped line of Intel Pentium chips. MMX processors contain additional instruction code sets that increase the processing speed of audio, video and graphical data by up to 60 percent, compared with traditional processors.

Intel released the Pentium chip to take advantage of the newly released Programmable Communication Interface (PCI) bus architecture. The new processor consisted of 3.1 million transistors and a new 64-bit data path. The chip was originally designed to operate at 66MHz but was scaled down to 60MHz to support the new transistor design, which was experiencing heat and power problems. The first chips deployed also suffered from a bug in the microcode that affected the processor's ability to calculate complex mathematical equations with precision. This problem was immediately fixed through a new batch of chips.

The most noticeable improvement introduced with the Pentium processor is its two-chips-in-one–type architecture. Encased within a single microprocessor chip are two processor chips. This type of architecture is referred to as superscalar, meaning that it can scale well to meet processing demands because of the ability of each processor chip to process independently of the other. This feature, combined with internal clock speeds up to 233MHz, made this processor quite an adversary.

Released with the Pentium family of processors was **MultiMedia Extension (MMX)** technology. MMX technology is often referred to as multimedia enhanced technology, but this is not completely accurate. MMX-equipped processors contained additional instruction code sets that increased the processing speed for audio, video and graphical data by up to 60 percent, compared with traditional Pentium processors. The MMX chips dramatically improved the response time of games and multimedia-based applications.

The different types of Pentium Processors include

- Pentium
- Pentium MMX
- Pentium Pro
- Pentium II
- PII Celeron

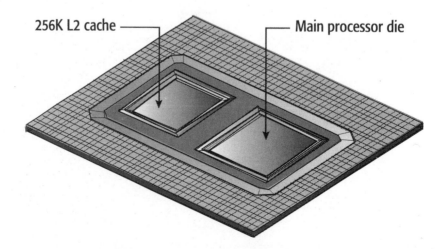

256K L2 cache — Main processor die

Pentium

The Pentium chip was introduced in 1993. The chips use a 64-bit data path and operate at internal clock speeds ranging from 60MHz to 200MHz. The Pentium was the first microprocessor chip designed to work with the PCI bus specification.

Pentium MMX

The Pentium with MMX technology was released in 1997. The new MMX chip included an expanded instruction code set with 57 new MMX microcode instructions. The new technology allowed the microprocessor to increase the processing speed of audio, video, and graphics by up to 60 percent.

Pentium Pro

Released in 1995, the Pentium Pro was the successor to Intel's Pentium processor. The microprocessor was unique in the Intel lineup because of the internal RISC architecture with CISC-RISC translator services.

Pentium II

The Intel Pentium II, or PII, processor is essentially an enhanced Pentium Pro processor with MMX extensions, cache memory and a new interface design. The PII was designed to fit into an SEC that plugs into a 242-pin slot.

PII Celeron

The only noticeable difference between the Celeron and regular Pentium II processors is the lack of cache memory within its cartridge.

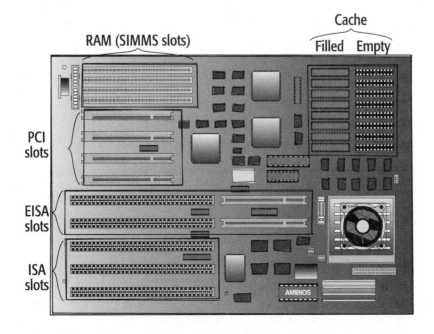

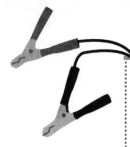

Considering the Clones

There are many manufacturers competing with Intel to produce microprocessor chips. For many years Intel's competitors produced clone copies of its chips, often slightly altering the original design to allow for faster processing speeds. A good example of this was when Advanced Micro Devices (AMD) released a 40MHz version of the 386 processor to rival the 33MHz version Intel was producing. Non-Intel, or clone, chips became popular because of the cheaper price and improved features.

When Intel released the Pentium generation of processors, the other manufacturers adopted their own unique naming conventions that steered away from the path Intel laid with this new release. Intel at the same time was experiencing problems with the early release of its Pentium line, with the discovery of a high-level mathematical division problem. Intel's competitors decided to take advantage of the situation by releasing their own chips to combat the Pentium processor.

An overview of these clones will be provided:

- ◇ Cyrix
- ◇ AMD
- ◇ PowerPC
- ◇ Alpha

WARNING

Be sure to check the Microsoft Hardware Compatibility List (HCL) before attempting to buy non-Intel processors.

NOTE

A number of clone manufacturers produce microprocessors that compete with Intel. There are several reasons for choosing their products. Two factors that stand out are the better performance and better pricing of models that some clone manufacturers offer.

Cyrix

Cyrix introduced a rival to the Intel Pentium processor in 1995. The first generation of its nonclone processor was named the M1 6x86 series. Early releases of the M1 encountered heat-related issues. Cyrix resolved the issues to produce a version that did not suffer from the earlier design problem. The improved chip offered lower power consumption requirements that allowed the chip to operate at cooler temperatures.

Although the chip was originally designed to rival the Pentium, its design included a number of additional features found in the Intel Pentium Pro processor. One of the important features of this processor was the ability to predict the next instruction to process before encountering it, thereby considerably boosting processor performance.

A follow-up to the M1 series of processors was the M2 series. The improved design included additional optimization, allowing instructions to process at faster speeds than other processors. The processors' improved capabilities were overshadowed by incompatibilities with software that made them unable to take full advantage of the improved timing. Cyrix later released software utilities and patches to address the timing issues.

This table shows the specifications for the more popular Cyrix processors currently available.

Model	Generation	Maximum Internal Clock Frequency (MHz)
Cyrix 233 MMX	M2	233
Cyrix 266 MMX	M2	266
Cyrix 300 MMX	M2	300
Cyrix 333 MMX	M2	333

Other notes on Cyrix processors include the following:

- ◇ The 6x86 received mixed reviews about its compatibility with Windows NT.
- ◇ The M2 features a set of 57 new instructions that are fully compatible with industry-standard MMX software.

AMD

In 1996 AMD introduced the K5 to combat the already released Intel Pentium processor. The K5 was released in a 64-bit version as a follow-up to the earlier K5x86, resembling a higher-performance 486-based processor. The performance of the K5 equals the Pentium at a reduced cost to the consumer.

AMD soon followed the K5 generation with the release of the K6 processor. The K6 offers a boost by accelerating the audio, video and 3-D capabilities of the chip in processing software.

One thing that sets this chip apart from its Intel and Cyrix counterparts is that it uses RISC technology. By using the reduced instruction set, it is able to process instructions at a more rapid rate. This capability and other improved implementations in design allow this chip to often outperform the Intel counterpart.

This table shows the specifications for the more popular AMD processors currently available.

Model	Generation	Maximum Internal Clock Frequency (MHz)
K6-2-3D 266 MMX	K6	233
K6-2-3D 300 MMX	K6	300
K6-2-3D 333 MMX	K6	333
K6-2-3D 350 MMX	K6	350

Other notes on AMD processors include the following:

❖ The AMD K6 processor competes with the latest PC processors equipped with MMX technology but offers a better "bang for the buck."

❖ Modern AMD processors still plug into K6 in motherboards using current technology with chipset and BIOS (Basic Input/Output System) support, without the need for special motherboards like the Intel Pentium Pro and Pentium II models.

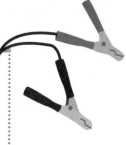

PowerPC

Apple, IBM, and Motorola developed the PowerPC as a new microprocessor technology. The PowerPC microprocessor uses RISC technology to produce a high processing rate. The innovative design of the PowerPC chip allows it to deliver high-performance computing power with lower power consumption than its counterparts.

The PowerPC design is much different from the traditional design of the Intel microprocessors. The term *PowerPC* refers to more than just a type of processor. It is more of an architecture standard that outlines specifications by which manufacturers can design processors. The resulting designs that follow the specifications offer performance advantages and innovative manufacturing techniques such as those IBM created.

IBM developed one of the most significant changes in processor manufacturing, which it called **Silicon-On-Insulator (SOI)** technology. The PowerPC 750 was the first chip released that used this new manufacturing method. SOI technology provided increased processor performance while using low power consumption. Low power consumption is important in implementations such as handheld devices, where low power is the key to producing a product that operates for longer periods of time powered by a battery.

This table outlines specifications for the more popular PowerPC processors currently available.

Model	SOI Technology	Maximum Internal Clock Frequency (MHz)
601	No	80
603e	No	250
604e	No	233
750	Yes	400

Other notes on PowerPC processors include the following:

- ❖ The PowerPC chip is used primarily in the IBM RS/6000 Unix-based workstation.
- ❖ Typically RISC-based systems process complex instructions using combinations of smaller instructions.

Silicon-On-Insulator (SOI)

The microchip manufacturing innovation that IBM invented. It is based on the ability to enhance silicon technology for improved performance through a new generation of chips manufactured using this technology.

Alpha

The Alpha is a high-speed microprocessor that Digital Equipment Corporation (DEC) developed. The Alpha processor is typically found in workstations and servers that need more processing power. You should not confuse the Alpha processor with the first line of DEC processors referred to as the Alpha, or **VAX**. The Alpha processor is unique and is much more advanced than the VAX.

One of the selling points of the Alpha chip is that it is the only other chip besides the Intel x86 generations of processors that can run the Microsoft Windows NT operating system. Alpha-equipped workstations are often characterized as the fastest NT workstations on the planet. NT takes advantage of the Alpha's ability to produce or generate graphics up to eight times faster than Intel Pentium-based systems. Alpha chips are also commonly found in Unix workstations.

There are several versions of the Alpha chip available that operate at speeds from 300MHz to 600MHz. The Alpha AXP is the newest generation of Alpha processors and is based on a true 64-bit design. The new Alpha chip accomplishes this design through a built-in **emulator**.

VAX
The Virtual Address eXtension technology built by Digital to run the VMS platform computers.

Emulator
A device that imitates computer operation through a combination of hardware and software that allows programs to run on otherwise incompatible systems.

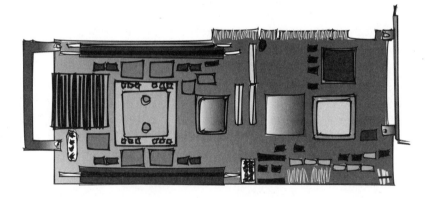

NOTE

The most notable feature of this new Alpha processor is its ability to run 32-bit Intel-based NT applications.

Using Multiprocessor Computers

Multiprocessor computers can use more than one processor installed in a single computer. Computers that contain more than one processor can scale to meet the needs of more demanding application programs. Microsoft Windows NT is an example of an operating system that can use multiple processors.

There are essentially two multiprocessing methods. Asymmetrical Multiprocessing (ASMP) is a method in which one processor is reserved to run the operating system and the input/output (I/O) devices. The second ASMP processor runs the application threads, including the other miscellaneous tasks that the first processor does not handle. This method is often inefficient, because one processor can become busier than the other.

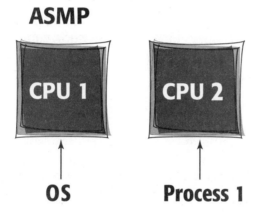

The other multiprocessing method is referred to as Symmetrical Multiprocessing (SMP). This method shares all the tasks equally. The tasks are split among each processor. The Microsoft Windows NT operating system supports this multiprocessing method.

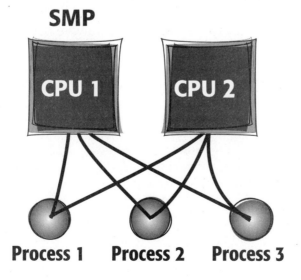

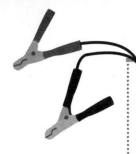

Understanding Memory

Memory is basically a series of cells with an address. Each memory cell stores a small piece information. Each memory cell is identified by a unique address location so the processor knows where the cell resides and can easily access it. Computers use several different types of memory, each serving a different purpose in their overall operation.

RAM

Random Access Memory (RAM), often referred to as main memory, is a temporary type of memory that the computer uses as a work area. This type of memory is dynamic, meaning that it is constantly changing because of the activity of the processor. When you shut off the power to the computer, RAM loses everything stored in it. RAM stores program instructions and related data for the CPU for quick access without the need for extracting data from a slower type of memory, like the hard disk.

The hard disk and floppy disk are more permanent forms of data storage. Programs and their output data are stored on disks for future use. When you shut off the power to the computer, the data on the storage media is intact. Accessing data and program instructions from storage media can take over a hundred times longer than from RAM.

ROM

Read-Only Memory (ROM) is a special type of memory in which data is written onto a chip during manufacturing. Information stored to ROM is permanent and cannot be changed. ROM stores the BIOS, the set of instructions a computer uses during the first stages of initialization. Without the BIOS, the computer would not have a mechanism to verify that the main hardware components are installed and functioning properly.

Memory Types

Here is a brief description of several types of memory.

SRAM

Static RAM (SRAM) is a type of computer memory that retains the information within it as long as power is supplied, allowing it to refresh. SRAM chips can store only about one-fourth the information a dynamic RAM chip can store. The typical application for SRAM is in cache memory.

DRAM

Dynamic RAM (DRAM) is a type of memory that uses capacitors and transistors to store electrical charges representing memory states. The capacitors that make up this type of memory need to be refreshed every millisecond and are unreachable by the processor during that time.

PROM

Programmable Read-Only Memory (PROM) is a special type of chip that is manufactured without any configuration. Manufacturers can then "burn in," or program, the chip to contain whatever configuration is needed.

EPROM

Erasable Programmable Read-Only Memory (EPROM) maintains its contents without the use of electrical power. The stored contents of an EPROM chip are erased and reprogrammed by removing the protective cover and using special equipment to reprogram the chip.

EEPROM

Electrically Erasable Programmable ROM (EEPROM) typically maintains the BIOS code, which can be updated through a disk that the BIOS manufacturer supplies.

Review Questions

Terms to Know
- ❑ Processor
- ❑ Megahertz
- ❑ Real Mode
- ❑ Protected Mode
- ❑ Emulator

1. Which processor was released in the first IBM PC?

_____

2. How did the 8086 differ from the 8088?

_____

3. What does CPU speed refer to?

_____

4. What does EPROM stand for?

_____

5. How does real mode differ from protected mode?

_____

6. What do clock cycles refer to?

_____

7. What is Virtual Real Mode?

_____

8. What does PROM stand for, and what is it?

_____

9. What does the term clock doubling refer to?

_____

10. How many transistors make up the original Pentium processor?

_____

11. How does asymmetrical processing differ from symmetrical?

_____

12. What is a numeric processor?

_____

13. What is the difference between a Pentium II and a PII Celeron?

_____

14. Which processor would you select if you wanted the best performance from an NT machine?

_____

15. What is the primary difference between RAM and ROM?

_____

Acronyms to Know
- ❑ SEC
- ❑ CISC
- ❑ RISC
- ❑ CPU
- ❑ MMX
- ❑ SOI
- ❑ VAX
- ❑ ASMP
- ❑ SMP
- ❑ RAM
- ❑ ROM
- ❑ SRAM
- ❑ DRAM
- ❑ PROM
- ❑ EPROM
- ❑ EEPROM

Chapter
2

Storing Your Files:
Data Storage

On every computer there is a collection of files. They include the files that run the operating system, the files needed to use applications, and the data files you create. All these files have to be saved somewhere, and that somewhere is called data storage. In this chapter, you will learn about these data storage options:

 Data storage overview

 Hard drives

 IDE drives

 SCSI drives

 Disk organization

 Boot partition and active partition

 Disk drive configurations

 Floppy drives

 CD drives

 Tape backup

Understanding Data Storage Basics

You can store data in a variety of formats. The format you choose depends on your needs. Some things to consider when choosing media, or types of storage devices, are:

- ◆ Should the media be fixed or removable? Fixed media stays with the computer. Removable media can be removed for use with another computer or for backup purposes.

- ◆ What capacity do you need? Are you storing a small amount of data or a large amount of data?

- ◆ How common is the storage media? If the storage media is not commonly used, it may be incompatible with other computer types. For example, if you received a 5¼-inch floppy disk, would it work on your computer? Would it work on most computers that are sold today?

- ◆ What is the cost of the storage media? Cost is often a primary concern. When read/write Compact Discs (CDs) first became available, most users considered them to be too expensive. Because prices have dropped so significantly, this is now a very common storage media.

Here are some storage quantities and their equivalents:

1,024 kilobytes (KB)	= 1 megabyte (MB)
1,024MB	= 1 gigabyte (GB)
1,024GB	= 1 terabyte (TB)
1,024TB	= 1 petabyte (PB)
1,024EB	= 1 exabyte (EB)

NOTE

Data is stored as a series of ones and zeros. In the early days of computing, data was transferred via punch cards. At that point, data was much more tangible and easy to understand. However, the trade-off for speed and accessibility is well worth it.

Here is a summary of the most common storage media.

Media	Description	Fixed or Removable	Data Capacity
Hard drive	Storage device that stores large amounts of data. Uses a series of magnetically coated disks to store ones and zeros.	Usually fixed, but some hard drives are removable.	New drives are in the gigabyte range.
Floppy disk	A removable plastic disk that stores small amounts of data. This is a popular media because of its low cost and wide availability.	Removable	Standard 3½-inch floppy disks can hold 1.44MB of data.
Compact disc	CDs are optical disks that store data. Most CDs can be written to one time but read many times.	Removable	CDs hold about 650MB of data.
Tape	Tape is a magnetic media that you commonly use for backup purposes. It is a slow media for accessing data, but its large capacity and low cost make it ideal for backup.	Removable	Depends on the tape, but can be in the gigabyte range.

TIP

Another popular form of disk storage is the Iomega Zip Drive, which you typically use for backups. The Zip Drive uses a Zip disk for storage. The Zip disk looks similar to a floppy but can hold up to 100MB of data.

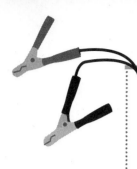

Understanding Hard Drive Basics

A **hard drive** is a series of magnetically coated disks that store data. A positive charge indicates a one, and the absence of a charge indicates a zero.

The hard drive consists of these pieces:

- Each hard drive contains a series of disks called platters.

- The platters are stacked together. Each platter has a hole in the middle, and a spindle is inserted through these holes. The platters rotate at a very high rate of speed.

- A read/write disk head sits on top of the disk surface and reads or writes to the disk as the disk rotates.

- An actuator arm, which is responsible for disk head movement, manages the disk head.

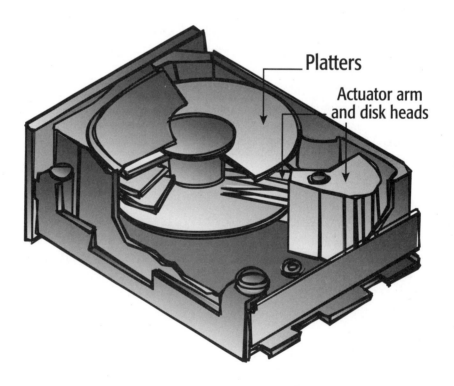

Platters

Actuator arm and disk heads

Selecting a Hard Drive

When choosing a hard drive, you should consider these options:

- ◆ Is the drive type a common standard?
- ◆ How much storage space do you need now and over the next year?
- ◆ What speed do you need?
- ◆ Does the drive need any additional hardware?
- ◆ How many drives can you chain together if you need more space in the future?
- ◆ How much will everything cost?

Two of the most common drive types are IDE and SCSI. We will cover these in more detail in the following sections.

WARNING

Because of the magnetic properties of disk drives, you should never place them near anything with magnetic properties.

NOTE

Hard drives are one of the most essential forms of data storage. As with most PC components, the technology has changed significantly over the last 20 years. In the early 1980s, an average hard disk stored 10MB of data and had an average disk access time of 87 milliseconds. In addition, hard drives were extremely expensive. Now in the late 1990s, you can buy hard drives in the gigabyte range for pennies a megabyte. In addition, access time is typically 8 milliseconds or less.

Considering IDE Drives

IDE stands for **Integrated Drive Electronics**. IDE drives are very popular, because the **disk controller** and drive are integrated into a single piece of hardware. This makes IDE drives less expensive than SCSI drives.

You can connect IDE drives to the computer in two ways:

❖ You can attach them directly to the motherboard if the IDE adapter is integrated as part of the motherboard.

❖ You can attach them to a paddleboard. The paddleboard is not a controller. It is a simple piece of hardware that facilitates the connection between the drive and the motherboard. This hardware is very inexpensive, usually costing under $20.

Traditionally IDE technology allows you to install two drives per paddleboard. You designate one drive as the master drive and the second drive as a slave drive. Jumpers on the hard drive usually determine the drive designation. You should refer to the drive's documentation to see how to configure your particular drive.

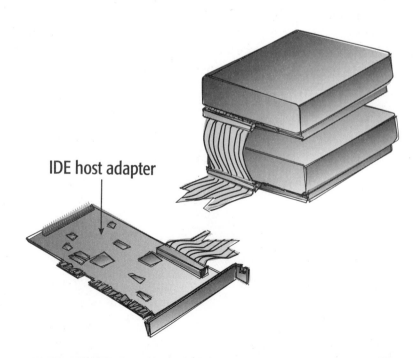

IDE host adapter

Integrated Drive Electronics, or IDE

A drive technology that integrates the drive and controller into a single piece of hardware. IDE drives are an inexpensive data storage solution.

Disk Controllers

Manage floppy and hard disks. Disk controllers can be a separate piece of hardware, or they can be integrated with the hard drive.

NOTE

You can start, or boot, your computer only from the master drive.

Here are some other notable facts about IDE:

❖ Most IDE drives that are used today are actually Enhanced IDE, or EIDE, drives. The original IDE specification supported drives only up to 528MB.

❖ You can easily distinguish an IDE drive from a SCSI drive, because IDE uses a 40-pin connector.

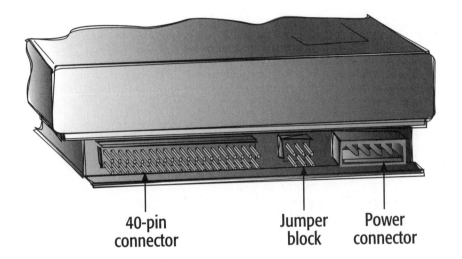

40-pin connector   Jumper block   Power connector

NOTE

In some hardware books and manuals, you will see references to RLL, MFM, and ESDI on the subject of hard drives. These standards have been obsolete for some time.

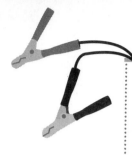

Considering SCSI Drives

SCSI stands for **Small Computer System Interface** and is pronounced "scuzzy." SCSI supports more than just drives. SCSI devices are attached to a SCSI adapter. SCSI devices include hard disks, CD-ROM players, tape backup devices, and other hardware peripherals. Because SCSI hard drives must be attached to an intelligent SCSI adapter, this is a more expensive disk storage solution overall when compared with IDE.

Small Computer System Interface, or SCSI

An interface that connects SCSI devices to the computer. This interface uses high-speed parallel technology to connect devices that include hard disks, CD-ROM players, tape backup devices, and other hardware peripherals.

These are some benefits of SCSI:

◆ With a SCSI adapter, you can easily add or remove SCSI devices to or from your computer.

◆ SCSI offers high performance.

◆ You can take advantage of new SCSI standards and adapters while maintaining compatibility with older SCSI devices.

◆ SCSI is a widely available, widely used, mature technology.

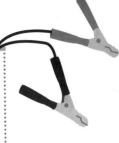

SCSI Standards

SCSI has many standards. This table defines them.

SCSI Standard	Bus Width	MBps Bus Speed	Max. # Supported Devices
SCSI-1	8-bit	5	8
Fast SCSI	8-bit	8	8
Fast and Wide SCSI	16-bit	20	16
Ultra SCSI	8-bit	20	8–16
Ultra Wide SCSI	16-bit	40	8–16
Ultra2 SCSI	8-bit	40	8
Wide Ultra2 SCSI	16-bit	80	16

Termination
Used at both ends of a bus to specify the beginning and end of a data bus and to keep data signals from bouncing back on the data chain once they reach the end.

SCSI or SCSI Wide refers to bus width, or the rate at which the computer can process information. A 16-bit bus can transfer twice as much information as an 8-bit bus. Regular SCSI uses an 8-bit bus width, and SCSI Wide uses a 16-bit bus width.

Fast SCSI refers to the faster data transfer speeds that exceed the original SCSI transfer rate of 5MBps.

SCSI Termination

Traditionally SCSI adapters allow you to daisy chain (connect in a linear fashion) up to seven devices off of each controller. The controller contains **termination**. You must also terminate the last device in the SCSI chain. The termination at the beginning and end forms the SCSI chain. Some devices use active termination, which means you don't have to do anything. Other devices require you to manually remove termination from devices in the middle of the chain and ensure that the last device is terminated.

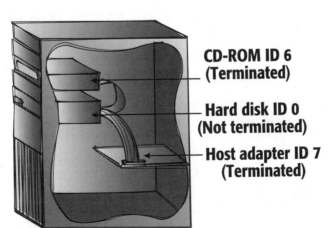

CD-ROM ID 6 (Terminated)

Hard disk ID 0 (Not terminated)

Host adapter ID 7 (Terminated)

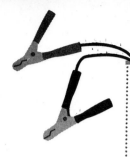

Organizing Disks

There are several ways to organize disk drives. The disk drives themselves are **physical**, and the usable space defined through partitions is considered logical. By using **logical drives**, you can define disk space however you want, regardless of the physical size of the disk. Consider this example:

Physical Hard Drives

The physical drives; for example, drive 0 or drive 1 in a two-drive configuration.

Logical Drives

Based on how you partition your physical drive. A logical drive is assigned a logical drive letter; for example, C:\.

Logical Drive C:\
1GB
Logical Drive D:\
1GB

Physical Disk 0
2GB

Physical Disk 0
1GB

Physical Disk 1
1GB

Logical Drive C:\
2GB

In the first example, you have a single 2GB physical disk that is logically partitioned into two logical drives. Each logical drive is 1GB in size.

In the second example, you have two physical disks that are each 1GB in size. In this case the two drives are defined as a single 2GB logical drive.

NOTE

In order to create logical drives, you can use utilities such as the DOS FDISK program, which is covered in Chapter 6, *DOS 101: DOS Basics Every MCSE Should Know*; third-party utilities like Partition Magic; or if you are using Windows NT, Disk Administrator.

Understanding Partition Types

Before you create your logical disk partitions, you should first understand these disk concepts:

- ◆ Active and boot partition
- ◆ Primary partition
- ◆ Extended and logical partitions

Active and Boot Partition

When you start your computer, the start-up process looks for the partition that is marked as active. This is almost always the C:\ drive. The active partition should have the operating system files your computer is using that are necessary to load the operating system. The partition that contains the operating system files is the boot partition. Normally the active partition and the boot partition are the same partition.

Primary Partition

Traditionally the first partition you defined was the primary partition. With the DOS operating system, you can have one primary partition. The primary partition is assigned all of the disk space you allocate to it. For example, if you were to create the first partition as a primary partition and allocate 1GB of space, the first drive by default (the primary drive) would be the C:\ drive and would consist of 1GB of usable space.

With the Windows NT operating system, you can have up to four partitions per physical disk. This can consist of four primary partitions, or three primary partitions and one logical partition.

Each physical partition can have only one drive letter assigned to it.

Extended and Logical Partitions

An extended partition is a logical drive that allows you to allocate the logical partitions however you wish. For example, you could create a single extended partition that was 1GB in size. Within the extended partition, you could then create four logical partitions, D:\, E:\, F:\, and G:\, that were each 250MB in size.

Understanding Disk Drive Configurations

In this section, you will learn about several disk drive configurations.

Volume Set

A volume set extends the size of a partition beyond a single physical drive.

Disk Stripe Set

A disk stripe set combines several logical partitions of the same size into a single logical disk. Stripe sets stripe data evenly over the entire set.

Mirrored Set

A mirrored set contains a primary partition and a secondary partition. Anytime data is written to the first partition, it is automatically written to the second partition. You use a mirrored set for fault tolerance.

Stripe Set with Parity Stripe

A stripe set with parity stripe is similar to a stripe set, but it contains a parity stripe across all drives. This gives you the benefits of a stripe set while also offering fault tolerance.

Stripe Set with Parity Drive

A stripe set with parity drive is similar to a stripe set with a parity stripe, except that the parity information is stored on a single drive as opposed to being striped.

Volume Sets

A volume set extends the size of a single partition. For example, assume that you created a single partition on your 1GB physical drive. You used the partition to store a database that is approaching 1GB in size. You can add a second physical drive and with the free space create a volume set.

In volume sets the data is written sequentially, so you can extend volume sets at any time without having to back up the data, create the volume set, and then restore the data. This makes volume sets an easy way to quickly and temporarily handle a shortage of disk space until you replace your disk drive with a larger drive.

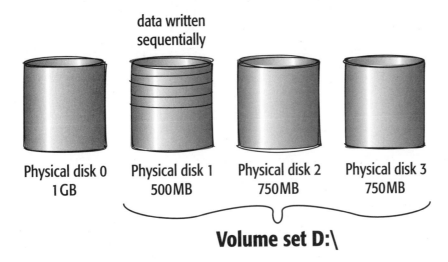

data written
sequentially

Physical disk 0
1GB

Physical disk 1
500MB

Physical disk 2
750MB

Physical disk 3
750MB

Volume set D:

Pros and Cons

Consider these factors when using volume sets:

Same-size partitions?	No. With volume sets, the partitions within the volume set do not have to be the same size.
Performance increase?	No. Volume sets write data sequentially, so there is no performance increase.
Fault tolerance?	No. Because volume sets contain no parity information, they are not fault tolerant. This means that if any physical drive within the volume set fails, the entire volume set is unusable.

NOTE

With Windows NT, you can have up to 32 partitions within a volume set.

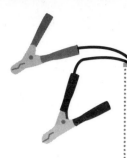

Disk Stripe Sets

In a disk stripe set, you define logical partitions of the same size as a stripe set. Once you create a stripe set, data is written across the set in stripes. The benefit of this disk configuration is that it allows you to take advantage of multiple disk **I/O channels** for improved performance.

I/O Channel, or Input/Output Channel

The channel between the computer and the disk drive. If you have more channels for data transfer, you have better performance.

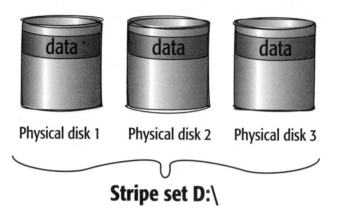

Physical disk 1   Physical disk 2   Physical disk 3

Stripe set D:\

Pros and Cons

Consider these factors when using stripe sets:

Same-size partitions?	Yes. Partitions have to be the same logical size in a stripe set.
Performance increase?	Yes. If the stripe set is located on multiple I/O channels, you will see a performance increase.
Fault tolerance?	No. Because stripe sets contain no parity information, if any drive within the stripe set fails, the entire stripe set will be lost. In this case you would restore your data from your most recent backup.

TIP

If you want fault tolerance, it is technically possible to mirror a stripe set.

Mirrored Sets

A mirrored set consists of a primary drive and a secondary drive. Anytime data is written to the primary drive, it is copied (or mirrored) to the secondary drive. The benefit of a mirrored set is that if a disk fails, you do not lose any data.

There are two types of mirrored sets:

◆ Disk mirroring is the use of one controller with two disks.

◆ Disk duplexing is the use of two controllers and two disks.

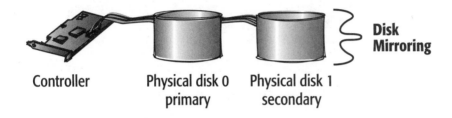

Controller   Physical disk 0   Physical disk 1   **Disk Mirroring**
                         primary   secondary

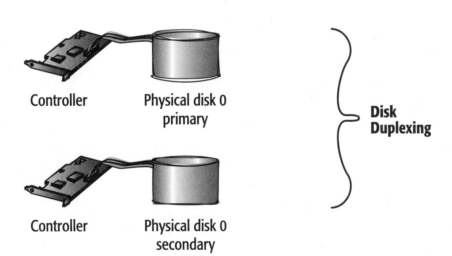

Controller   Physical disk 0
                         primary

                                                                        Disk Duplexing

Controller   Physical disk 0
                         secondary

Pros and Cons

Consider these factors when using mirrored sets:

Same-size partitions?	Yes. In a mirrored set, both of the logical partitions have to be the same size.
Performance increase?	Yes and no. With disk mirroring, performance decreases on writes, because one controller must write to both drives. With disk duplexing, you actually see a slight performance increase, since you are using two separate I/O channels.
Fault tolerance?	Yes. Mirrored sets are fault tolerant.

Stripe Sets with Parity Stripe

A stripe set with a **parity** stripe arranges logical drives of equal size into a stripe set. In addition, each drive within the set has a parity stripe. Parity involves mathematical calculations that can reconstruct data if one of the drives within the set fails.

Parity

In the context of a stripe set, a series of mathematical calculations based on the data stored. If a disk fails, the stored parity information can be used to rebuild the data.

RAID, or Redundant Array of Inexpensive Disks

A method of using a series of hard disks as an array of drives. Some implementations of RAID improve performance. Other implementations of RAID provide fault tolerance and improve performance.

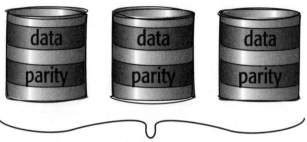

Stripe set with parity stripe

Pros and Cons

Consider these factors when using stripe sets with parity stripe:

Same-size partitions?	Yes. Within any stripe set, partitions must be equal in size.
Performance increase?	Yes. Each I/O channel that the stripe set uses increases the performance of the stripe set.
Fault tolerance?	Yes and no. As long as only one drive fails, the stripe set with the parity stripe is fault tolerant. If two or more drives fail, you must re-create the stripe set with the parity stripe and then restore the data from the most recent backup.

NOTE

This drive configuration is supported by Windows NT software and is considered a software implementation of RAID 5. With software implementations of **RAID**, you can use any disk drives you want.

Stripe Sets with Parity Drive

A stripe set with a parity stripe drive arranges logical drives of equal size into a stripe set. A separate drive stores parity information. Parity involves mathematical calculations that can reconstruct data if one of the drives within the set fails.

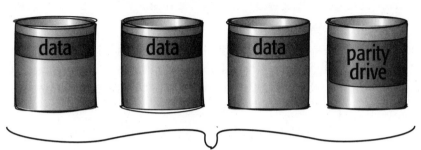

Stripe set with parity drive

Pros and Cons

Consider these factors when using stripe sets with parity drive:

Same-size partitions?	Yes. Within any stripe set, partitions must be equal in size.
Performance increase?	Yes. Each I/O channel that the stripe set uses increases the performance of the stripe set.
Fault tolerance?	Yes and no. As long as only one drive fails (assuming that the parity drive isn't the failed drive), the stripe set with the parity drive is fault tolerant. If two or more drives fail, you must re-create the stripe set with the parity drive and then restore the data from the most recent backup.

NOTE

This type of disk configuration is associated with hardware RAID, which is usually implemented as a proprietary vendor solution.

Understanding Types of Offline Data Storage

Online Data Storage

Data is readily available at high speed. You do not need to do anything special to access online storage.

Offline Storage

Data is currently unavailable. You use offline storage to store large amounts of infrequently accessed data or to store computer backups.

Hard drives are considered to be **online data storage**. This means that data is readily available at high speed. You do not need to do anything special to access online storage.

Another type of storage is called offline storage. **Offline storage** means that the data is not readily available without some type of user intervention. Offline storage is useful for transferring data between computers, storing large amounts of data, or providing a means of backup.

Some common forms of offline storage are floppy disks, compact discs, and tape drives.

NOTE

There is also a concept of near-line storage. Near-line storage accessibility is somewhere between online and offline storage. For example, a magneto-optical drive that uses a jukebox to store data is not as readily available as hard drives but can access data without user intervention.

Distribution Media for Applications

In the not so recent past, almost all applications were distributed on floppy disks. Now the most common distribution media is CD. If you don't have a CD player (which you should upgrade to) and you buy an application that comes on a CD, look for a card that allows you to order the application on disk. You can usually do so for a minimal fee.

Note that not all applications have this option. For example, the types of applications with 100,000 pieces of clip art that come on four CDs would be impractical to distribute on floppy disks.

Floppy Drives

Floppy disks, which are used in floppy drives, provide a convenient way of transferring small amounts of data from one computer to another. Traditionally floppy disks came in two sizes: 3½-inch format and 5¼-inch format.

High-density 3½-inch floppy disks can hold up to 1.44MB of data, and high-density 5¼-inch floppy disks can hold up to 720KB of data. For the most part, 5¼-inch floppy disks are obsolete now and are very rarely seen. There is also a standard for low-density disks, but this standard is also obsolete.

NOTE

For transferring small amounts of data, the floppy disk is still an extremely popular option. Floppy disks are very inexpensive. The standard is mature, and the media is very fault tolerant. Not that anyone recommends it, but some IS professionals toss them about like Frisbees, without any damage to the disk or data.

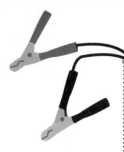

CD Drives

Compact discs, or CDs, have become a very popular storage media. Compact discs use an optical drive to read data. This is different from the magnetic media that standard hard disks use. This means that CDs are not susceptible to magnetism as hard drives and floppy disks are.

Traditionally CD devices were read-only. Now CD-Recordable (CD-R), or CD read/write devices, have decreased dramatically in price and are increasing in popularity. They are considered WORM, or Write Once-Read Many, devices.

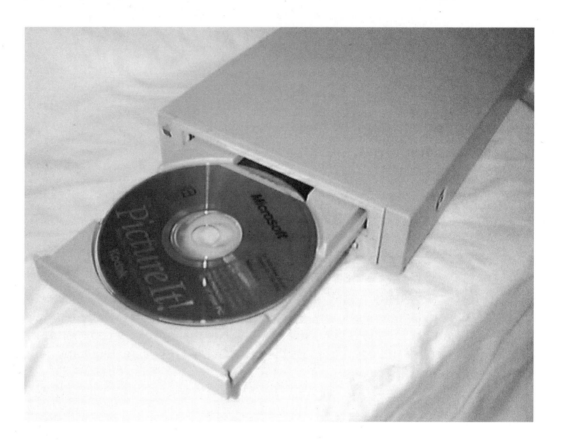

These are some of the advantages of CDs:

    ◇ They can store up to 650MB of data.

    ◇ They are inexpensive to reproduce.

    ◇ They are a lightweight media.

    ◇ If handled properly, they are a durable media.

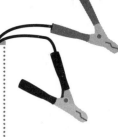

Tape Drives

Tape drives use a tape cartridge to store data. Tapes are a popular form of backup, since a single tape can hold huge amounts of data. **Backups** are critical for any computer, because you value your data. Any computer professional can tell you many horror stories of failed drives with outdated or no backups. The good news is, there are places that usually can recover your data. The bad news is, this method of data recovery is terribly expensive.

While tape provides high-capacity storage, it is a slow medium to read and write to. This is not typically a problem when doing backups, because backups are often scheduled for periods of inactivity. When choosing a tape backup device, you should consider these questions:

◆ How much storage space do you need?

◆ What throughput (data transfer speed) do you need for the backup?

◆ What is the cost of the tape device and the tapes themselves?

◆ What backup software is compatible with the drive you select?

◆ Does your computer operating system have a driver for the tape drive, and is the drive on the operating system's hardware compatibility list (a list that specifies what hardware can be used with the software)?

Backups

Copy all of your data to a secondary storage option. If your primary storage option becomes unavailable, you can use backups to restore the operating system, application, and data files.

Review Questions

Terms to Know
- ❏ Hard Drive
- ❏ Floppy Disk
- ❏ Tape
- ❏ Disk Controller
- ❏ Terminator
- ❏ Physical Drive
- ❏ Logical Drive
- ❏ Active Partition
- ❏ Boot Partition
- ❏ Primary Partition
- ❏ Extended Partition
- ❏ Logical Partition
- ❏ Volume Set
- ❏ Disk Stripe Set
- ❏ Mirrored Set
- ❏ Stripe Set with Parity Stripe
- ❏ Stripe Set with Parity Drive
- ❏ Parity
- ❏ Online Data
- ❏ Offline Data
- ❏ Tape Drive
- ❏ Backup

1. The two most common types of hard drives are:

   _____

   _____

2. True or false: IDE drives require a separate IDE adapter for installation.

3. You can easily identify an IDE hard drive because it uses a _____ pin adapter.

4. You can easily identify a SCSI hard drive because it uses a _____ pin adapter.

5. Which drive type offers better performance, IDE or SCSI?

   _____

6. What is the difference between a physical drive and a logical drive?

   _____

   _____

7. Define a volume set.

   _____

   _____

8. List three disk drive configurations that are fault tolerant.

   _____

   _____

   _____

9. What is the difference between disk mirroring and disk duplexing?

   _____

10. True or false: If two drives in a stripe set with parity fail, you can still recover the stripe set if it consists of six or more drives.

11. True or false: In a stripe set using a parity drive, all of the partitions within the stripe set must be the same size.

12. What is the difference between online and offline storage?

_____

_____

13. How much data can be stored on a CD?

_____

14. How much data can be stored on a 3½-inch floppy disk?

_____

15. True or false: You should make sure to keep all floppy disks away from any magnetic field.

Acronyms to Know
❑ KB
❑ MB
❑ GB
❑ TB
❑ PB
❑ EB
❑ CD
❑ IDE
❑ SCSI
❑ RAID

Chapter

3

Data Movement: Input/Output Devices

Computers process, manipulate, and send data according to instructions from a user. Each computer has input and output interfaces to allow you to connect input or output devices. The input device allows information to enter the computer, and the output device allows information to exit the computer. Without providing the ability to enter or extract information, the computer is nothing more than a box with colored lights. In this chapter, you will learn about these input/output ports and devices:

 Serial and parallel ports

 Monitors

 Keyboards

 Mouse

 Modems

 ISDN adapters

 Printers

 PC cards

Understanding Serial Ports

A serial port is either an input or output port that supports **serial communication**. Serial communication is the process of transmitting and processing data one **bit** at a time.

Data transmitted in a serial fashion can be sent using one of two methods: synchronous data transmission and asynchronous data transmission.

Synchronous data transmission is the method in which a **clock signal** regulates the flow of data over a cable or wire. This transmission method is used when large amounts of data must be transferred in a short period of time.

Asynchronous data transmission uses a small bit of information, referred to as the **start bit,** to tell the computer when to start transmitting data and a **stop bit** telling it when to stop. This method is used when transferring smaller amounts of data. Both the computer sending the data and the one receiving the data must agree on the number of start and stop bits for communication to take place.

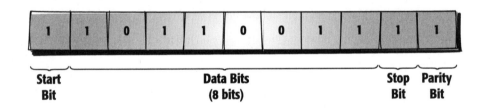

| | Start Bit | Data Bits (8 bits) | Stop Bit | Parity Bit |

Other Notes on Serial Ports

Other notes on serial ports include the following:

❖ Serial port cables connect directly to serial ports on the personal computer.

❖ Most PCs are manufactured with two serial ports that connect serial devices, such as a mouse, modem, or line printer.

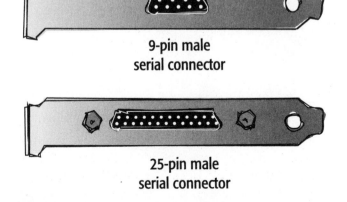

9-pin male
serial connector

25-pin male
serial connector

Serial Communication

The process of transmitting and processing data one bit at a time.

Bit

A binary digit. The digit is the smallest unit of information and represents either an off state (zero) or an on state (one).

Clock Signal

Controls the rate at which synchronous data is transmitted.

Start Bit

The bit that synchronizes the clock on the computer receiving the data being sent. In asynchronous data transmission, the start bit is a space.

Stop Bit

The bit that identifies the end of the character being transmitted so that the character is clearly recognized.

Understanding Parallel Ports

A parallel port is either an input or output port that supports **parallel communication**. Parallel communication occurs when data is transmitted and processed 1 **byte** (8 bits) at a time. Eight separate transmission lines carry the signal. Parallel communication is typically faster than serial communication.

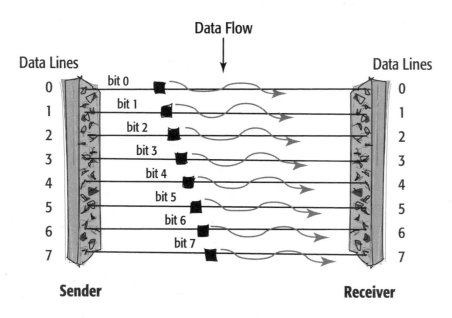

Data Flow

Data Lines | Data Lines
Sender | Receiver

Other Notes on Parallel Ports

Other notes on parallel ports include the following:

- Most parallel ports today are based on the **ECP** or **EPP** standards that support data transfer speeds of more than 2MBps.

- You can easily identify a parallel port by its 25-pin female connector.

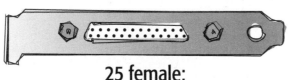

25 female:
a parallel port.

NOTE

The original parallel port was designed to send information to a printer in one direction. Standards were later developed to improve the capabilities of the parallel port by allowing communication to occur in both directions and supporting multiple devices on the same port.

Parallel Communication

The process of transmitting and processing data 1 byte (8 bits) at a time.

Byte

A single binary character, or 8 bits.

ECP (Extended Capabilities Port)

The standard developed for parallel communication by Hewlett-Packard and Microsoft to allow for data transfer rates of more than 2MBps. In addition to the high data transfer rates, it allows for bidirectional operation.

EPP (Enhanced Parallel Port)

The standard developed for parallel communication by Intel, Xircom and Zenith Data Systems to allow for data transfer rates of more than 2MBps. It supports bidirectional operation of attached devices and an addressing scheme.

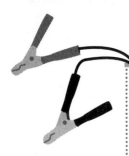

Understanding Monitors

The monitor is the most common type of output device. It may look like a simple television, but it is not. The monitor allows the human eye to interact with the computer. Without a monitor, the computer's output capabilities would be very limited. Imagine if the only output available were in printed or audible form. The monitor allows the computer to translate computer data into text and graphics and display them on a screen.

There are several types of computer monitors available based on different technology standards. The internals of the devices are essentially the same. They all contain an **electron gun** that shoots electrically charged particles called electrons toward the back of the monitor screen. The screen is coated with a phosphorous material that glows when an electron runs into it. A beam is made up of these electrons that span across and down the screen, forming an image.

Electron Gun

The device that shoots electrically charged particles called electrons toward the back of the monitor screen.

Refresh Rate

Signifies the number of times the beam of electrons shot from the electron gun redraws the screen in one second.

Dot Pitch

Measures the distance, in millimeters, between two dots of the same color on the monitor.

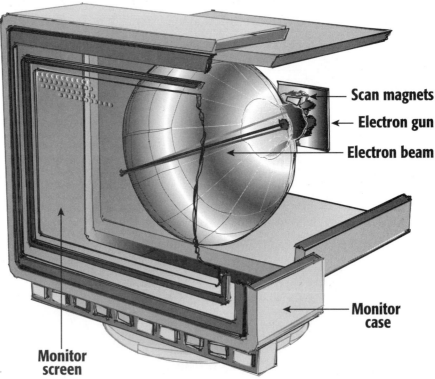

Scan magnets
Electron gun
Electron beam
Monitor case
Monitor screen

NOTE

Two ways of measuring a monitor's quality are the **refresh rate** and **dot pitch** characteristics. The refresh rate signifies the number of times the beam of electrons shot from the electron gun redraws the screen in one second. The dot pitch measures the distance between two dots of the same color on the monitor.

Video Display Adapter Standards

Video display adapters (the adapter inside your computer that connects to the monitor) have many standards. Each standard consists of specifications for the maximum supported resolution, colors supported for the maximum resolution, and connector type. Each video display adapter type has a different interface to allow for easier identification.

This table defines the standards.

Video Standard	Resolution	Supported Colors
Monochrome Display Adapter (MDA)	80 x 25	Monochrome (text only)
Hercules Graphics Controller (HGC)	720 x 350	Mono (text and graphics)
Color Graphics Adapter (CGA)	320 x 200	4
	640 x 200	2
Enhanced Graphics Adapter (EGA)	640 x 350	16
Video Graphics Adapter (VGA)	640 x 480	16
	320 x 320	256
Super VGA (SVGA)	800 x 600	256
	1024 x 768	16
Extended Graphics Array (XGA)	800 x 600	65,536
	1024 x 768	256
IBM 8514/A	1024 x 768	256

Resolution refers to the sharpness of a screen image and is often expressed in dots per square inch (dpi). The higher the resolution, the higher the number of dots on the screen it takes to produce that image.

Supported colors refer to the number of colors available from a palette of maximum colors that make up an image. The number of supported colors can range from two to several million.

Other Notes on Monitors

Other notes on monitors include the following:

◆ Your video display adapter and monitor must support the selected range of supported resolutions and maximum colors to function properly.

◆ Adapters with larger amounts of installed memory will support more colors and higher resolutions.

◆ Monitors are available in many sizes, including 14-inch, 15-inch, 17-inch and 21-inch.

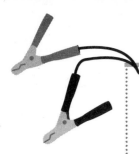

Using a Keyboard

The keyboard is the most common type of input device. The keyboard takes in information in the form of letters and numbers. The letters and numbers are translated into instructions that the computer must perform. The computer translates literally what is entered, so any typing mistakes will result in an error.

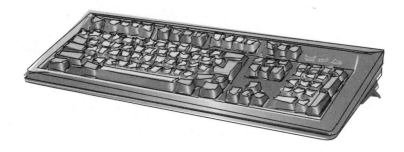

Other Notes on Keyboards

Other notes on keyboards include the following:

- ◇ Choose a keyboard that is comfortable for you, because you will interact with the device almost the entire time you are performing a computing task.

- ◇ Special cleaners are available to clean your keyboard, although replacing it is usually easier than the time and effort needed to clean it.

- ◇ Its connector type easily identifies a keyboard.

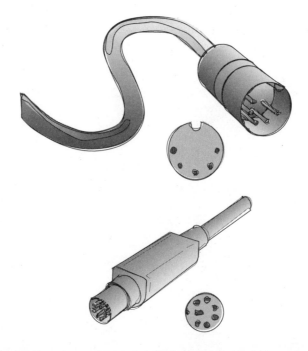

Using a Mouse

The mouse is the second most common type of input device. You use the mouse for navigating, selecting, or drawing in the user environment. The mouse movements are translated into computer instructions in the form of motion and button selection. To start a mouse operation, simply move the mouse pointer on the screen until it is in the correct position and click one of the mouse buttons.

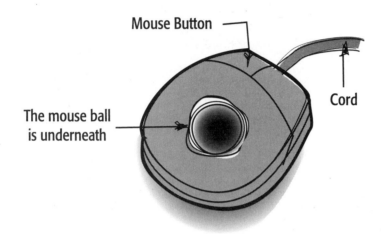

Mouse Button

Cord

The mouse ball is underneath

Other Notes on the Mouse

Other notes on the mouse include the following:

- Many people use a mouse pad to provide a nonslick service to roll the mouse on. They are available in many styles and decorative themes.
- Its connector type and number of buttons easily identify a mouse.

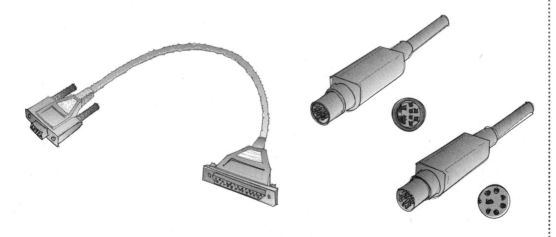

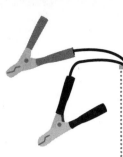

Understanding Modems

Modems function as input and output devices. Modems allow computers to communicate with one another over great distances. They convert digital signals from a computer into analog audible tone signals that can be transmitted over phone lines.

Digital signals are made up of discreet values. The values represent an on or off state. Discreet voltages represent the on or off conditions. An on condition is represented by +5 volts, and an off condition by −5 volts. The values do not change over time; they change instantaneously from one state to another.

Analog signals are constantly changing values. The values represent fluctuations in voltage or sound. An analog signal can consist of an infinite number of possible values.

The process of converting digital signals to analog signals is called modulation. When the receiving computer gets the data, the signals received from the modem are translated from the analog tone signals to the original digital data before the sending computer converted it. The process of converting analog signals to digital is called demodulation. This is where the term modem (modulate-demodulate) comes from.

Modulation/Demodulation

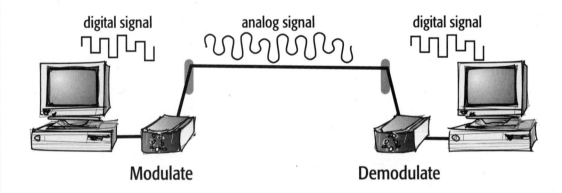

Other Notes on Modems

The speed at which a modem communicates is measured in bits per second. Modems can communicate at speeds from 300bps to over 56,000bps.

Modems come in two distinct types: internal and external. External modems require a connection to an available serial port on the back of a computer using an **RS-232C** cable. Internal modems plug into an expansion slot inside a computer.

Modems are backward compatible and slow down their transmission speed to communicate with slower modems.

Cable Modems

Cable modems allow high-speed access to the Internet over cable TV (CATV) lines. The cable modem requires two connections: one to the cable outlet and the other to the computer. Cable modems are more economical than ISDN, and you do not need to install an additional phone line. There is no need to dial; it is always active.

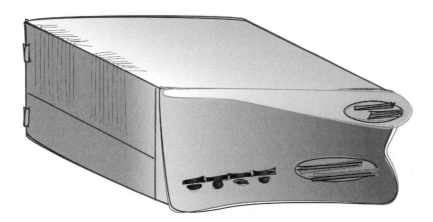

The range at which a cable modem operates varies from 200Kbps to 10Mbps. The typical range is more like 2Mbps to10Mbps. Data that is downloaded from the Internet is transmitted at a higher rate than data that is uploaded.

Cable modems typically connect via a **10BASET** connection to a network card installed in your computer. They are currently manufactured only as external devices.

RS-232C
An interface standard for use between data communications equipment (DCE) and data terminal equipment (DTE).

10BASET
The representation of a 10Mbps signal transmitted over twisted-pair using baseband signaling. It is the IEEE 802.3 standard for unshielded twisted-pair Ethernet.

Understanding ISDN Adapters

ISDN stands for **Integrated Services Digital Network**. ISDN is a digital dial service that transmits digital data at a higher transmission rate than a standard modem. This makes ISDN more expensive than using a modem. ISDN is still cost effective, considering that the rate for one ISDN line is less than two business lines, and it can support data, voice, and faxing capabilities.

You can connect ISDN adapters to the computer in two ways:

◇ Internal ISDN adapters plug into an available expansion slot inside a computer.

◇ External ISDN adapters need a connection to an available serial port on the back of a computer via a null-modem cable.

Other Notes on ISDN

The most typical ISDN user is the **telecommuter**, who uses the high-speed service to interact with the office from home.

ISDN adapters often link small branch offices that do not transmit large amounts of data to one another. A connection begins when data needs transmission.

You can identify the speed of an ISDN adapter by the number of signal bearer, or B, channels. An ISDN adapter configured with a single B channel can support 64Kbps, whereas a D channel supports only 16Kpbs.

Here is a summary of available ISDN services.

ISDN Service	Channel Type	Speed
BRI	2 B + 1 D channel (2 x 64K + 16K)	64Kbps
HO	6 B channels (6 x 64K)	384Kbps
PRI	23 B + 1 D channel (23 x 64K + 16K)	1.48Mbps

Integrated Services Digital Network (ISDN)

A technology that combines digital and voice transmission onto a single wire.

Telecommuter

Someone who remotely connects to their office to work from home or a remote location.

Choosing a Printer

Printers are output devices that produce a hard copy result in the form of printed text and graphics. Printers differ from other types of devices because they not only transfer an image to paper, they must also move the paper through the process.

Printer Types

Several types of printers are available based on different technology standards. Most printer types operate basically the same way. This table defines printer types. *Method of imprint* refers to the method of transferring information to paper.

Printer Type	Method of Imprint
Dot matrix	Tiny pins impact an ink-filled ribbon.
Inkjet/bubble jet	Ink squirts at the paper, following a pattern to create an image.
Laser	A laser beam spans across and down the screen, forming an image, using a special ink and heat to create an image.
Thermal	Similar to a dot matrix printer, but instead using heat to strike a special ribbon.

Other Notes on Printers

Printers have two operating modes: text mode and graphics mode. Text mode involves the simple lookup of ASCII characters, such as letters and numbers, from a character table and then produces the result. Graphics mode involves sending instructions to the printer to control the print operation to produce a custom character or result.

Photo-quality printers have recently emerged to provide a method for printing photos taken by digital cameras.

Printers are networked to provide many users with access to a single device, thus saving the money needed to purchase a print device for every user. Modern printers include an expansion slot to plug in a network printer card or have one built in.

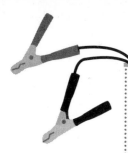

Choosing PC Cards

The purpose of the PC card is to enhance the capabilities of a computer. Adding a card to your computer allows you to customize it for your needs. Without this feature, the computer would not be as modular and would not allow you to add devices chosen to meet your specific needs.

There are several types of PC cards, such as those providing sound, network, video, and input/output capabilities. Regardless of the type of PC card, they attach to the computer by plugging into an available expansion bus slot on the motherboard. The expansion bus provides a pathway that links the device with the CPU and memory inside the computer.

There are several expansion bus design standards. It is important that you identify the slot type before purchasing a new PC card. Each bus design standard has a primary connector and may have one or more extension connectors to allow for additional capabilities. Other differences include the operating speed, interface, and method of configuration.

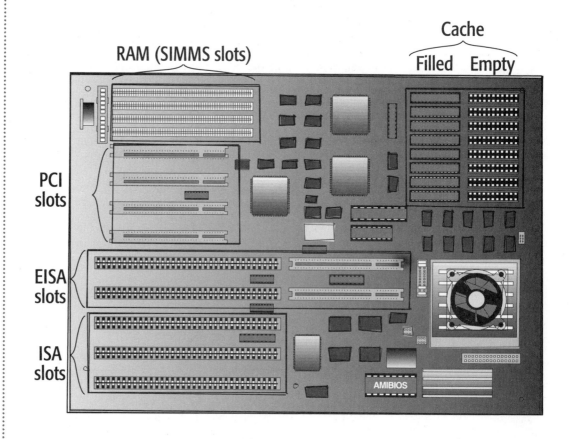

Bus Standards

Bus standards have evolved over time to take advantage of other PC technologies, such as faster microprocessor types. Most motherboards contain several bus standard types to accommodate the many add-in components available in the market today.

Bus standards provide manufacturers with a common specification by which to manufacture. This table defines the standards.

Bus type	Interface	Speed	Configuration
ISA	8-bit	8MHz	Hardware
MCA	16-bit or 32-bit	10MHz	Hardware or software
EISA	32-bit	8MHz	Software
VL-Bus	32-bit	Speed of CPU	Hardware
PCI	32-bit or 64-bit	Speed of CPU	Plug-and-Play
PCMCIA	16-bit	33MHz	Software
SCSI	8-, 16-, 32-, or 64-bit	8MHz–20MHz	Hardware or software

Most PC cards today are configured through software. The software includes a driver that tells the computer's operating system how to talk to the card and interpret information coming from the card. Some cards need hardware jumpers or switches for configuration.

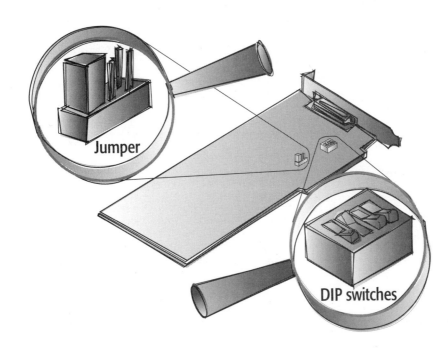

Jumper

DIP switches

Review Questions

1. Define serial communication.

   _____

   _____

2. What is the difference between data that is transmitted serially and data that is transmitted in parallel?

   _____

   _____

3. True or false: The refresh rate determines how many dots of the same color are drawn on the screen.

4. Which display adapter type is the best choice to display the maximum resolution and most colors?

   _____

5. Name the three mouse interface types.

   _____

   _____

   _____

6. True or false: Digital signals represent constantly changing voltages.

7. What is the difference between a modem and a cable modem?

   _____

   _____

8. True or false: ISDN transmits data at a higher rate than a standard modem.

9. True or false: Motherboards are manufactured to accommodate only one bus specification.

10. Why are printers attached to the network?

_____

Acronyms to Know
❑ ECP
❑ EPP
❑ ISDN

Chapter

4

Hardware Configuration: Putting It All Together

Configuring your computer hardware can be an easy or difficult task to complete. Each hardware device is configured with unique system resource settings. The resource settings allow the device to communicate with the computer's processor and memory without competing or conflicting with other devices. Most devices have the ability to accept various combinations of resource settings.

In this chapter, these hardware configuration topics are covered:

 Hardware installation

 Software drivers

 Interrupts

 Base memory

 I/O memory

 Direct Memory Access (DMA)

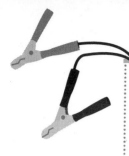

Installing Hardware

You install new hardware through a multistep configuration process. The fundamental steps are to configure the device at a physical level and at one or more logical levels so that the system can communicate with the device. A device will not function properly unless it is properly installed.

When you install a piece of hardware, you should properly configure it. You can determine configuration settings by reviewing the documentation that comes with the device. Traditionally, older hardware was configured through **DIP switches** and **jumpers**. Now this technology is fairly obsolete. Most hardware configuration is now done through software.

Each hardware device is unique and has its own specific items that you need to configure. Common configuration settings include interrupts, base memory, I/O memory, and DMA. These items are covered in more detail in the following subsections.

Completing the physical configuration of the device allows you to plug it in. Be sure that you have all of the necessary accessories, such as screws or cables, when completing this step. If the device is a PC card, carefully plug it into an available bus slot of the same type, and secure it by screwing it into the case. It usually does not matter which slot you place the card into unless it is a Programmable Communication Interface (PCI), Extended Industry Standard Architecture (EISA), or MicroChannel Architecture (MCA) card; then it is identified by slot number.

Once you have securely attached the device, you can begin the logical configuration. You install the device drivers and any other parameters that a particular operating system might need in order to communicate and interact with a device.

DIP Switch

Stands for Dual In-line Package switch. It contains parallel rows of contacts that can configure computer components and peripheral devices.

Jumper

A cable or wire that establishes or completes a circuit. It can also be defined as a shorting block to connect adjacent pins that are exposed on an expansion card.

NOTE

One reason Plug-and-Play technology is so important is that it automatically configures hardware devices for you.

TIP

If you install a new piece of hardware and your computer does not work or another piece of hardware fails, you probably have a hardware conflict. You can verify this by removing the new piece of hardware and seeing if everything works again.

Understanding Software Drivers

Software drivers are special programs that tell the computer how to communicate with and control a hardware device. Each device has a driver that allows it to communicate with the computer. The driver is written to operate only within a certain operating system. For instance, a Windows 3.1x driver will not work for that device if Windows NT is installed.

Most software drivers are not usually generic in nature. Each piece of hardware contains unique components, and these components might not reside on a similar device, even by the same manufacturer.

The software driver must communicate with that device to accurately interpret the instructions issued to the device from the operating system. Some devices, such as the mouse, are generic in that most do not contain special features or chips that need customized instruction code.

When you install a device, you should have the driver disk in hand and install it when the operating system prompts you. Operating systems such as Windows 95 detect the presence of a new device and install the driver, provided they properly recognize the device. This is possible because Windows 95 contains an archive of the most common device drivers.

Other Notes on Software Drivers

Other notes on software drivers include the following:

- ❖ You should install the latest driver available for your device for a particular operating system, because they are typically updated if issues are reported.

- ❖ DOS-based drivers are loaded through a DEVICE= statement in the CONFIG.SYS file.

TIP

You might think of a software driver as the bridge between a piece of hardware and a specific operating system's software.

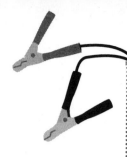

Handling Interrupts

Each device interacts with the computer based on its ability to interrupt the processor so that it can send or retrieve data or carry out a function. A device must have a method for telling the computer's processor that it needs attention. A hardware device tells the processor that it needs attention through an **interrupt request (IRQ)** line. By using this method of interruption, the processor can function without the need to ask a device every few seconds if it needs service.

When a device interrupts the system processor, the processor stops what it is doing and handles the interrupt request. Because each device is assigned a number when the device is configured, the system knows which device needs attention. Once the processor has attended to the device, it returns to the function it was performing before the interruption.

Each device must have a unique IRQ so that the processor knows what to attend to when a service request is called. There are exceptions to this rule; for instance, serial ports (also referred to as COM, or communication ports) can share the same IRQ, but they must be assigned another unique identifier (I/O address). If any other devices share the same interrupt and need attention from the processor, the machine will hang or immediately reboot in the confusion of determining what requested service.

Interrupt Request (IRQ)

The method a device uses for informing the microprocessor (CPU) that the device needs attention. Through this method of interruption, the microprocessor can function without needing to poll each device to see if it needs service.

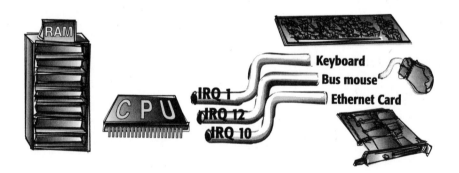

The following table shows the standard interrupts that most systems use.

- ◆ *System device* refers to the device that is configured to use the specified interrupt.
- ◆ *IRQ* refers to the interrupt request line that the hardware device uses to notify the processor that it needs attention.

System Device	IRQ
System timer	0
Keyboard	1
Reserved	2
COM 2, 4	3
COM 1, 3	4
LPT2 (usually available for other devices)	5
Floppy disk controller	6
LPT1	7
Real-time clock	8
Redirected or cascaded to IRQ2	9
Available (also used for PCI common interrupt)	10
Available	11
PS/2 or bus mouse port (available if not used)	12
Math coprocessor	13
Hard disk controller	14
Available (also used for PCI secondary IDE controller)	15

Other Notes on Hardware Interrupts

Other notes on hardware interrupts include the following:

❖ The PCI bus standard allows devices connected to a PCI bus to communicate using one common interrupt (IRQ 10).

❖ Some COM ports can share the same interrupt.

❖ Plug-and-Play devices scan the system and determine an available interrupt request to assign to a new device during installation.

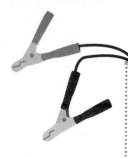

Using Base Memory

Base memory refers to the reserved area in memory where devices can store data so that the processor can directly access the data. Some devices need this allocated memory range located in the system **RAM**. The area is typically located in the upper area of RAM memory called the **Upper Memory Area (UMA)**.

RAM

Stands for Random Access Memory. RAM is the main, or system, memory that runs the operating system and application programs.

Upper Memory Area (UMA)

The area of memory between 640KB and 1MB in an IBM-compatible computer. This area of memory was originally reserved for system and video use.

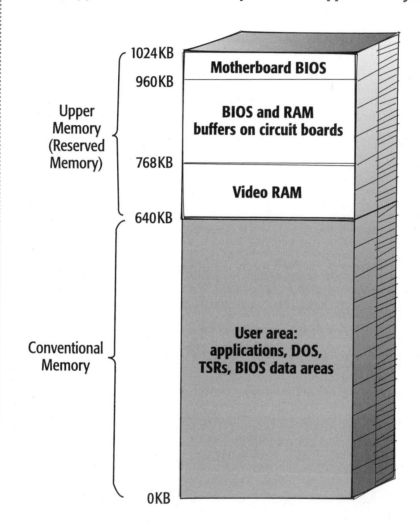

This table shows the typical base memory address assignments.

System Device	Memory Range
Video RAM	A0000–BFFFF
Available	C0000–CFFFF
Available	D0000–DFFFF
System ROM	E0000–EFFFF

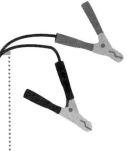

Other Notes on Base Memory

Other notes on base memory include the following:

- ❖ When configuring address ranges, be sure that they do not overlap.
- ❖ When assigning a memory address range to a DOS-based device, be sure to exclude the range in the **CONFIG.SYS** file.

What Do You Have There?

If you want to check what resources are already in use on a Windows 95 computer, you do this by going to the Start ➤ Control Panel, double-click the System icon, click the Device Manager tab, click Computer, and click the Properties button. From this screen, you click the appropriate radio button: IRQ, I/O, DMA, or Memory.

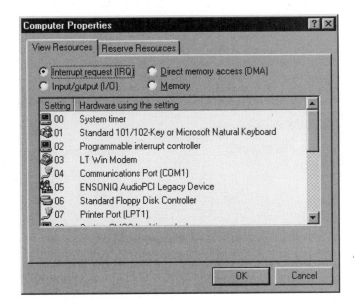

CONFIG.SYS

A DOS or OS/2 file that contains special configuration settings in the form of line statements. The file is stored in the root of the C drive and is one of the key files read when an operating system boots.

Using I/O Memory

Each device has a memory address called an I/O address. The address acts like a mailbox for the processor to send instructions to the device. The I/O address is also commonly called the port address.

When instructions are sent to this address, the device reads the instructions and carries them out. The device does not talk to the processor through the same mechanism. It uses the interrupt assigned to it to request service or additional instructions from the processor.

Each device must have a unique I/O address so that the correct device receives the instructions from the processor. Most PCs are designed to support more than one I/O address for a device. This feature helps prevent a conflict between two similar devices, such as the COM ports that share the same interrupt. The two ports would have separate I/O addresses, thus preventing a clash between them.

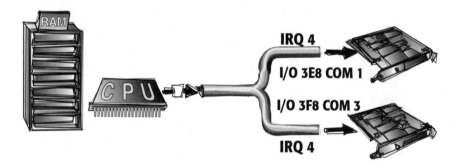

This table shows the typical I/O address assignments.

SYSTEM DEVICE	MEMORY ADDRESS
DMA controller	000–01F
Interrupt controller	020–03F
Timer	040–05F
Keyboard	060–06F
Real-time clock	070–07F
DMA page register	080–09F
Second interrupt controller	0A0–0BF
DMA controller 2	0C0–0DF
Math coprocessor	0F0–0FF
Primary hard disk controller	1F0–1F8

SYSTEM DEVICE	MEMORY ADDRESS
Joystick controller	200–20F
XT expansion unit	210–217
FM synthesis interface	220–22F
CD-ROM I/O port	230–233
Bus mouse	238–23B
Plug-and-Play I/O port	274–277
LPT2 (second parallel port)	278–27F
COM 4 (serial port 4)	2E8–2EF
COM 2 (serial port 2)	2F8–2FF
Available	280–31F
XT hard disk controller	320–32F
MIDI port	330–33F
Alternate floppy controller	370–377
LPT1 (primary printer port)	378–37F
LPT3 (third parallel port)	3BC–3BF
Color graphics adapter (CGA, EGA, VGA)	3D0–3DF
COM 3 (serial port 3)	3E8–3EF
Floppy disk controller	3F0–3F7
COM 1 (serial port 1)	3F8–3FF

Other Notes on I/O Memory

Other notes on I/O memory include the following:

- ❖ Some older devices are coded to use only one I/O address and cannot be changed.

- ❖ If your device does not support an I/O address that is available (not in use by another device), you may select an address used by another device, provided you can change the other device's address to an available I/O address.

- ❖ Always note the addresses your system uses, to make life easier when troubleshooting or adding a new device.

Using DMA

DMA stands for **Direct Memory Access**. DMA allows a device to transfer data directly to RAM without using the attention of the processor for the entire transfer period. The result is a faster and more direct method for data transfer. This was especially useful in older PCs, allowing the DMA channel to transfer data in the background, thus freeing the processor to tend to other duties.

This graphic shows the CPU intervention for the transfer of data.

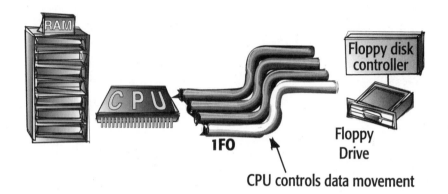

CPU controls data movement

This graphic shows the use of DMA for direct transfer of data.

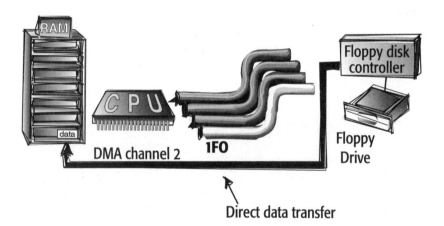

Direct data transfer

Direct Memory Access (DMA)

The method of transferring data directly from a device, such as a storage device, directly to memory without involving the processor.

NOTE

The term *channel* is often used in describing DMA. In older PCs, a DMA controller chip handled DMA activities. The chip contained four DMA channels that were numbered 0–3. Technology enhancements allowed the inclusion of up to eight channels. Each bus standard type allows a different number of DMA channels.

This table shows the standard DMA channels that most systems use.

System Device	DMA Channel
Available	0
Available	1
Floppy disk controller	2
Available	3
Not available (used for internal purposes or second DMA controller)	4
Available	5
Available	6
Available	7

Other Notes on DMA

Other notes on DMA include the following:

- ❖ DMA is typically used by devices such as floppy disks, hard disks, tape devices, and network cards.

- ❖ The only available DMA channel on older PCs is DMA channel 3.

- ❖ When two devices are configured to the same DMA channel, neither device can transfer the data to memory correctly.

- ❖ If your device does not operate correctly using various combinations of DMA channel assignments, try the Disable DMA option.

TIP

If you install a piece of hardware and your computer does not work, remove the last piece of hardware that you installed. Then, if the computer works, you know that the new piece of hardware conflicts with an existing piece of hardware.

Review Questions

Terms to Know
- ❏ DIP Switch
- ❏ Jumper
- ❏ Software Driver
- ❏ Base Memory
- ❏ CONFIG.SYS

1. How do you accomplish the physical configuration of a device?

_____

2. What are the four hardware settings that you use to configure computer hardware?

_____

_____

_____

_____

3. How does an interrupt work?

_____

4. Which interrupt does LPT2 typically use?

_____

5. True or false: All devices need a reserved area of memory in which to operate.

6. What I/O address range is typically assigned to the primary hard disk controller?

_____

7. How does DMA typically work?

_____

8. Which DMA channel is typically assigned to the floppy disk controller?

_____

9. What is a software driver?

_____

10. True or false: A software driver will work with any operating system as long as it follows the Software Driver Association guidelines.

11. True or false: Two hardware devices can share the same IRQ.

12. What does DMA stand for?

_____

13. What does I/O stand for?

_____

14. What does IRQ stand for?

_____

Chapter
5

Local Operating Systems: A Comparison

Every computer consists of hardware and software. In the previous chapters, you learned about hardware. In this chapter, you will learn about local operating systems, which are the heart and brains of the computer's software. The local operating system manages system hardware and resources. In the past 20 years, operating systems have changed dramatically. This chapter will provide an overview of common operating systems. Some of the information is provided as a historical overview to give you an idea of the evolution that has occurred in operating system development. These local operating systems and operating system concepts will be covered:

 DOS

 Windows

 Windows 95

 Windows 98

 Windows NT Workstation

 Unix and Linux

 OS/2

 Dual booting between operating systems

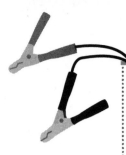

Understanding DOS

If you used a computer between 1981 and the early 1990s, chances are, the computer ran DOS as its operating system. DOS stands for Disk Operating System. Microsoft originally licensed DOS to IBM as an operating system to be used with IBM's personal computers. This version of DOS was called PC-DOS.

In what has become one of the smartest moves in the computer industry, Microsoft licensed DOS, as opposed to selling DOS to IBM. Microsoft also retained the right to license other versions of DOS. This version of non-IBM DOS was called MS-DOS and was used by other hardware vendors who made PCs with the same Intel CPU that IBM used with its PCs. These computers were referred to as IBM clones and typically were more competitively priced than their IBM counterparts.

The following subsections describe the major features that the various evolutions of DOS offered.

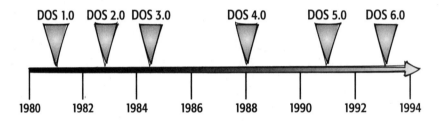

DOS 1.*x*

This version provided

- A very limited ability to use system resources
- The ability to support floppy disks

DOS 2.*x*

This version provided

- Support for 10MB hard drives
- Support for serial interface
- The hierarchical tree structure used to store data within directories and subdirectories

DOS 3.x

This version provided

- Support for larger hard drives
- Networking capabilities
- Support for two partitions on a single physical drive
- Enhancements to many utilities

DOS 4.x

This version provided

- The DOS shell, which was more graphical in appearance
- Support for a mouse

DOS 5.x

This version provided

- The EDIT, DOSKEY, UNFORMAT, and UNDELETE programs
- The ability to load drivers into upper memory (memory beyond the 640K range)

DOS 6.x

This version provided

- Disk utilities such as virus scanner and disk defragmentation, compression software, and backup software
- The EMM386.EXE utility, which allowed memory to be better managed

NOTE

DOS 6.22 was the last version of DOS to be released. At this point, DOS is not a commonly used operating system, because it lacks a truly graphical interface. However, many DOS commands continue to be supported under the Windows 9x platform, and advanced users find knowing DOS commands very useful. You will learn more about DOS in Chapter 6, *DOS 101: DOS Basics Every MCSE Should Know.*

Understanding Windows

While DOS provided many functions, users wanted these functions combined with a user-friendly interface. This led to a Graphical User Interface (GUI) operating system based on top of DOS (meaning that Windows is not an operating system by itself and requires DOS to be running). The Windows platform was based on technology that supported 16-bit processing.

The first version of Windows was version 1.0. This version broke new ground (in the PC market) by allowing more than one application to run at the same time. It also supported windows that you could tile (meaning that you could view many windows at the same time). Windows also had full mouse support, which made this operating system easier to use than DOS, which primarily used a keyboard for user input. Version 1.0 of Windows supported the Intel 80286 processor.

Windows 2.0 was the second version of Windows to be released and introduced icons to the Windows desktop. It also supported Program Information Files (PIFs), which allowed users to better configure Windows. An enhanced version of Windows 2.0, called Windows/386, added support for the Intel 80386 processor.

The first commonly accepted version of Windows was Windows 3.0, which introduced the File Manager and the Program Manager utilities. It changed the way memory was managed and offered the option to run Windows in Enhanced mode. In Enhanced mode, you could use part of the hard drive as virtual RAM. This feature offers better performance, and, in fact, Windows 95 and 98 and Windows NT include this concept as the page file.

The last versions of Windows to be released were Windows 3.1 and 3.11. Windows 3.1 added better graphical and multimedia support. This version of Windows had better error protection and supported Object Linking and Embedding (OLE). OLE is a technology that lets applications work together and share information. Windows 3.11, also known as Windows for Workgroups, added support for networking capabilities.

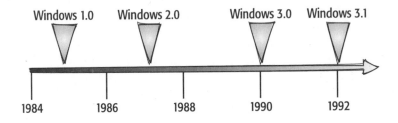

Understanding Windows 95

Released in the fall of 1995, the Windows 95 operating system is Microsoft's 32-bit operating system that supports preemptive multitasking of applications.

Windows 95 acts as its own operating system and does not run on top of DOS. It is also compatible with DOS and Windows 16-bit applications. In addition, Windows 95 provides backward compatibility with existing hardware devices.

The key features added to Windows 95 over the Windows 3.x platform include

- A new, more intuitive user interface
- Introduction of the Explorer utility, which makes file management easier for users
- More dynamic configuration that does not require as much user interaction
- A more reliable and robust operating system
- Plug-and-Play capability, which means that hardware is much easier to install
- Support for long filenames up to 255 characters, instead of eight characters with a three-character extension for DOS and Windows 3.x
- Built-in fax and electronic messaging capabilities
- Access to the Internet through Internet Explorer
- Improved memory management
- Better support for video and CDs

TIP

With Windows 95 and Windows 98, you have the option of purchasing the Microsoft Plus! package (for Windows 95 or Windows 98). The Plus! pack offers additional enhancements for the Windows platform. A popular feature of the Plus! package allows you to customize your Desktop through additional sounds, mouse pointers, screen savers, color schemes, and wallpaper. Additional games also ship with the Plus! pack.

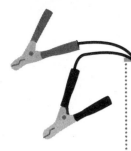

Understanding Windows 98

Released in 1998, Windows 98 follows Windows 95 as the next evolutionary step in desktop software. The Windows 98 operating system improves the Windows 95 interface in several ways.

◆ The Desktop has been simplified to reduce clutter. You can access most options via the Start button.

◆ Windows 98 focuses on Internet integration. With Windows 98, you can use an Active Desktop. The Active Desktop functions like a Web page. With Active Desktop, you can view Web pages and link documents. By right-clicking the Desktop, you can turn the View as Web Page option off. Windows 98 provides an Internet Connection Wizard to help you connect to the Internet. FrontPage Express is also bundled with Windows 98 to help you create your own Web pages.

◆ Windows 98 includes utilities to make your computer perform better and to optimize resources. The Tune-Up Wizard optimizes your hard drive, scans disks for errors, deletes unnecessary or unused files, and optimizes performance for applications.

◆ An Update Wizard checks the Microsoft Web site for system and driver updates for your computer.

◆ The Help system is more comprehensive by connecting you to Microsoft's online help through the Internet.

◆ There are better accessibility features for users with disabilities.

◆ The multimedia capabilities have been improved to take advantage of new hardware standards.

◆ Multiple display support is provided for users who want to view multiple monitors (connected to a single computer) simultaneously.

NOTE

The next major version of Windows will be Windows 2000, which merges the Windows 9x platform with the Windows NT platform.

Understanding Windows NT Workstation

Windows NT Workstation provides the highest level of performance and security of the Microsoft desktop operating systems. It is easy to use and uses the same desktop interface as Windows 95. With NT Workstation, you get these features:

- ◆ A 32-bit multitasking operating system.

- ◆ The ability to support Intel and Alpha platforms.

- ◆ Support for multiple processors and preemptive multitasking.

- ◆ Internet support as a client through Internet Explorer and support as a server through Peer Web Services, which allows the workstation to act as a World Wide Web (WWW) and File Transfer Protocol (FTP) server. With the WWW service, users can access Web documents from the Web server. With the FTP service, users can transfer files to and from the Web server.

- ◆ High security through mandatory logon and the NT File System (NTFS), which lets you apply security to users and groups, and view resource access through auditing. NTFS is covered in more detail in Chapter 17, *NT Resources: File and Print Management.*

- ◆ Support for applications written to work with DOS, 16-bit Windows, 32-bit Windows, OS/2, and POSIX.

- ◆ Full networking capabilities.

- ◆ Network services by sharing file and print resources, and support for up to 10 concurrent client connections.

- ◆ Support for up to 4GB of RAM and 16EB of disk space.

- ◆ One of the most reliable operating systems, because applications run in separate memory spaces, preventing a failed application from affecting other applications.

NOTE

The main disadvantages of NT Workstation over Windows 95 and Windows 98 are that it has greater hardware requirements and is not as backward compatible. It is also a more expensive software platform.

Understanding Unix and Linux

Unix is another popular operating system. It is a 32-bit, multiuser, multitasking operating system. Linux is a derivative of the Unix operating system.

Unix

Unix was first developed in the late 1960s as an operating system for mainframe computers. The original development team consisted of Bell Telephone Laboratories, General Electric, and MIT. During the early development of Unix, many universities were able to obtain the Unix operating system by signing nondisclosure agreements that allowed them to use the software for educational purposes. Computer science students gained experience with Unix and contributed to its development.

Today two major versions of Unix exist:

- ◆ Unix System Laboratories (USL) System V UNIX
- ◆ Berkeley Software Distribution (BSD) Unix

In addition, there are many other flavors of Unix, but most are derivatives of the versions listed above.

The differences in Unix include different versions produced as commercial software, shareware, and freeware. Each variation has its own features and offers different levels of hardware and software support. Different versions of Unix are also designed to support specific hardware platforms—for example, Intel, RISC, Alpha, and PowerPC.

Because the Unix operating system was designed for engineers by engineers, it has a stigma of being difficult to use and is not as user-friendly as other operating systems. A standard for Unix called X Windows provides a graphical interface for Unix, making it easier to use.

NOTE

You may notice that Unix is referred to as both *Unix* and *UNIX*. When *Unix* is used, it specifies Unix in general. When *UNIX* is used, it specifies the Unix used by USL and is a trademark name.

Linux

Linux is a popular version of Unix, because it is offered as **shareware** and **freeware**. Many of the utilities included with the distribution of Linux are also freeware or shareware. This makes Linux an attractive offer for people who want a powerful desktop operating system at little or no cost.

Linux supports all of the major software that is produced for the Unix operating system. It is mostly compatible with System V, BSD, and POSIX. It is primarily designed to run on an Intel platform but has been ported to other platforms.

The advantages of Linux include the following:

- ✧ It is a true 32-bit operating system.
- ✧ It supports preemptive multitasking, which is the ability to run more than one application or task at one time.
- ✧ It offers the ability to support multiple users and includes networking capabilities.
- ✧ Security features are included, such as login/password, and directory and file permissions.
- ✧ The distribution software includes development software.

The disadvantages of Linux include the following:

- ✧ The software that ships with Linux tends to be very basic.
- ✧ Text-based versions of Linux are difficult to learn. X Windows Linux is easier to use.
- ✧ Linux accesses hardware directly, as opposed to going through a software interface, so hardware problems are more common under Linux.

NOTE

POSIX is a standard designed to standardize Unix implementations.

Shareware
Software that is generally available for trial use. If you like the software, you should pay a small licensing fee.

Freeware
Software that you can use without payment.

Understanding OS/2

OS/2 was originally going to be the second-generation operating system, thus the name OS/2. The development of OS/2 was originally a joint project between Microsoft and IBM. The partnership did not last long. Microsoft decided to leave the partnership and concentrate on the Windows 3.1 and LAN Manager operating systems.

The first version of OS/2 to support 32-bit processing was OS/2 2. This operating system was more powerful than Windows 3.1. However, the hardware requirements were considerably higher to run OS/2, and most users stayed with Windows 3.x. IBM now owns and supports OS/2.

OS/2 version 3 was renamed OS/2 Warp. This version of OS/2 required a 386 processor but in reality needed a 486 processor. This version was very graphical in nature and provided true multitasking capabilities.

The current version of OS/2 is OS/2 Warp 4. This product is marketed as a desktop operating system and as a server through OS/2 Warp Server. While OS/2 is very functional, it has never enjoyed high market share.

The features of OS/2 Warp 4 include the following:

❖ The operating system is scalable and can support up to 64 processors.

❖ OS/2 is easy to use and provides a stable operating system platform.

❖ It is compatible with DOS, Windows, and OS/2 applications.

❖ There is heterogeneous support for existing industry standards.

❖ OS/2 can run on platforms ranging from laptop computers to mainframe computers.

❖ There is full Internet support, including TCP/IP, Telnet, and FTP. There is also full support for Java applications.

Dual Booting between OSes

You may want your computer to run more than one operating system. This is especially useful in test environments where you want to maximize equipment usage. For example, you have one computer at home, and you want to learn Windows NT Workstation and Linux. You cannot run both operating systems concurrently, but you can load both operating systems on the same computer and, depending on how you start your computer, access one operating system or the other.

Tips for Creating a Dual-Boot Configuration

You might want to install each operating system on its own disk partition to avoid any conflicts.

Check the vendor documentation to see if there are any recommendations for configuring the dual boot. For example, if you will boot between DOS and NT, you should install DOS first.

Windows 98 can dual-boot with

- ◆ MS-DOS 5.x or later
- ◆ Windows 3.x
- ◆ Windows NT

Dual boot is not supported for Windows 95 and Windows 98.

Windows NT can dual-boot with

- ◆ MS-DOS
- ◆ Windows 3.x
- ◆ Windows 95
- ◆ Windows 98
- ◆ OS/2
- ◆ POSIX

Review Questions

1. What does DOS stand for?

   _____

2. What does GUI stand for?

   _____

3. Which version of Windows 3.*x* first supported networking capabilities?

   _____

4. True or false: Windows 3.*x* acted as its own operating system and did not require DOS to be installed.

5. True or false: OS/2 is a nonproprietary operating system, and the source code is freely available to developers.

6. Which Microsoft operating system offers the highest performance and security options for desktop computers?

   _____

7. Which Microsoft desktop operating system first offered 32-bit processing?

   _____

8. What was the last version of DOS to be released?

   _____

9. Which Microsoft desktop operating system first offered the Active Desktop?

   _____

10. Which Unix service offers a graphical interface?

    _____

11. What are the two major versions of Unix?

_____

_____

12. What is the popular shareware/freeware version of Unix called?

_____

13. True or false: You can dual-boot between Windows 95 and Windows 98.

14. What is the Unix standard called that standardizes Unix implementations?

_____

Chapter

6

DOS 101: DOS Basics Every MCSE Should Know

I f you are new to the computer field, you may be asking yourself why you need to know DOS. At times DOS may be the
fastest and easiest way to complete a specific task. You don't
need to be a DOS expert, but you should know the basics. This
chapter will cover the important commands and DOS concepts that
every MCSE should know. They include

 DOS disk organization

 The directory structure

 Commands to manipulate the directory structure

 The DIR command

 Commands to manipulate files

 The COPY and MOVE commands

 The ATTRIB command

 Commands to manipulate date and time

 The DOSKEY command and the F3 key

Organizing Your Disks

As they say on television, this isn't something you want to try at home just for the heck of it. **Disk partitioning** and organization is usually set up for you when you buy a new computer. But if the setup doesn't meet your needs or you want to start from scratch, these DOS commands are useful:

❖ FDISK

❖ FORMAT

❖ SYS

Assume that you need this configuration:

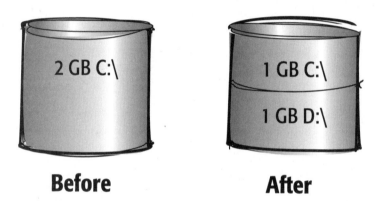

Disk Partitioning

The process of creating logical disks from a physical disk. You can then format the logical disks and use them to store data.

Originally the drive is configured as a single 2GB partition. You need to logically divide the hard drive into two partitions, each 1GB in size. You can do this with the DOS commands shown here:

Command	Purpose
FDISK	The FDISK command defines primary and extended partitions, deletes partitions, marks the active partition, and displays partition information.
FORMAT	The FORMAT command initializes a hard drive or floppy disk. Formatting a disk erases any previously stored data and prepares it as a new media on which you can store data.
SYS	The SYS command copies the DOS system files and the command interpreter to the floppy or hard disk that you specify. You need these files to boot DOS.

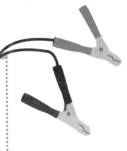

Partitioning Your Hard Drive

FDISK is the program you use to configure and display information about your physical disk(s). With FDISK you can

- ◇ Create DOS partitions or **logical drives**.
- ◇ Set the **active partition**.
- ◇ Delete partitions or logical drives.
- ◇ Display partition information.
- ◇ Change the current fixed drive. (This option appears only if you have more than one physical drive.)

To access the FDISK program, type **FDISK** at the command prompt. Here is the main FDISK screen:

```
                              FDISK Options

Current fixed disk drive: 1

Choose one of the following:

1. Create DOS partition or Logical DOS Drive
2. Set active partition
3. Delete partition or Logical DOS Drive
4. Display partition information


Enter choice: [1]




Press Esc to exit FDISK
```

Logical Drives

Are based on how you partition your physical drive. Each is assigned a logical drive letter; for example, C:\.

Active Partition

Has the operating system files that your computer needs to load the operating system. The active partition is usually located on the C:\ drive.

Dual Booting

Having two or more operating systems on your computer. At system startup, you can select which operating system you will boot.

TIP

If you want to **dual-boot** between DOS and NT, you should install DOS before installing NT.

WARNING

If you use FDISK to partition your disk and you use the option to make the entire physical disk the logical disk, it is automatically configured as the active partition. The active partition is used to boot your operating system. If you do not use the entire physical disk, you must manually specify which partition will be the active partition.

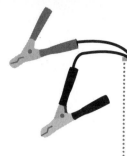

Formatting Your Disks

The FORMAT command prepares a floppy or hard disk for use with DOS. When you **format** a disk, you create a File Allocation Table (FAT) that keeps track of where data is stored on the disk. Formatting also creates the tracks and sectors on the disk that are needed to store data.

Format

The process of initializing a floppy disk or logical drive and preparing it so that you can store data on it.

 TEST IT OUT

Try these steps to format a floppy disk:

1. Access a DOS prompt.

2. Place a floppy disk in the floppy drive.

3. From the command prompt, type **A:**

4. At the A:\> prompt, type **FORMAT A:**

    You will see this line:

        Insert new diskette for drive A: and press ENTER when ready...

5. Press Enter. The disk will be formatted.

6. The next line will prompt you for a volume label with this text:

        Volume label (11 characters, ENTER for none)?

    At this point you can type a label for the disk. Type whatever label you want to identify the disk.

7. The last question will prompt

        Format another (Y/N)?

    Press N for no.

There are two important FORMAT options you should know. These are:

FORMAT Option	Description
FORMAT /S	Copies the DOS system files to the disk so that it can be bootable.
FORMAT /Q	Performs a quick format.

 **WARNING**

Formatting a disk erases any data that was previously stored on the disk. Use the FORMAT command with extreme caution.

Using SYS to Prepare a Boot Disk

The SYS command copies the DOS system files to a disk so that it can be bootable. When you SYS a drive, these files are copied to the disk:

- ♦ COMMAND.COM
- ♦ IO.SYS (This is a hidden file.)
- ♦ MSDOS.SYS (This is a hidden file.)

TEST IT OUT

On the previous page, you formatted a blank floppy disk. In this exercise, you will use the SYS command to copy the DOS system files to the floppy.

1. To access the floppy, type **A:**

2. From A:\>, type **DIR**

3. You will see this message:

       File not found

4. Type **C:**

5. From C:\>, type **SYS A:**

6. You will see this message:

       System transferred

7. Type **DIR A:**

8. You will see that COMMAND.COM is stored on the floppy disk.

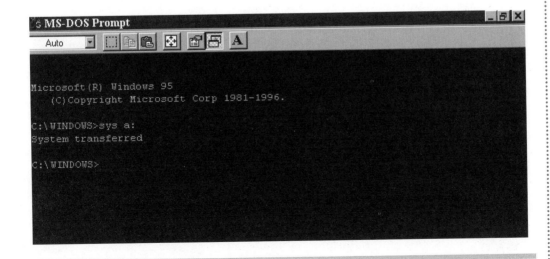

Creating a Directory Structure

The directory structure is like a filing cabinet for your hard disk. It allows you to logically group files with similar functions. When creating your directory structure, a little planning can really pay off in terms of productivity. Think of your filing system. If you just threw everything into one drawer, it would be difficult to find a specific document. The same thing would occur on your computer if you put all your documents into one directory or folder.

Consider the logic of this sample directory structure. In this case, there are separate folders for applications and data. Each application and data folder is further divided with subdirectories to organize data even better.

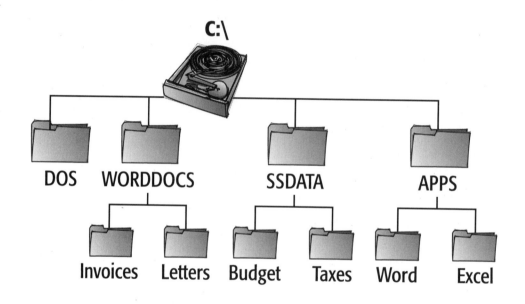

NOTE

The directory structure is like an upside-down tree. It is hierarchical in nature.

NOTE

You can use the terms *folder* and *directory* interchangeably.

Manipulating the Directory Structure

There are several commands you can use to manipulate the directory structure. The tasks that are based on these commands include

- ❖ Listing the contents of directories and subdirectories
- ❖ Creating new directories
- ❖ Removing directories you no longer need
- ❖ Navigating the directory structure
- ❖ Deleting entire branches of your directory structure

This table summarizes the most useful commands for directory structure manipulation.

Command	Description	Example
DIR	Directory shows the directory listing, including files and subdirectories of the current directory.	C:\>DIR
MD	Make Directory creates a new directory or subdirectory.	C:\>MD WORDDOCS
RD	Remove Directory removes a directory or subdirectory.	C:\>RD WORDDOCS
CD	Change Directory traverses the directory structure.	C:\>CD WORDDOCS
DELTREE	Delete Tree deletes the specified directory as well as the files and subdirectories within the directory.	C:\>DELTREE WORDDOCS

TIP

With any DOS command, you can type /? at the command prompt for additional information and syntax options.

Listing Directories, Subdirectories, and Files

To show a listing of all the files and directories on your logical drive, you use the DIR command. This is perhaps the most commonly used DOS command.

When you issue the DIR command, you see this information about the files and directories that are relative (in the same folder) to the path you are in:

- ◆ Directory name or filename and extension
- ◆ Date and time you created the directory or file
- ◆ Size of the file in bytes
- ◆ Total number of files and the space used by the folder as well as the remaining disk space in bytes

```
Command Prompt                                            _ □ ×

D:\test>dir
 Volume in drive D has no label.
 Volume Serial Number is 3896-802D

 Directory of D:\test

11/04/98  04:50p       <DIR>          .
11/04/98  04:50p       <DIR>          ..
11/04/98  04:47p       <DIR>          apps
11/04/98  04:46p       <DIR>          data
11/04/98  04:47p       <DIR>          exceldocs
11/04/98  04:50p                    9 joke.txt
11/04/98  04:49p                   13 textfile
11/04/98  04:46p       <DIR>          worddocs
               8 File(s)            22 bytes
                          3,434,388,480 bytes free

D:\test>_
```

Use **DIR /P** if you have more than one screen of information and you want to pause between screens.

Use **DIR /W** to see a wide list format.

Use **DIR /S** to see all of the information within the subdirectories of the directory.

Creating and Deleting Directories

To define your directory structure, you use commands to create and delete directories.

To create a directory, you use the MD, or Make Directory, command.

To delete a directory, you use the RD, or Remove Directory, command.

NOTE

Before you can remove a directory with the RD command, the directory must be empty of all files and subdirectories.

TEST IT OUT

1. From the C:\> prompt, type **MD WORDDOCS**

   Press Enter.

2. From the C:\> prompt, type **MD SSDATA**

   Press Enter.

3. From the C:\> prompt, type **MD TEST**

   Press Enter.

4. From the C:\> prompt, type **DIR**

   Press Enter. You should see a directory listing that includes the directories you just created.

5. From the C:\> prompt, type **RD TEST**

   Press Enter.

6. From the C:\> prompt, type **DIR**

   Press Enter. You should now see a directory listing that includes the directories you just created, with the exception of the TEST directory.

TIP

To delete directories that contain files or subdirectories, you should use the DELTREE command.

Using the Change Directory Command

You use the CD command to change directories. This allows you to move fairly easily from one branch of the DOS hierarchical structure to another. Assume you have this directory structure:

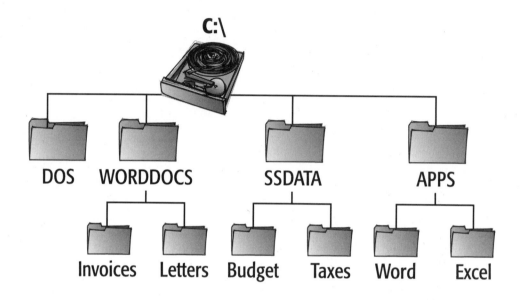

To move down a level—in this case, to the WORDDOCS directory—type this command from the C:\> prompt:

```
CD WORDDOCS
```

To move back up one level of the directory structure, use the CD.. command like this:

```
C:\WORDDOCS>CD..
```

If you are more than one level down the tree and want to return to the root drive, you specify CD\ like this:

```
C:\WORDDOCS\LETTERS>CD\
```

TEST IT OUT

To test directory manipulation, you will complete the directory structure shown on the previous page. If you completed Test It Out on page 99, skip steps 1–2.

1. If you are not already at the C:\> prompt, type **C:** at the command prompt and press Enter.

2. From C:\> type **MD WORDDOCS**

    Press Enter. Type **MD SSDATA**

    Press Enter.

3. From C:\> type **MD DOS**

    Press Enter. Type **MD APPS**

    Press Enter.

4. Change to the WORDDOCS directory by typing **CD WORDDOCS**

5. From C:\>WORDDOCS> type **MD INVOICES**

    Press Enter. Type **MD LETTERS**

    Press Enter.

6. To return to the root level of C:\, from C:\>WORDDOCS> type **CD**

7. Take the steps needed to complete the directory structure shown on the previous page.

NOTE

Make sure that when using DOS, you use a backslash (\) when specifying a path or using the CD\ command. The forward slash (/) is associated with file options.

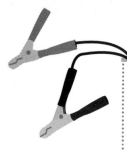

Manipulating Files

Once you have set up your directory structure, the next step is to place files into directories. Most of your files will be programs and application files, or data created from the application programs.

In addition, sometimes you will need to create or edit a text file.

For example:

- ◆ You need to create a file called LOGON.BAT that specifies that ABC.EXE should run whenever the .bat file is called.

- ◆ You have a file called ACCT.TXT that needs to be renamed ACCT99.TXT.

- ◆ You have a text file that needs to be updated through editing.

These commands are useful in file manipulation:

Command	Description
COPY CON	COPY CON lets you create a text file by capturing whatever data is written to the console (screen). This command works well for quickly creating text files.
TYPE	The TYPE command displays the contents of a text file.
EDIT	The EDIT command brings up a text editor that has a user-friendly interface for creating and editing text files.
DEL	With the DEL command, you can delete files that you no longer need.
REN	The REN, or RENAME, command renames a file.

These commands are covered in greater detail in the following subsections.

NOTE

If you are creating a small text file, COPY CON can be a time-saver. If you need to create a larger text file or edit an existing text file, use EDIT. If you are trying to create a text-only file, these commands are better than a word processor, which includes formatting information within the file.

Creating a Text File from the Console

You can use the COPY CON command to very quickly create a text file from the command prompt. This command is useful if you need to create a small file. The COPY CON command uses this syntax:

COPY CON *filename* Press Enter.

Type the text that the file will contain. Press Enter.

Press the Ctrl key and the Z key at the same time. This will appear as ^Z.

For example:

COPY CON TEST.TXT Press Enter.

This is a sample text file.

^Z. Press Enter.

The system will verify with a message saying, "1 file(s) copied."

```
Command Prompt                                          _ □ ✕
Microsoft(R) Windows NT(TM)
(C) Copyright 1985-1996 Microsoft Corp.

D:\>copy con test.txt
This is a sample text file^Z
        1 file(s) copied.

D:\>
```

TEST IT OUT

1. From the C:\WORDDOCS directory, type **COPY CON DATA.TXT**
   Press Enter.

2. Type any data you want.

3. Press the Ctrl key and the Z key at the same time. Press Enter.

4. You should receive the following verification:

   "1 file(s) copied."

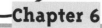
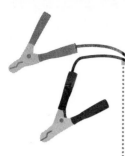

Displaying the Contents of a File

To display the contents of a text file, you can use the TYPE command. TYPE redirects the data within the file to the console screen. TYPE uses this syntax:

```
TYPE drive letter:\directory\filename
```

Or if the prompt is on the correct drive and directory where the file exists, type:

```
TYPE filename
```

ASCII Files

Contain data from the ASCII character set. ASCII is a standard for encoding letters and numbers into the ones and zeros that the computer understands.

NOTE

You usually use the TYPE command to see the contents of a text or **ASCII file.** It does not produce readable information if you use it to display the contents of an executable file or a file generated by most applications.

TIP

If the text file you are trying to read contains more than a screen of information, the TYPE command can be somewhat frustrating, because it simply scrolls through the file at what seems like light speed. If this is the case, consider reading the file with the EDIT command.

Editing Text Documents

One of the easiest ways of editing and creating text files is through the use of the EDIT program. EDIT is the DOS user-friendly editing program.

You can call up the EDIT program and then specify which file to open for editing, or you can call up the path and filename you wish to edit when you invoke the EDIT program.

TEST IT OUT

1. From the C:\> prompt, type **EDIT**.

2. The EDIT program will start.

3. Type whatever you want the text file to say.

4. Press the Alt key and the F key to access File ➤ Save.

5. The Save As dialog box will appear. Save the file as SAMPLE.TXT, and select the OK button.

6. Press the Alt key and the F key to access File ➤ Exit.

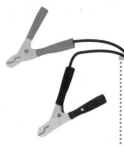

Deleting a File

Once you no longer need a file, you can delete it with the DEL command. DEL is an easy command to use. The syntax is

    DEL *drive letter:directory\filename*

Or if you are already in the directory in which the file exists, the syntax is

    DEL *filename*

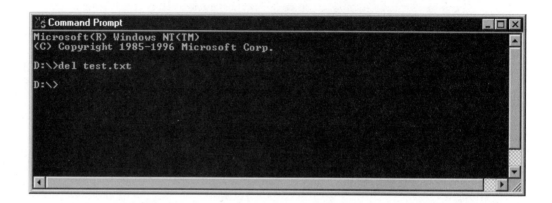

```
Command Prompt                                          _ □ ✕
Microsoft(R) Windows NT(TM)
(C) Copyright 1985-1996 Microsoft Corp.

D:\>del test.txt

D:\>
```

NOTE

Third-party DOS utilities—for example, Norton Utilities—can sometimes recover files that have been deleted.

NOTE

If you delete a file in Windows 95 or Windows 98, you can recover the deleted file from the Recycle Bin.

WARNING

Do not delete files if you are unsure of what they are. They might be program, application, or configuration files you need.

Renaming a File

Use the REN command to rename files, using this syntax:

REN *oldname newname*

For example, assume that you have a file called ACCT.TXT that you want to
rename ACCT99.TXT. You would use this command:

 TEST IT OUT

In this exercise you will create, rename, and then delete a file.

1. At the root of C:\, create a text file, using EDIT or COPY CON, called
   OLD.TXT.

2. At the C:\> prompt, type **REN OLD.TXT NEW.TXT**.

3. Use the DIR command to verify that your file has been renamed.

4. At the C:\> prompt, type **DEL NEW.TXT**.

5. Use the DIR command to verify that your file has been deleted.

Using the DOS Wildcards

DOS uses wildcard characters to represent specific letters or numbers as a variable. This is useful when you are looking for a series of files or you want to perform an action on many files at the same time.

The * (asterisk) wildcard represents any number of characters that you are looking for.

The ? (question mark) wildcard represents a single character or number. You can use multiple ? wildcards in a single query. This wildcard is not as commonly used as *.

Assume you have this structure:

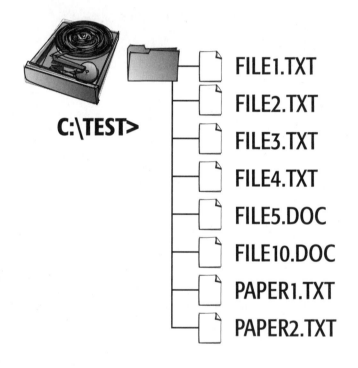

C:\TEST>

FILE1.TXT
FILE2.TXT
FILE3.TXT
FILE4.TXT
FILE5.DOC
FILE10.DOC
PAPER1.TXT
PAPER2.TXT

TEST IT OUT

1. Create the directory structure and files that were shown on the previous page. Refer to page 105 for help on creating the DOS directory structure and page 100 for help on creating the text files.

2. Access the C:\TEST directory and type the commands listed in the following steps in bold.

3. **DIR *.TXT**

   You should see FILE1.TXT, FILE2.TXT, FILE3.TXT, FILE4.TXT, PAPER1.TXT, and PAPER2.TXT.

4. **DIR *.DOC**

   You should see FILE5.DOC and FILE10.DOC.

5. **DIR FILE?.***

   Notice that FILE10.DOC does not show up, because the ? wildcard indicates only a single placeholder.

6. **DIR P*.TXT**

   You should see PAPER1.TXT and PAPER2.TXT.

7. **REN F*.DOC F*.TXT**

   Type **DIR *.DOC** to see if any .doc files remain.

8. **DEL P*.***

   Type **DIR P*.*** to see if any of the files beginning with *P* remain.

NOTE

As you can see, wildcards make DOS management a lot easier and more efficient than managing files on an individual basis.

Copying and Moving Files

If you do not like the location of your files or you want to rearrange your file structure, you can use the COPY and MOVE commands.

The COPY command copies the file(s) from the source directory to the destination directory. A copy of the file then exists in both the source and destination directories.

The MOVE command moves the file(s) from the source directory to the destination directory. The file then exists only in the destination directory.

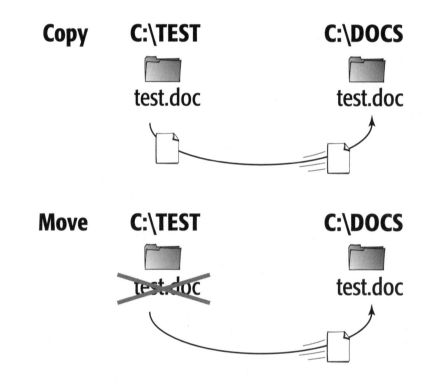

The syntax for performing a COPY is

    COPY source path and file destination path and file

For example:

    COPY C:\TEST\TEST.DOC C:\DOCS\TEST.DOC

The syntax for performing a MOVE is

    MOVE source path and file destination path and file

For example:

    MOVE C:\TEST\TEST.DOC C:\DOCS\TEST.DOC

TEST IT OUT

1. On C:\TEST, create files TEST1.DOC, TEST2.DOC, TEST3.DOC, and MOVEME.DOC. Create the directory C:\DOCS.

2. From C:\TEST, type **COPY TEST1.DOC C:\DOCS**.

3. Do a DIR on C:\TEST and C:\DOCS. Does TEST1.DOC exist in both directories?

4. **MOVE MOVEME.DOC C:\DOCS**

5. Do a DIR on C:\TEST and C:\DOCS. Does MOVEME.DOC exist in both directories?

6. **COPY T*.DOC C:\DOCS**

Working with Filenames

There are different types of file systems. You can use FAT, which allows the names of files and folders to be only 8 characters with a 3-character extension. With Windows 95 and Windows 98, you can use FAT32. FAT32 allows the names of your files and folders to be up to 255 characters long with multiple spaces and periods.

If your filename or folder name is longer than 8 characters, it is automatically assigned a short name. Sometimes the short names are not very intuitive. For this reason, it's a good idea to try to keep your filenames fairly short.

You should also note that DOS utilities do not understand spaces in filenames. If you have a filename with spaces or a long filename, use quotation marks around the filename when using DOS utilities.

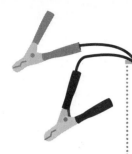

Setting File Attributes

Each DOS file has attributes that define the properties of the file. You can manipulate these attributes by using the ATTRIB command. The DOS attributes are

❖ Read-only

❖ Archive

❖ System

❖ Hidden

Incremental Backup

Backs up only the files that have the archive bit set. After the incremental backup is complete, the archive bit is cleared. If you have to restore data, you must use your last full backup and each incremental backup that you have done.

Differential Backup

Backs up all files with the archive bit set. The archive bit is not cleared when you complete the backup. If you have to restore data, you need only your last full backup and your last differential tape.

Attribute	Description
Read-only	If you set the read-only attribute, you cannot modify or delete a file unless you remove the read-only attribute. This attribute safeguards a file from being accidentally modified or deleted.
Archive	You use the archive attribute with backups. A file that is marked with the archive attribute indicates that it is a new file or a file that has been modified since the last backup. Use this attribute when you perform **incremental** or **differential backups**.
System	The system attribute indicates that the file is a system or program file. To manipulate any of the other attributes, you must first remove the system attribute. This attribute implies that a file is read-only.
Hidden	The hidden attribute keeps a file from being listed through the DIR command or from being accidentally deleted.

The syntax for the ATTRIB command is

```
ATTRIB drive letter:\directory\file [+attribute|-attribute]
```

❖ +*attribute* indicates that you are applying an attribute.

❖ −*attribute* indicates that you are removing an attribute.

Assume that you have a directory, D:\TEST, and that the directory contains a file called TEST.DOC.

To see the file attributes, you would type **ATTRIB TEST.DOC**.

Note that the archive bit is set. This attribute is applied to all new files.

To apply the hidden attribute to the TEST.DOC file, you would type **ATTRIB TEST.DOC +H**.

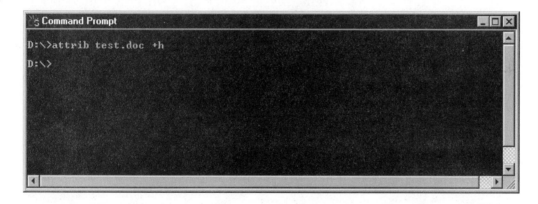

To remove the hidden attribute from the TEST.DOC file, you would type **ATTRIB TEST.DOC -H**.

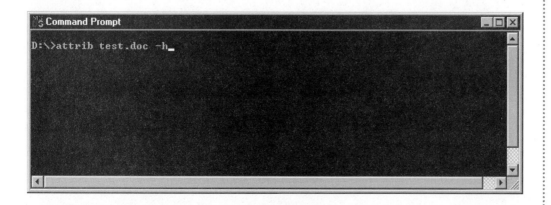

Manipulating the Time and Date

You can see what time your computer is set to or you can change the time with the TIME command. Use the DATE command to display the date or change the date.

To see the time, type **TIME** at the command prompt. To change the time, type this at the command prompt:

TIME *time*

```
Command Prompt                                          _ □ ×

D:\>time
The current time is: 17:30:27.71
Enter the new time:

D:\>
```

To see the date, type **DATE** at the command prompt. To change the date, type this at the command prompt:

DATE *date*

```
Command Prompt                                          _ □ ×

D:\>date
The current date is: Wed 11/04/1998
Enter the new date: (mm-dd-yy)

D:\>
```

Using Some Timesavers

Two options that can help you save time are the F3 key and the DOSKEY command.

The F3 key displays the last command that you typed.

The DOSKEY command keeps a history of the commands that you have typed. You access it by pressing the up-arrow (↑) and down-arrow keys (↓) on the keypad.

TEST IT OUT

1. From a DOS prompt, type **DOSKEY**

   Press Enter. You will see the message "DOSKey installed" displayed.

2. Type several of the commands that you have learned about in this chapter.

3. Press the F3 key to display the last command that you typed.

4. Use the up-arrow (↑) and down-arrow (↓) keys on the keypad to view the history of the commands you have issued since you invoked DOSKEY.

5. From a DOS prompt, type **TIME**

   If the time is correct, press Enter. If not, type in the correct time and press Enter.

6. From a DOS prompt, type **DATE**

   If the date is correct, press Enter. If not, type in the correct date and press Enter.

TIP

Another useful DOS command is CLS. When you type CLS at the command prompt, it clears the current screen and leaves you with a DOS prompt.

Using the DOS Configuration Files

If you boot your computer using DOS as your operating system, DOS looks for two files during start-up. These files customize the configuration for your computer:

- ◆ CONFIG.SYS
- ◆ AUTOEXEC.BAT

The main function of the CONFIG.SYS file is to configure system hardware and set the computer's environment parameters.

The main function of the AUTOEXEC.BAT file is as a batch file that runs every time you start your computer. Common items in AUTOEXEC.BAT include programs that should run every time you start your computer and customization commands for your computer.

CONFIG.SYS

CONFIG.SYS configures your computer's memory management, DOS configuration, and hardware configuration. Here is a sample CONFIG.SYS file with commonly included items:

```
DEVICE=C:\DOS\HIMEM.SYS
DEVICE=C:\DOS\EMM386.EXE NOEMS
DOS=HIGH,UMB
FILES=20
BUFFERS=30
DEVICE=C:\FUJITSU\ATAPI.SYS /D:OEMCD001
```

The first three lines represent memory management configuration options. DOS does not use the same memory management scheme as Windows 95, Windows 98, and Windows NT. This means that without some type of memory manager, your computer can recognize only 640K of memory. For more information on memory management, you should consult a DOS manual.

The FILES=x option specifies how many file handles DOS can keep open at any time. *File handles* is a fancy way of saying open files. You should limit the number of open files to conserve memory.

The BUFFERS=x option specifies how many buffers (which is memory) will be available to store information in RAM as opposed to disk. This is called caching. Requests that are handled through cache as opposed to disk are processed much more quickly.

The last line in the sample file represents a CD-ROM driver that is being loaded. Any other device drivers that need to be loaded would also be included.

AUTOEXEC.BAT

The AUTOEXEC.BAT file is a special batch file that loads or configures, without user input, any options that should be configured each time you start the computer or any programs that should be run. Here is a sample AUTOEXEC.BAT file:

```
PATH=C:\DOS;C:\WINDOWS;C:\WORD
C:\DOS\SMARTDRV
STARTNET
```

In this sample file, the first line sets up the path the computer will use. PATH tells the computer that it should look for executable files in other folders. For example, if you were in the C:\DOCS folder and you tried to execute WORD.EXE, the system would look in memory, then in the current folder, then in the folders listed in the PATH statement.

The second line specifies that the SMARTDRV program should be loaded. SMARTDRV improves system performance by taking advantage of the computer's memory.

The final line calls another batch file, STARTNET, which loads network services.

Review Questions

Terms to Know
- ❏ Disk Partitioning
- ❏ Logical Drive
- ❏ Active Partition
- ❏ Dual Booting
- ❏ Format
- ❏ ASCII files
- ❏ Incremental Backup
- ❏ Differential Backup
- ❏ DOS Wildcard
- ❏ AUTOEXEC.BAT
- ❏ CONFIG.SYS

1. Which DOS command do you use to erase data on a floppy disk or hard drive so that the media is initialized and you can now store new data?

   _____

2. Which DOS command do you use to copy the DOS system files and the command interpreter to the floppy disk or hard disk that you specify?

   _____

3. List four options that are presented (and represent the main tasks) when you use the FDISK command.

   _____

   _____

   _____

   _____

4. Which FORMAT option performs a quick format?

   _____

5. Which FORMAT option also transfers the system files as the format is performed?

   _____

6. List three files that are transferred when you SYS a drive.

   _____

   _____

   _____

7. If you were at C:\TEST\DOCS and you wanted to go to the root of C:\, which command would you use?

_____

Acronyms to Know
❑ DOS
❑ ASCII File

8. Which command would you use from the C:\ prompt to delete the TEST.DOC file that is located in C:\TEST?

_____

9. What is the purpose of the COPY CON command?

_____

10. Which command do you use to change the contents of an existing text file?

    A. CHANGE

    B. EDIT

    C. COPY CON

    D. EDITOR

11. True or false: You use the DISPLAY command to see the contents of a text file.

12. You use the _____ command to rename a file.

13. What is the difference between the DOS * and ? wildcards?

_____

14. What is the difference between the DOS COPY and MOVE commands?

_____

15. What are the command and syntax to specify that TEST.DOC should have a hidden attribute?

_____

Chapter

7

Graphical Interface:
Windows Basics

In this chapter, you will learn the fundamentals of the graphical interface through Windows 95. As far as the fundamentals go, Windows 95 and Windows 98 are very similar, so if you are using Windows 98, this information still applies.

This chapter covers these topics:

 The Windows 95 opening screen

 The Start button

 My Computer

 Network Neighborhood

 The Recycle Bin

 Customizing your Desktop

 Creating shortcuts

 Using Wizards

 Windows Explorer

 Internet Explorer

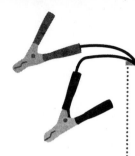

A Quick Introduction

The Windows 95 operating system was designed with these goals:

◇ It had to be easy for people to use.

◇ It needed to be a usable system so that people could perform the tasks they needed to do.

◇ The platform needed to be stable so that users would feel comfortable storing data on the computer.

◇ The interface needed to be visually pleasing so that users would like Windows 95 and feel comfortable using it.

Windows 95 uses a Graphical User Interface (GUI), which makes it easier for users than the old DOS command-line environment. Windows 95 is designed to be a *discoverable* operating system, which means that users can intuitively complete necessary tasks.

In order to use Windows 95, you should first become proficient with a mouse. In Windows 95, using the left mouse button, sometimes called the primary mouse button, allows you to complete basic tasks, such as launching a program or opening a folder. The right mouse button, or secondary mouse button, allows you to perform more advanced tasks, such as changing a file's properties.

In this chapter, you will learn about some Windows 95 basics, which include

◇ Common terms

◇ Using the Desktop

◇ Using the Taskbar

◇ Using common features in Windows 95

TIP

When introducing new users to a GUI and the mouse, letting them play the game Solitaire allows them to feel more comfortable with a mouse. The only drawback is that most users become addicted to this game!

Brand-new users of Windows 95 should first learn

- ❖ To use the mouse. You do this through practice.

- ❖ To be able to open windows to easily complete common tasks. To open windows, you simply point and click what you want to open. To access items, you use a single click. You typically open items with a double click.

Once a window is open, you will see something similar to this screen.

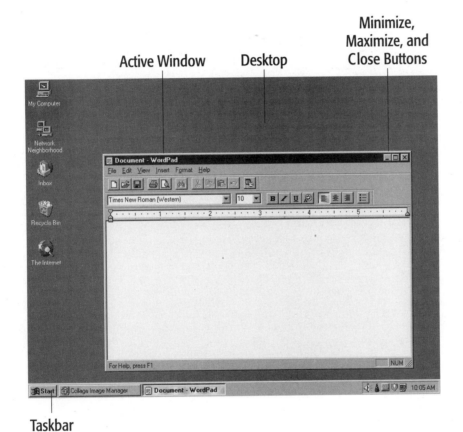

Minimize, Maximize, and Close Buttons

Active Window   Desktop

Taskbar

There are several things you can learn from this screen. The active window (the one you are using) has three buttons in the upper right-hand corner.

- ❖ The _ button minimizes the window. The application is still running while minimized, and you can easily reaccess it by clicking the item on the Taskbar.

- ❖ The ❑ button maximizes the window so that it takes up the entire screen.

- ❖ The X button closes the application.

You can see which applications are running by looking at the Taskbar. By clicking a button on the Taskbar, you specify the active window.

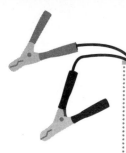

Using the Windows 95 Opening Screen

When you start Windows 95, you see a screen similar to this.

From this screen, there are options for

- ◆ The Taskbar and Start button
- ◆ My Computer
- ◆ Network Neighborhood
- ◆ The Inbox
- ◆ The Recycle Bin
- ◆ The Internet

Graphical Interface: Windows Basics

This table provides an overview of each of the Windows 95 opening screen options.

Option	Description
The Taskbar and Start button	The bottom of the screen contains the Start button and Taskbar. From the Start button, you can run applications, access documents, configure your computer, and shut down your computer. The Taskbar shows you which applications are running and allows you to switch between applications.
My Computer	My Computer shows you what disk resources your computer is using and allows you to access folders and files. You can also access the Control Panel, Printers, and Dial-Up Networking folders through My Computer.
Network Neighborhood	If your computer is attached to a network, Network Neighborhood allows you to browse the network for computers that offer network resources.
Inbox	The Inbox icon allows you to use Microsoft Exchange for e-mail and fax services.
Recycle Bin	The Recycle Bin allows you to store files that you have deleted so that you can undelete them if necessary.
The Internet	The Internet initially calls up the Internet Connection Wizard, which allows you to connect to the Internet. After Internet connection has been configured, it calls up the Internet Explorer program.

The main topics will be covered in more detail throughout this chapter.

NOTE

If your computer came with Windows 95 already installed, your Desktop may contain differences because of customization from the hardware manufacturer. As you use Windows 95, you can customize the Desktop to reflect your personal preferences.

Using the Start Button

You can do almost anything from the Windows 95 Start button. When you click Start, you see this menu.

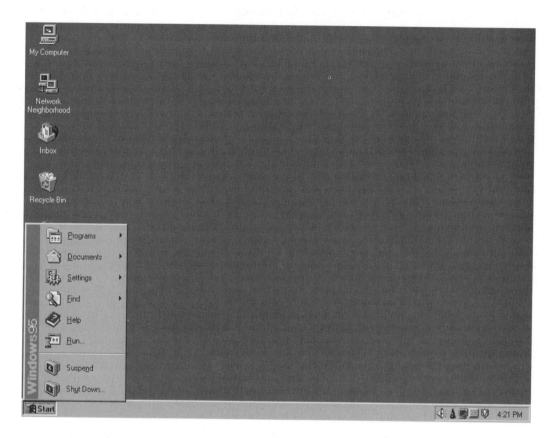

From Start, you can access

- ◆ Programs
- ◆ Documents
- ◆ Settings
- ◆ Find
- ◆ Help
- ◆ Run
- ◆ Suspend
- ◆ Shut Down

Each of these options is covered in more detail in the following subsections.

Programs

When you point to the Programs menu within the Start button, you see all of the programs that have been installed on your computer.

Within the menu pointed to by Programs, the top options display a folder icon with an arrow to the right of the screen. This arrow indicates that there is a cascading menu for this option. The bottom options without folders and arrows indicate that this is the application and there is no cascading menu.

This screen shows an example of the Programs menu.

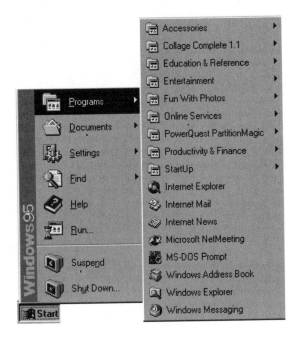

Documents

The Documents menu allows you to quickly access the last 15 documents that you worked with.

Settings

Through the Settings menu, you can configure the Control Panel, Printers, and the Taskbar.

Control Panel

Through Control Panel, you configure most options for your computer. This includes hardware, software, and network settings, among other items.

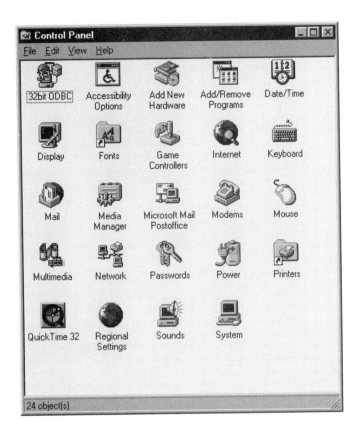

Printers

You can use the Printers folder to create, delete, and manage printers.

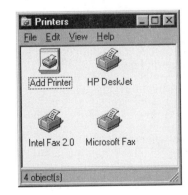

Taskbar

Through the Taskbar Properties dialog box, you can configure how Windows displays the Taskbar, and you can add, remove, or configure which items appear on the Start menu.

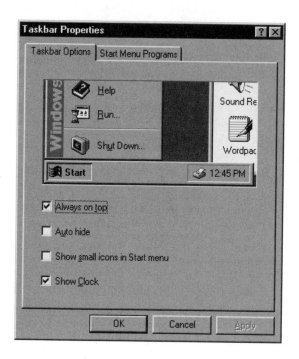

Find

Find allows you to search files and folders based on name, location, or when the file was created or modified. If you use Find for advanced searches, you can search for files based on file type, text within the file, and the size of the file.

If your computer has been added to a network, you can also search for computer names through the Find option.

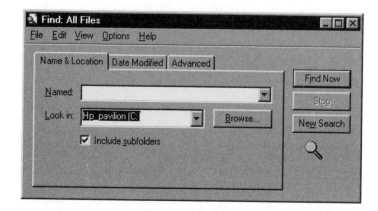

Help

Help provides online help for Windows 95. Help is arranged so that you can read it like a book using the Contents tab, or you can use the Index and Find tabs to search for information on a specific topic.

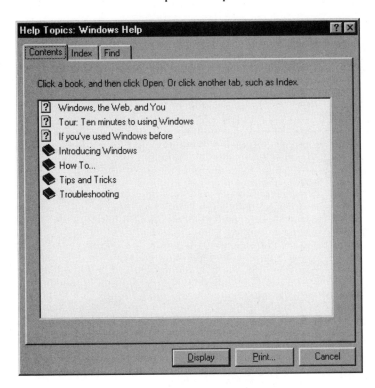

TEST IT OUT

If you are not familiar with Windows 95, the Help Topics dialog box provides a tutorial to help get you up and running.

1. Select Start ➤ Help.

2. From the Help Topics dialog box, click the icon that reads, "? Tour: Ten minutes to using Windows."

3. The tour will load; follow the directions. The entire tour should take about 10 minutes.

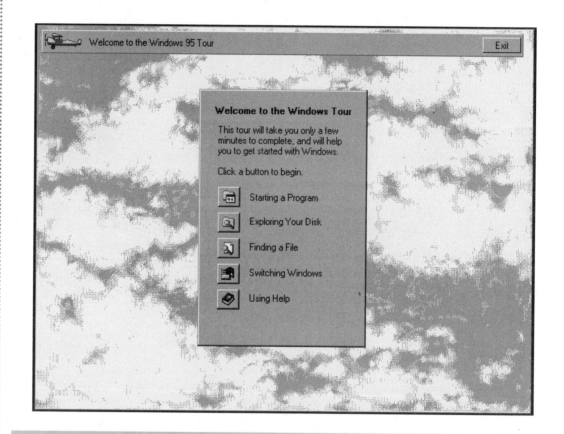

Run

The Run option allows you to run command-line utilities or to launch applications. Within Run, you can browse for files by using the Browse button.

Using Run can be a faster way of launching programs or a way to launch programs that are not defined as part of the Start menu.

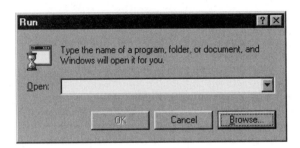

Suspend

If your computer hardware supports the Suspend option, this allows you to suspend operation, which conserves power. When you return your computer to a running state, you should be able to start at the point where you suspended your computer.

Shut Down

The Shut Down menu offers four choices, as defined in this table.

Shut Down Option	Description
Shut down the computer	Saves any changes that you have made and prepares the computer to be turned off.
Restart the computer	Saves any changes that you have made and restarts your computer. Many changes to your computer require you to restart the computer for the changes to be effective.
Restart the computer in MS-DOS mode	Allows you to restart the computer in DOS mode, which may be needed to run specific DOS applications.
Close all programs and log on as a different user	Disconnects any network connections and closes all of your programs so that another user can log on.

Accessing My Computer

The My Computer icon on the Desktop contains information about your computer's installed drives and allows you to configure your computer. From My Computer, you see icons that represent

- ◆ Floppy drives
- ◆ Logical drives (the logical disk partitions you have created, like C:)
- ◆ CD-ROM drives
- ◆ The Control Panel folder
- ◆ The Printers folder
- ◆ The Dial-Up Networking folder

The contents of the My Computer window depends on your computer's configuration. Here is a sample screen.

NOTE

The Control Panel and Printers folders are the same items you see under Start ➢ Settings. They also exist in other locations. Making these items more accessible enables users to easily access them.

By left-clicking an item within My Computer, you can get more information. For example, if you click a floppy drive, logical drive, or CD-ROM drive, you see the contents of those drives, which includes folders and files.

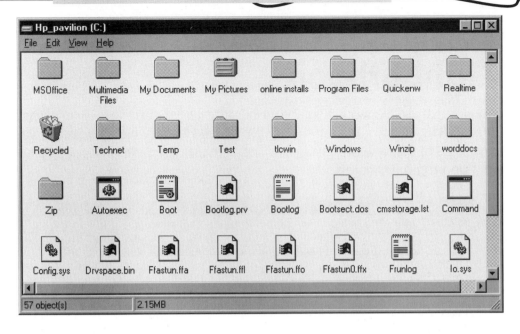

Defragmentation
The process of reorganizing your files on a disk so that they are arranged contiguously. This process better uses disk space.

By right-clicking an item within My Computer, you get a menu that allows you to open the item, explore the item, find information within the item, scan for viruses, format the drive, create a shortcut for the item, and use the Properties option.

If you choose to see Properties, you can get detailed information about capacity and use tools that manage disk drives, such as error checking, backup, and **defragmentation**.

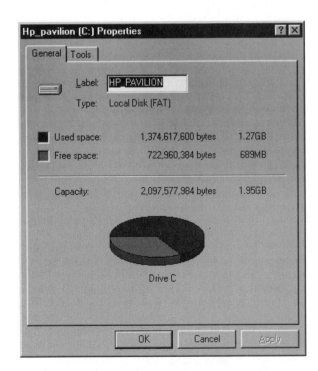

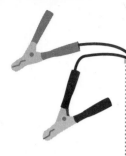

Accessing Network Neighborhood

Network Drive

A mapping to a network path that appears to the user as a drive letter. You access it the same way you access a local drive.

You typically use Network Neighborhood only if your computer is connected to a network. By clicking the left mouse button on Network Neighborhood, you can see all of the network resources. They are arranged hierarchically by network and computer name.

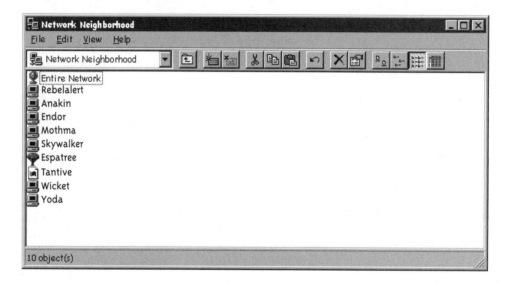

If you right-click the Network Neighborhood icon, you can

- ◇ Find computers on the network
- ◇ Map **network drives**
- ◇ Disconnect network drives
- ◇ Create a new shortcut
- ◇ Rename the icon
- ◇ See network properties, which brings up Control Panel ➢ Network

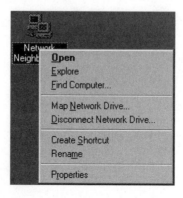

Using the Recycle Bin

If you've ever thrown anything away and then pulled it out of the trash, you already know how the Recycle Bin works. When you delete files, they are placed in the Recycle Bin. You recover the files by removing them from the Recycle Bin and specifying the destination of the files.

When you open the Recycle Bin, you see

- ◆ The name of the files that you deleted
- ◆ The original path the files existed in
- ◆ The date and time you deleted the files
- ◆ The type of the files
- ◆ The size of the files

If you click the File menu within the Recycle Bin, you can restore files, empty the Recycle Bin (at which point, you cannot recover those files), delete specific files, and see file properties.

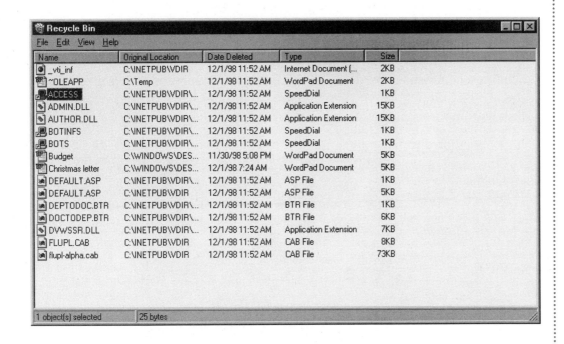

Name	Original Location	Date Deleted	Type	Size
_vti_inf	C:\INETPUB\VDIR	12/1/98 11:52 AM	Internet Document (...	2KB
~OLEAPP	C:\Temp	12/1/98 11:52 AM	WordPad Document	2KB
ACCESS	C:\INETPUB\VDIR\...	12/1/98 11:52 AM	SpeedDial	1KB
ADMIN.DLL	C:\INETPUB\VDIR\...	12/1/98 11:52 AM	Application Extension	15KB
AUTHOR.DLL	C:\INETPUB\VDIR\...	12/1/98 11:52 AM	Application Extension	15KB
BOTINFS	C:\INETPUB\VDIR\...	12/1/98 11:52 AM	SpeedDial	1KB
BOTS	C:\INETPUB\VDIR\...	12/1/98 11:52 AM	SpeedDial	1KB
Budget	C:\WINDOWS\DES...	11/30/98 5:08 PM	WordPad Document	5KB
Christmas letter	C:\WINDOWS\DES...	12/1/98 7:24 AM	WordPad Document	5KB
DEFAULT.ASP	C:\INETPUB\VDIR\...	12/1/98 11:52 AM	ASP File	1KB
DEFAULT.ASP	C:\INETPUB\VDIR	12/1/98 11:52 AM	ASP File	5KB
DEPTODOC.BTR	C:\INETPUB\VDIR\...	12/1/98 11:52 AM	BTR File	1KB
DOCTODEP.BTR	C:\INETPUB\VDIR\...	12/1/98 11:52 AM	BTR File	6KB
DVWSSR.DLL	C:\INETPUB\VDIR\...	12/1/98 11:52 AM	Application Extension	7KB
FLUPL.CAB	C:\INETPUB\VDIR	12/1/98 11:52 AM	CAB File	8KB
flupl-alpha.cab	C:\INETPUB\VDIR	12/1/98 11:52 AM	CAB File	73KB

1 object(s) selected   25 bytes

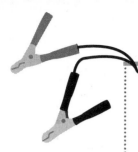

Customizing Your Desktop

The ability to customize your Desktop allows you to personalize it to suit your needs and personality. This section will show you how to change the appearance of items on your Desktop, which include

❖ The background colors your computer uses

❖ Whether or not you use a screen saver

❖ Other aspects of the Desktop appearance

To easily change your computer's Desktop appearance, right-click an open space on the Desktop, as shown in this screen.

When you choose Properties, you see a Display Properties dialog box similar to this screen (the options you see depend on the hardware and software that is installed on your computer).

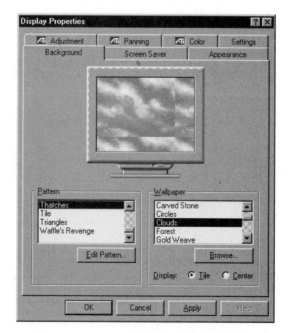

Background

The Background tab allows you to choose the wallpaper that your computer uses. There are many choices available through the Windows 95 software. In addition, you can add your own pictures that can serve as your background.

If you don't choose wallpaper, you can choose a pattern to give your desktop color some texture.

Screen Saver

The Screen Saver tab allows you to specify that your computer should use a screen saver if there is no activity for a specified amount of time. The original intent of the screen saver was to prevent screen damage. Through this tab, you can configure

- ❖ Which screen saver to use
- ❖ Whether you need a password to disable the screen saver
- ❖ The amount of time without any activity before the screen saver starts

Appearance

The Appearance tab specifies the color scheme that the Desktop, windows, and icons use. Here you can be really creative and assign each item its own color, size, and font.

WARNING

Through Properties, there is a tab called Settings. You should not modify the settings without understanding what you are doing. You should also test any changed settings before they are applied. If you configure settings incorrectly, you may not be able to see your display properly or you may not be able to see it at all.

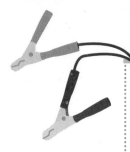

Creating Shortcuts

Shortcuts point to any object within Windows 95. You can place shortcuts on the Windows Desktop or within any folder. The main advantage of shortcuts is that they allow you to quickly access resources.

Some examples include applications, files, folders, disk drives, and Control Panel items. You can recognize a shortcut by the small arrow in the left-hand corner of the icon.

To Create a Shortcut

To create a shortcut, you select an object and from the File menu choose Create Shortcut. You can also create shortcuts by right-clicking an object and choosing Create Shortcut. After you create a shortcut, you can drag and drop it anywhere you like (for example, the Desktop).

You can also create a shortcut by right-clicking the Desktop and choosing New ≻ Shortcut. This brings up the Create Shortcut dialog box.

 TEST IT OUT

1. From an empty place on the desktop, right-click and choose New ≻ Shortcut.

2. In the Command Line box, type **Write**.

3. In the Select a Name for the Shortcut dialog box, click the Finish button to accept the name Write.

4. The shortcut will appear on your Desktop.

Using Wizards

Wizards are built into Windows 95 as an easy way for you to perform specific tasks. For example, if you want to install a printer in Windows 95, you open the Printers folder and click Add Printer. This starts the Printer Wizard, which asks you a series of questions that allow you to install the printer.

Some of the Windows 95 Wizards are

- The Printer Wizard
- The Internet Connection Wizard
- The PC Card Wizard
- The Add New Hardware Wizard
- The Dial-Up Networking Setup Wizard

This is the beginning screen for the Add Printer Wizard.

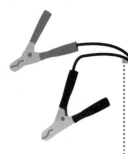

Using Windows Explorer

Windows Explorer accesses and manages folders and files. From Explorer, you can manage

- ◆ Floppy drives
- ◆ Logical drives
- ◆ CD-ROM drives
- ◆ The Control Panel
- ◆ The Printers folder
- ◆ The Dial-Up Networking folder
- ◆ Network Neighborhood
- ◆ The Recycle Bin

Within Explorer, the left side of the dialog box shows you a hierarchical structure of all objects. The right side of the dialog box shows you details on what you have highlighted on the left side of the screen.

Through Explorer, you can manage objects by adding, deleting, or manipulating the properties of an object. You can also use drag-and-drop to copy or move objects within Explorer.

If your computer is connected to a network, you can also map network drives, which allows you to access network resources in the same way you access a local resource on your C: drive. You can also disconnect network drives.

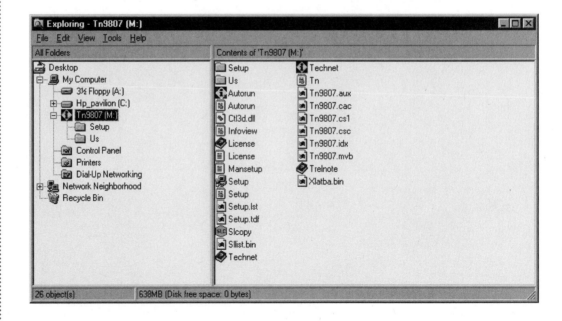

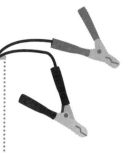

Using Internet Explorer

Internet Explorer is Microsoft's Web client software. You can access Internet Explorer by clicking The Internet on the Windows 95 Desktop. In order to take full advantage of Internet Explorer, you should first connect to the Internet.

This screen is an example of using Internet Explorer.

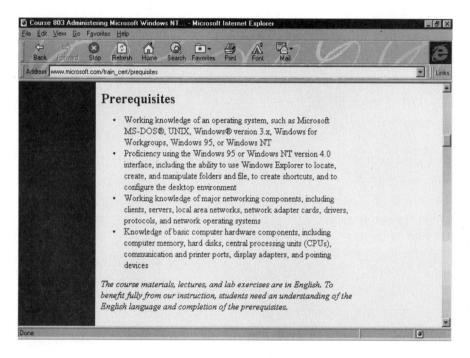

URL
A Uniform Resource Locator. It is the way addresses are accessed on the Internet.

From the main screen you can specify the **URL,** or address, that you want to access. You can also use these buttons:

- ◆ The Back and Forward buttons allow you to go back and forth between pages you have already accessed.

- ◆ The Stop button halts the loading of a page, which is useful when you have a slow connection and the page you are trying to access is very large.

- ◆ The Refresh button allows you to reload the current page you are viewing.

- ◆ The Home button takes you back to your default home page.

- ◆ The Search button connects you to Internet search engines.

- ◆ Favorites allows you to bookmark your favorite sites and pages so that you can quickly access them.

- ◆ With the Print button, you can get a hard copy of the page you are viewing.

- ◆ The Font button allows you to customize font information.

- ◆ The Mail button allows you to compose e-mail, read e-mail, and access news services.

Review Questions

1. Which item on the Windows Desktop allows you to recover files that you have deleted?

   _____

2. Which item on the Windows Desktop allows you to access Internet resources?

   _____

3. Which item on the Windows Desktop allows you to access disk resources?

   _____

4. Which item on the Windows Desktop allows you to see which applications are running?

   _____

5. Which item on the Windows Desktop provides a starting point for accessing almost anything in Windows 95?

   _____

6. You go to Start ➢ _____ to see the last documents that you accessed.

7. Through Start ➢ _____, you can access Control Panel, Printers, and Taskbar Properties.

8. Through Start ➢ _____, you can access online help information.

9. What are the four Shut Down options?

   _____

   _____

   _____

   _____

10. True or false: You can access the Control Panel program from My Computer, Windows Explorer, and Start ➤ Settings.

11. What is the advantage of using shortcuts?

_____

12. What is a Wizard?

_____

13. What is the difference between the Windows Explorer and the Internet Explorer?

_____

14. Which mouse button do you click on an object if you want to configure advanced properties?

_____

Chapter
8

Beyond OS:
Common
Applications

Previous chapters have given an overview of the hardware and operating systems that computers use. This chapter will focus on applications, which are software designed to perform specific tasks.

When choosing an application, you should note that applications are platform specific. That means that an application written to run on a Macintosh will not run on an Intel computer running Windows 95.

A few of the most common applications that people use the computer for on a regular basis are outlined in this chapter.

 Word processors

 Spreadsheets

 Databases

 E-mail

 Desktop publishing

 Internet browsers

 Virus scanners

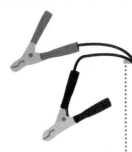

Using Word Processors

Word processing applications have to do with creating, editing, and printing documents via an electronic medium rather than by handwriting or using a typewriter. Rather than slave over a typewriter and deal with correction fluid and stuck keys, people now use word processing applications such as Corel WordPerfect or Microsoft Word to write their personal or business correspondence, résumés, papers, etc.

A basic word processing program provides the ability to type in text and then save it as a text file. It gives you the option to edit the work you've done and to print it. A basic word processing program should also perform word wrap for you. Unlike using a typewriter, where you must manually set the end of each line and reset it to the next, word wrap takes whatever does not fit on a single line and automatically continues it on the next line.

This screen shot shows the Microsoft Word application.

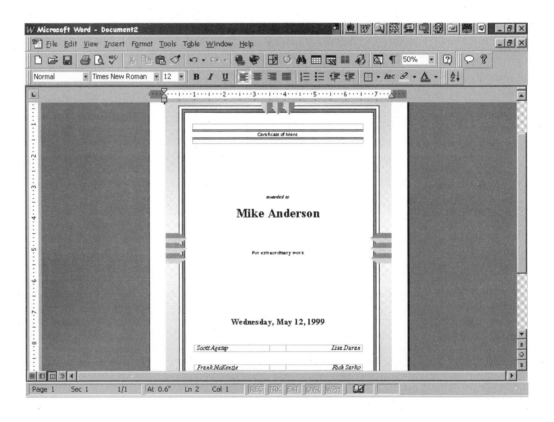

Features of Word Processors

A full-featured word processing program not only contains the basic abilities listed previously, such as the ability to edit, print, save, and have word wrap, but also includes these options:

Fonts and sizing   You often can choose from a variety of fonts, which are different styles of uniform sets of text that you also have the option of sizing.

Search and replace   You can input a word or phrase, and the word processor searches for and replaces it with text you specify. For example, search for *NT 5* and replace with *Windows 2000*.

Move and copy   You can move or copy words or blocks of text within the same document or into other documents.

Layout settings   You can center the text and designate the width of the margins and the page.

Headers, footers, and page numbers   You can specify what text goes at the top and bottom of each page. Page numbers are automatically inserted in the header or footer in the format you specify.

Preview and print   You can view the document in **WYSIWYG** format and send the document to a print device.

Spelling, grammar, and thesaurus   You can check your document for spelling and grammatical errors. If a mistake is detected, the word processor will make suggestions. The thesaurus option gives you optional words to use in place of a word you have used.

Templates   You can import a template with predefined text styles.

Common examples of word processors include

- Microsoft Word
- Corel WordPerfect

WYSIWYG
Stands for What You See Is What You Get and is a view within an application that lets you see the final document while you are creating or editing the document.

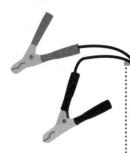

Using Spreadsheets

Spreadsheets are the delight of the accountant and are useful for anyone who needs to keep track of numbers and do analysis. Spreadsheet applications, such as Microsoft Excel and Lotus 1-2-3, are used in such fields as tax accounting, real estate, investment, banking, and many others. They have the ability to track information and do analysis on the data input into them. By extrapolating data, people can do long-term planning and modeling based on the results of spreadsheet calculations and statistical analysis.

Spreadsheet Organization

Spreadsheets follow the format of rows and columns. Spreadsheets appear as a series of cells, which are the boxes at the intersection of a row and a column.

Cells can contain labels, numeric values, and formulas.

- A label is descriptive text; for example, Dec. Sales or Inventory.
- A numeric value is the actual data. For example, under Dec. Sales, the numeric value could be 10,000.
- A formula is a powerful feature within a spreadsheet that allows you to reference other cells by using mathematical calculations. For example, a formula might be Sum Cells A1 to A10.

The real power of a spreadsheet is gained through the calculations based on defined formulas. Whenever you add, delete, or modify data, calculations are automatically made to update cells that have defined formulas based on the cell that you edited. The manpower needed for manual recalculation would be much greater than using the automated spreadsheet formulas. This capability allows number crunchers to play the "what if" game much more easily.

With many spreadsheets, you can display data results in a multitude of forms, either textual or visual. Spreadsheets are capable of creating very visually effective pie charts and bar graphs, colorful and rich in information.

Features of Spreadsheets

Most spreadsheets include these features:

- The ability to chart data for informational purposes, statistical analysis, and trend forecasting

- The option of formatting text and cells with a variety of options, including the width and height of cells; fonts; positioning data within the cell; and any borders, colors, or patterns that will be part of the spreadsheet

- Support for complex formulas based on data within cells

- The ability to import data from other sources, such as other spreadsheets or databases

Common examples of spreadsheets include

- Microsoft Excel

- Lotus 1-2-3

- Borland Quattro Pro

This screen shot shows the Microsoft Excel application.

	Bagel Day	Pickup	Cleanup
3	18-Sep	Davina Baum	Lisa Duran
4	25-Sep	Malka Geffen	Liz Paulus
5	2-Oct	Kate Kaminski	Molly Sharp
6	9-Oct	Laura Arendal	Raquel Baker
7	16-Oct	Emily Wolman	Rebecca Rider
8	23-Oct	Grey Magauran	Robin Kibby
9	30-Oct	Davina Baum	Susan Berge
10	6-Nov	Malka Geffen	Tory McLearn
11	13-Nov	Kate Kaminski	Barbara Gordon
12	20-Nov	Laura Arendal	Blythe Woolston
13	4-Dec	Grey Magauran	Brianne Agatep
14	11-Dec	Emily Wolman	Charlie Mathews
15	18-Dec	Davina Baum	Chris Meredith
16	8-Jan	Malka Geffen	Cyndy Johnsen
17		Kate Kaminski	Dan Schiff
18		Laura Arendal	Dann McDorman
19		Grey Magauran	Dave Nash
20		Emily Wolman	David Zielonka

Using Databases

Databases are collections of data organized so that users can easily add, edit, or access data. Databases can be used for personal use on a desktop computer or can exist as distributed databases throughout a network.

Databases resemble spreadsheets in style and function as a place to store and cross-reference data. They do not perform the complex calculations that spreadsheets do. They do allow more complex search and retrieval of data than spreadsheets.

In business, common uses of databases include inventories, sales tracking, and customer lists. For personal use, you might use a database to track a home inventory or a Christmas card mailing list.

Database Organization

Databases are commonly organized by files, records, and fields.

A file is a collection of records. A record is a complete set of fields, and a field is a single piece of information within a record. An analogy for a file is a telephone book. In this case, a record is an entry within the book for a person or business, and a field is a specific address or phone number.

This graphic shows an example of database organization.

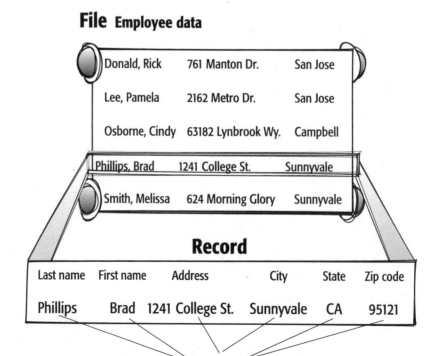

File Employee data

Donald, Rick	761 Manton Dr.	San Jose
Lee, Pamela	2162 Metro Dr.	San Jose
Osborne, Cindy	63182 Lynbrook Wy.	Campbell
Phillips, Brad	1241 College St.	Sunnyvale
Smith, Melissa	624 Morning Glory	Sunnyvale

Record

Last name	First name	Address	City	State	Zip code
Phillips	Brad	1241 College St.	Sunnyvale	CA	95121

Fields

Features of Databases

Most database software (referred to as database management systems) includes these features:

- ◇ The ability to store and organize data.
- ◇ The option of controlling user access. For example, some users may have read access to portions of the database, while other users have write access.
- ◇ The ability to create detailed reports.
- ◇ The ability to query specific information in the database.

The ability to create queries of database information is a powerful feature. The language that creates the query is called query language. A common query language is Structured Query Language (SQL). An example of a query is

```
SELECT ALL WHERE STATE=CA and AGE>21
```

This query would search for all records where the state was California and the age of the user was over 21.

Common examples of database management system software include

- ◇ Microsoft Access
- ◇ Microsoft SQL Server
- ◇ Oracle8i

This screen shot shows the Microsoft Access application.

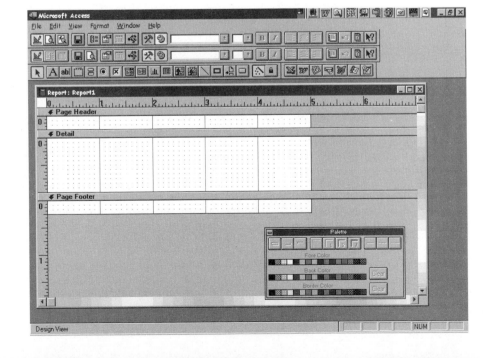

Using E-mail

The word *e-mail* is short for electronic mail. E-mail is probably the most commonly used application. At its heart, e-mail is basically text messages transmitted and stored over communication networks. It has evolved to be able to send varied media images, such as pictures, audio files, and video files.

The main benefit of e-mail is that it is a fast, reliable, and easy way of sending messages to others. You can send an e-mail message to an individual or to many users at once, which is called broadcasting. While broadcasting can be a legitimate use of e-mail—for example, through a personal mailing list—some people take advantage of this option to send unwanted advertising material to masses of other users. This technique is known as spamming.

Local E-mail Systems and Internet Gateways

Traditionally e-mail was confined to a single network. With the common acceptance of the Internet, most networks now use a gateway (which connects two different network environments) to connect to the Internet. This approach allows e-mail to be sent to any place in the world that also has an Internet connection.

To send e-mail on the Internet, you send a message that is addressed to a specific person via their e-mail address.

For example, consider this e-mail address: username@server.com

  ⬧ The part before the @ sign designates the username of the person the mail is being sent to. This name must be unique for the domain in which the user is registered.

  ⬧ The part after the @ is the name of the domain that the mail recipient uses.

Overview of Mail Exchange

When you compose e-mail, it is sent to the local mail server on a local network or at the **Internet Service Provider (ISP)**. The message is sent and perhaps forwarded through a series of gateways. The message arrives at the receiver's local mail server, where it waits until the recipient logs on and retrieves the message.

Internet Service Provider (ISP)

Provides a point of access to the Internet for users who do not need or cannot afford a direct Internet connection.

Common Features of E-mail Applications

Common features of e-mail applications include

- ◆ A text editor for creating text messages
- ◆ The ability to attach files, which may contain more text, pictures, audio, or other information
- ◆ The option to send messages to multiple users and to send a copy of the message to users other than the direct recipient
- ◆ The option to create an address book, which allows you to easily store commonly used names and e-mail addresses
- ◆ A spell-check feature that allows you to check for spelling errors before mail is sent

There are many different options for sending e-mail. Some e-mail programs are included with groupware applications (client-server software that consists of a variety of applications), while other e-mail applications are part of an Internet browser.

This graphic shows a common way of sending e-mail through Microsoft Outlook.

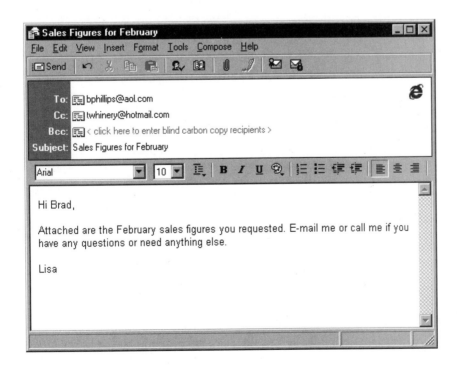

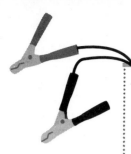

Using Desktop Publishing

From your desk at home, you can now create newsletters, Christmas cards, wedding invitations, and a host of other things. Desktop publishing uses software to produce high-quality page designs.

This popular application integrates word processing and graphics programs. The main difference between a word processor and a desktop publishing application is that the word processor is usually more powerful for creating text-oriented documents, and the desktop publishing software is oriented toward artistic layout of documents. Most desktop publishing applications are not as powerful as graphics programs. For complex graphics, it is best to create the graphic through a graphics program, then import the graphic into the desktop publishing application.

NOTE

As word processors become more complex, the line between word processors and desktop publishing software is beginning to blur.

Traditionally the cost of creating high-quality production documents has been very high. With the widespread use of the personal computer and the high availability of desktop publishing software, it is now affordable for most users. To produce a document, you can design your own document or use predefined style sheets included with most software. Style sheets are usually provided for things such as newsletters, invitations, brochures, and a variety of other documents.

TIP

After you create the document, you can send it to a printer. You should use a printer with 1,270dpi (dots per inch) or 2,540dpi resolution.

Common Features of Desktop Publishing Software

Some of the features of desktop publishing software include

- ❖ Page design
- ❖ Magazine-style columns
- ❖ Page and chapter auto-numbering
- ❖ Snap-into-place alignment services
- ❖ The ability to manage documents through WYSIWYG style

Popular desktop publishing applications include

- ❖ Adobe PageMaker
- ❖ QuarkXPress

This graphic shows an example of a document created with PageMaker.

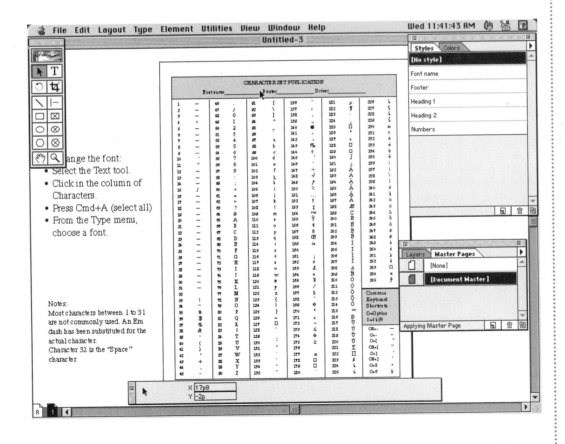

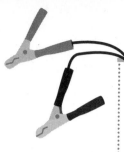

Using Internet Browsers

Internet browsers are the medium through which users navigate the Internet World Wide Web (WWW).

The WWW is a collection of Internet servers that are arranged in a hierarchical structure of domains. Each domain is registered through InterNIC. When a server is installed in the domain, it contains a series of Hypertext Markup Language (HTML) documents. HTML supports text, graphics, audio, and video documents. HTML documents can also contain links to other documents, which are called hyperlinks.

To access an Internet server, you use an Internet browser, which is special software that searches for and displays Web pages. The leading Internet browsers are Netscape Navigator and Microsoft Internet Explorer. Both are graphical browsers and support text and graphical information.

To access a Web site, you type in the Uniform Resource Locator (URL) in the address field of your browser. A URL looks like this:

```
HTTP://www.sybex.com
```

HTTP specifies that you are using the Hypertext Transfer Protocol, and www.sybex.com specifies that you are accessing a domain called sybex.com that is part of the World Wide Web.

TIP

You may notice that different Web sites recommend that you should view them with a specific viewer. For example, you should view microsoft.com with Internet Explorer. If you use Netscape Navigator, some parts of the site are not accessible. For this reason, many users now load both browsers on their computers.

NOTE

If you want to host your own Web site, you can use Web server software such as Microsoft Internet Information Server or Netscape Enterprise Server.

Common Features of Internet Browsers

Most Internet browsers offer these features:

◇ The ability to display graphical information

◇ The option to create a list of favorite sites that you can quickly and easily access

◇ A history file that keeps track of all the sites that you have visited

◇ The option to limit access to sites that indicate they contain material that may be inappropriate for younger users

◇ Secure communication options that encrypt information you send; for example, a credit card number

◇ The ability to print content

◇ File Transfer Protocol (FTP) client software that lets you download files from FTP servers

This graphic shows an example of an Internet Explorer window.

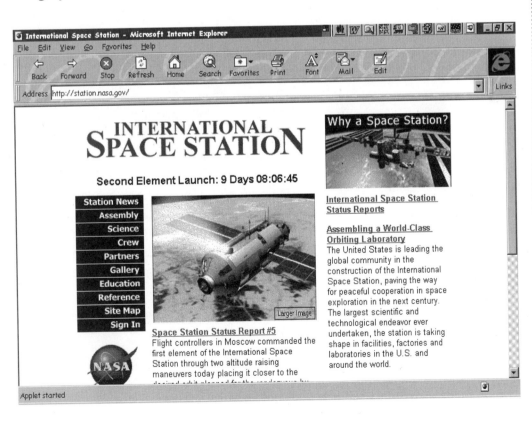

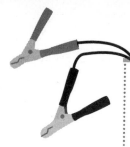

Using Virus Scanners

Viruses are software that affects the way your computer works without your permission or knowledge. Viruses do not exist naturally and are written by programmers with specific agendas.

Viruses have two main characteristics. The first is that they spread without user knowledge and are able to spread from one file to another. This technique is called self-propagation. The second characteristic is that the virus has some action that it performs, which is called the payload. The payload may be something fairly harmless, such as displaying a message, or it might be more malicious, such as erasing your entire hard drive.

This table defines the four major categories of viruses.

Virus Type	Description
File infector virus	This virus type works by attaching itself to or replacing executable files or files with certain types of extensions. When these viruses are in memory, they infect files that you run or access.
Boot sector virus	A boot sector virus infects the boot sector of your hard drive or a bootable floppy disk. When a virus infects the boot sector, it is loaded whenever you boot the computer. This technique allows the virus to reside in memory and then infect files on your hard drive.
Master boot record virus	The master boot record is located on side 0, track 0, sector 1 on every hard disk. This location tells the computer where the bootable partition is so that the computer's operating system can be loaded. Once the master boot record is infected, it loads the virus into memory each time that you start the computer, leaving the virus to infect the hard drive.
Multipartite virus	A multipartite virus is a combination of virus types.

Preventing Viruses

To prevent viruses, you should use virus-scanning software. Virus-scanning software works by scanning your computer's memory and hard disk for any viruses that may be present. If a virus is detected, the program should have an option to remove the virus.

Make sure that you are running the most current version of virus-scanning software. Vendors update their virus definition files on a regular basis to scan for the newest viruses. It is even recommended that you use two virus-scanning programs, because one vendor may have virus definitions not defined by another vendor.

Use virus-scanning software that can dynamically scan for viruses as you open or download files. It's best to catch the virus before it infects your computer.

Download software only from Web sites that are run by commercial organizations. You should still scan the software before you load it on your computer.

Make sure that you scan for viruses before doing backups. This ensures that you have a virus-free version to restore from, should you ever need it.

When choosing virus-scanning software, consider how many viruses the scanner checks for, what options are available for virus cleanup, how automated the scanner is, how easy it is to update the scanner, and how often updates are posted.

Some examples of commonly used virus-scanning software include

- ✧ Norton AntiVirus
- ✧ McAfee VirusScan
- ✧ ThunderBYTE Anti-Virus

Review Questions

- Word Processor
- Spreadsheet
- Database
- E-mail
- Desktop Publishing
- Internet Browser
- Virus
- Virus Scanner

1. Which application type tracks data and allows you to perform complex formulas and calculations based on the data?

   _____

2. Which application do you use to access the Internet and view Web sites?

   _____

3. Which application is the best choice for creating, editing, and printing documents?

   _____

4. Which application do you use to transmit messages over communication networks?

   _____

5. Which application type integrates the qualities of word processing applications and graphics programs?

   _____

6. What are the two most commonly used Internet browsers?

   _____

   _____

7. What does URL stand for?

   _____

8. Databases use files, records, and fields to organize data. Define a file, record, and field.

   _____

   _____

   _____

9. True or false: SQL is a common query language associated with spreadsheets.

10. What does HTML stand for, and what does it specify?

_____

Acronyms to Know
❑ WYSIWYG
❑ ISP

11. What protocol is used with Internet browsers to support file transfer?

_____

12. List four categories of viruses.

_____

_____

_____

_____

13. What is WYSIWYG?

_____

Chapter
9

The Networking Model: OSI Overview

The Open Systems Interconnection (OSI) model provides a framework for understanding networking models. The OSI model is made up of seven layers. In this chapter, you will learn about

 The OSI model in general

 An example of OSI flow

 The Physical layer

 The Data-Link layer

 The Network layer

 The Transport layer

 The Session layer

 The Presentation layer

 The Application layer

 The OSI model and connectivity devices

Understanding OSI Model Basics

The **International Standards Organization (ISO)** specified the OSI model in 1977. The OSI model is not an actual product. It is a theoretical model that defines how networks work from the ground up. By understanding the OSI model, you can apply it to different networking standards. Even though networks are implemented differently, they all use the same core concepts for data transfer. The OSI model defines seven layers and the function of the data flow within each layer.

There are two main advantages to using this type of model:

> ❖ Breaking down a large concept like a network into smaller parts (in this case, layers) makes it easier to understand.

> ❖ Modularizing network functions enables you to easily replace specific technologies without having to replace the entire network.

The smallest unit of data begins at the Application layer. As data moves down the OSI model, more information is added at each layer to allow network communication to take place. At the receiving computer, the layers are stripped off at corresponding peer layers. The process is then reversed for the reply.

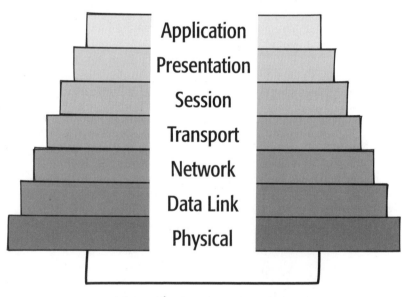

Physical Connection

ISO, or International Standards Organization

An international standards organization dedicated to defining global communication and informational exchange standards. ANSI is the American representative to the ISO.

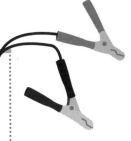

The Networking Model: OSI Overview

The functions of the seven layers of the OSI model are:

OSI Layer	Function	Example of Layer Function
Application	The Application layer supports file and print services. It also manages whether requests are processed locally or remotely.	An example of Application layer services is file and print application services.
Presentation	The Presentation layer formats and translates data.	An ASCII character being converted to symbolic text is an example of Presentation layer services.
Session	The Session layer manages communication sessions between service requesters and service providers. This layer manages communications by establishing, synchronizing, and maintaining the connection between sender and receiver.	Session functions include managing security, logging, and administration.
Transport	The Transport layer is usually associated with reliable end-to-end connections. It is the layer responsible for managing connections, error control, and flow control between sender and receiver.	The TCP and SPX protocols are Transport Layer protocols.
Network	The Network layer is responsible for moving packets over an inter-network so that they can be routed to the correct network segment.	IP and IPX are Network layer protocols. Routers work at the Network layer of the OSI model.
Data-Link	The Data-Link layer includes information about the source and destination hardware addresses of the communicating devices. It also specifies lower-layer flow control and error control.	Devices that use Data-Link layer protocols are network cards and bridges.
Physical	The Physical layer is responsible for the transmission of data over a physical medium.	Cables and physical connections are defined at the Physical layer.

ASCII, or American Standard Code for Information Interchange
A 7-bit coding scheme that translates symbolic characters into the ones and zeros that are stored as data on a computer. Extended ASCII uses an 8-bit coding scheme.

Protocol
A specification that defines a set of rules or procedures that hardware or software uses for communication.

Looking at an Example of OSI Flow

This graphic highlights the flow of data through the OSI model.

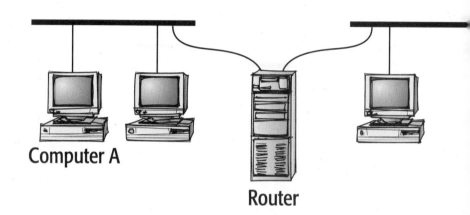

Computer A

Router

Assume you have a file that you want to send from computer A to computer B. There are many things that must occur.

1. You have to create the file using some type of application, like e-mail, that offers file services. The underlying file service is part of the Application layer. This might be a simple message like "hello."

2. The next step is to translate the message into something that the computer will understand. As humans, we see "hello," but the computer wants to see ones and zeros. The Presentation layer translates "hello" into ASCII code, which uses ones and zeros.

3. At the higher levels of communication, a connection, or session, is established and maintained. This connection determines when requests are made so that appropriate responses can be made. Just like human conversations, computer communications are usually a series of requests and responses that must be answered sequentially.

4. If you want to make sure that the connection is reliable (for example, like a telephone conversation as opposed to a letter), you might use connection-oriented services that guarantee reliable delivery.

5. In this example, computer A and computer B are on different network segments. The Network layer routes the packets to the correct network segment by identifying network addresses and calculating the best route the packet should take.

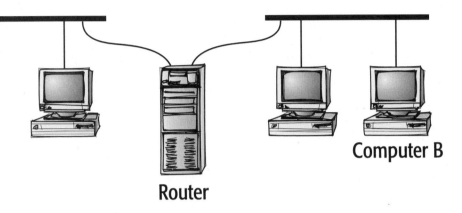

Router   **Computer B**

6. Once data gets to the correct segment, it must be delivered to the correct computer (sometimes called a node) on the segment. Looking at the physical address of the network card accomplishes this. This happens at the Data-Link layer.

7. The only physical connection that actually exists between the two computers is at the Physical layer of the OSI model. This is where all of the cables and network connections come into play.

Here are some mnemonics to help you remember the seven layers.

Layer	Memory Trick Top to Bottom	Memory Trick Bottom to Top
Application	All	Abdul
Presentation	People	Paula
Session	Seem	See
Transport	To	To
Network	Need	Need
Data-Link	Data	Don't
Physical	Processing	People

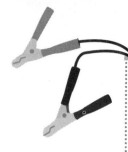

Using the Physical Layer

When you get down to the nitty-gritty details of actually spitting the ones and zeros onto a cable, you are dealing with the Physical layer.

The Physical layer of the OSI model determines:

10BASE2

An Ethernet standard that defines 10Mbps Ethernet using thin coaxial cable in a linear bus topology.

10BASET

An Ethernet standard that defines 100Mbps Ethernet using unshielded twisted-pair cabling in a star topology.

Topology

Can be physical or logical. A physical topology defines the way that a network is physically laid out, and a logical topology defines the way that data is transferred through the network.

❖ The physical network structure you will use. For example, **10BASE2** Ethernet requires a bus **topology**; **10BASET** Ethernet requires a star topology.

❖ The mechanical and electrical specifications of the transmission media that will be used. For example, 10BASE2 Ethernet requires a coaxial cable using the RG-58 standard, which has a 50-ohm resistance.

❖ How data will be encoded and transmitted. There are all kinds of schemes used for encoding data, which specifies how the ones and zeros will be transmitted. For example, Ethernet networks use a scheme called Manchester encoding.

Terminator

Cable   T-connector

NOTE

Topologies, Ethernet, and Token Ring are covered in greater detail in Chapter 11, *Connecting the Computers: Networking Hardware.*

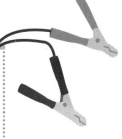

Physical Layer Technologies

The technologies that the Physical layer uses include:

The connection type. Connections can be point-to-point or multipoint. Point-to-point assumes that there are only two devices connected. Multipoint connections mean that three or more devices are connected.

The physical topology. Topologies define the physical layout of the network. Common topologies include star, bus, and ring.

The type of signal. Signals can be analog or digital. Local computer networks use digital signals, and the standard telephone system uses analog signals for transmission.

The ype of bit synchronization. You can send data by asynchronous or synchronous means. Asynchronous communication requires less expensive equipment but is less efficient when transferring large blocks of data. Synchronous equipment is more expensive but provides better efficiency.

The transmission signaling technology. You can use baseband or broadband bandwidth for transmission of data signals. Baseband is associated with digital signals, and broadband is associated with analog signals.

Physical Layer Hardware

Examples of Physical layer hardware are

- ◇ Network cards
- ◇ Network cables
- ◇ Concentrators
- ◇ Hubs
- ◇ Repeaters
- ◇ Modems
- ◇ **ISDN** adapters

> **NOTE**
>
> At the Physical layer, data is referred to as bits.

Synchronous Communication

Transmits data by synchronizing the data signal between the sender and receiver and sending data as a continuous stream. This is the most efficient way of sending large amounts of data but requires expensive equipment between the sender and the receiver.

Asynchronous Communication

Begins transmission of each character with a start bit and ends transmission of each character with a stop bit. This method of communication is not as efficient as synchronous communication but is less expensive.

ISDN

Stands for Integrated Services Digital Network. It is a communication standard that uses a digital transmission channel as opposed to regular phone service, which uses an analog transmission channel.

Using the Data-Link Layer

The Data-Link layer of the OSI model has three primary responsibilities:

◆ Establishing and maintaining the communication channel

◆ Identifying computers on the network segment by physical address

◆ Organizing the data into a logical group called a frame

Establishing and maintaining the communication channel is very low-level work. At the Data-Link layer, it just means confirming that a data channel exists and that it is open. At the Session layer, there is higher-level communication management.

Each computer on the network is identified with a unique physical address, which is called the MAC, or Media Access Control, address. On Ethernet and Token Ring cards, this is a 6-byte hexadecimal address that is burned into an **EPROM** chip on the network card. This address uniquely identifies computers when you send data from a source to a destination.

Data is logically grouped into a frame. A frame logically organizes the bits from the Physical layer. Here is an example of a frame:

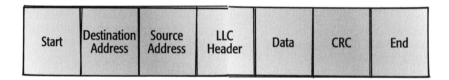

| Start | Destination Address | Source Address | LLC Header | Data | CRC | End |

Frame Description

In the preceding frame:

◆ The start field identifies the beginning of the frame. This might be 10101010.

◆ The destination address is the MAC address of the computer to which the frame is being sent.

◆ The source address is the MAC address of the computer from which the frame is being sent.

◆ The Logical Link Control (LLC) header manages the LLC connection.

◆ The data field contains the data from the upper-layer protocols.

◆ The **CRC** is a **cyclic redundancy check** and is used for low-level error control. For example, is the connection valid?

◆ The end field indicates that this is the last field of the current frame.

EPROM

Stands for Electrical Programmable Read-Only Memory and is a type of computer chip.

CRC, or cyclic redundancy check

A form of error detection that performs a mathematical calculation on data at both the sender's end and the receiver's end to ensure that the data is received reliably.

Sublayers of Data-Link

The Data-Link layer has two sublayers

- ◆ LLC sublayer
- ◆ MAC sublayer

The LLC sublayer defines the flow control, and the MAC sublayer is used for addressing.

Data-Link Layer	LLC (Logical Link Control)
	MAC (Media Access Control)

NOTE

Data is referred to as a frame at the Data-Link layer.

Data-Link Layer Technologies

Examples of Data-Link layer technologies are

- ◆ Bridges
- ◆ Intelligent hubs
- ◆ Network Interface Cards (NICs)

Using the Network Layer

The primary responsibility of the Network layer is to move data over an **internetwork**. This is called routing.

At the Data-Link layer, addressing is physical. At the Network layer, addressing is logical. Each network segment must have a unique network address. This address routes packets to the correct network segment.

The main functions of the Network layer are to:

Internetwork
Two or more network segments that are connected.

♦ Logically define network segments based on unique network addresses.

♦ Determine how packets should be delivered based on current routing information. Route discovery accomplishes this.

♦ Choose the best path for a packet to take as it is being passed through the network.

♦ Pass the packets through the network using some type of switching mechanism.

♦ Provide network-level connection services.

Sending data through the Network layer is considered to be connectionless service. This is like sending a message through the regular mail. You drop the mail in a postbox and assume that it will reach its destination. The Network layer is similar in that you send a packet and assume that it will reach its destination.

Just as with the post office, there is a mechanism for detecting failure. If you don't hear from them, you assume that the letter was received. If you don't put enough postage on the letter or the recipient is not there, the post office returns the letter. Most protocols at the Network layer have similar fault tolerance built in. This means that if a packet is undeliverable, even with connectionless service, you should receive error notification.

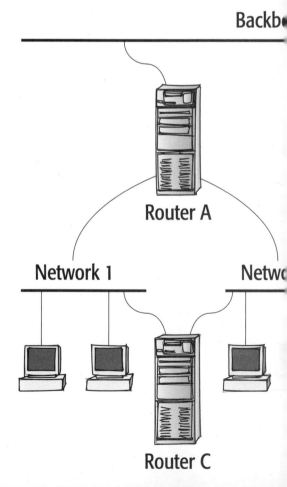

Backb

Router A

Network 1   Netw

Router C

Network Layer Example

In the network example below, assume that you want to send a packet from network segment 1 to network segment 4. These are the steps that occur:

- ⬥ Each router contains route tables that define the best path to all known network segments.

- ⬥ If the packet is routed from router C to router D to router E, the packet will take three hops. Each pass through a router is considered a hop.

- ⬥ If the packet is routed through the backbone, it will pass through router A and router B for a total of two hops.

- ⬥ The routers calculate which path is more efficient. In this case, the packet is routed through the backbone, because it is more efficient.

- ⬥ If one of the backbone routers becomes unavailable, the packet will be rerouted through whichever path is next in efficiency.

NOTE

Data is referred to as datagrams or packets at the Network layer.

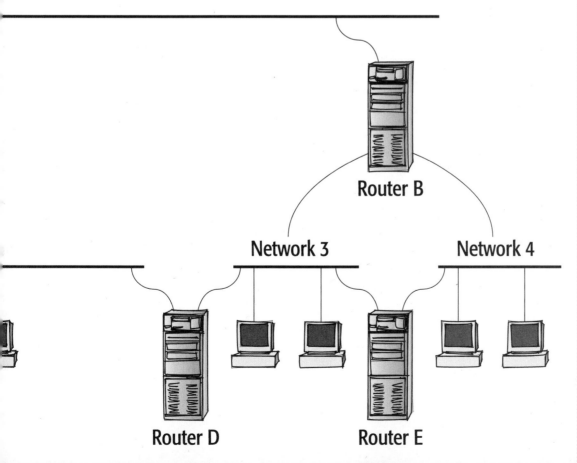

Router B

Network 3   **Network 4**

Router D   **Router E**

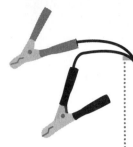

Using the Transport Layer

The Transport layer of the OSI model is associated with reliable delivery. With reliable delivery, the sender and receiver establish a connection, and the receiver acknowledges receipt of the data by sending an acknowledgment packet to the sender. The closest human analogy is transferring information through a telephone conversation as opposed to transferring information through a letter.

Most protocols have two mechanisms for sending data through the Transport layer: connection-oriented transmission and connectionless transmission.

Connection-oriented transmission

- ◇ Is more reliable
- ◇ Involves more overhead, so is slower and less efficient
- ◇ Can provide guaranteed file transfer. For example:

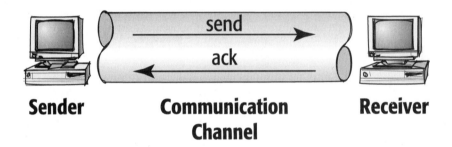

Sender   **Communication Channel**   **Receiver**

Connectionless transmission

- ◇ Is less reliable
- ◇ Involves less overhead, so is faster and more efficient
- ◇ Can provide network broadcasts. For example:

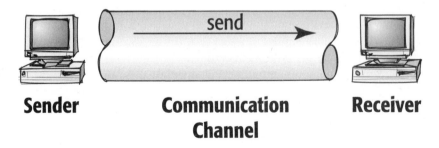

Sender   **Communication Channel**   **Receiver**

Other Transport Layer Functions

If the data that is being sent exceeds the maximum packet length, the Transport layer divides the data into chunks that can then be sent according to the maximum packet length. The Transport layer is responsible for dividing, then reassembling the data chunks into the original data at the receiver's end.

The Transport layer has the ability to perform some error control. If a particular data chunk does not arrive at the receiver's end, this layer can request that the missing data be retransmitted.

This layer of the OSI model also performs some flow control. The sender and receiver determine how much data can be sent before an acknowledgment is required.

NOTE

Data at the Transport layer is referred to as a datagram, segment, or packet.

Network and Transport Layer Technologies

The Network and Transport layers of the OSI model work very closely together. The following protocols are defined at these layers:

- ◆ TCP/IP, the leading industry protocol. With TCP/IP, TCP functions at the Transport layer, and IP functions at the Network layer.

- ◆ IPX/SPX, a proprietary protocol that NetWare uses. With IPX/SPX, IPX functions primarily at the Network layer, and SPX functions at the Transport layer.

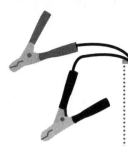

Using the Session Layer

The Session layer of the OSI model is responsible for managing communications between a sender and a receiver. Some of the communication tasks performed at this layer include

◇ Connection establishment

◇ Maintenance of connections

◇ Synchronization of communication

◇ Dialog control

◇ Connection termination

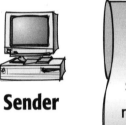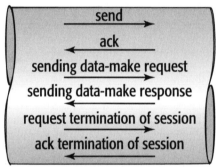

Sender

send

ack

sending data-make request

sending data-make response

request termination of session

ack termination of session

Receiver

Communication Channel

Three main functions of the Session layer are

◇ Creation of the connection

◇ Data transfer and dialog control

◇ Termination of the connection

Creation of the Connection

Creation of a connection involves

◇ Authenticating through a username and password that are valid on the receiving computer

◇ Determining which computer will be the sender, which will be the receiver, and which will send first

◇ Figuring out what type of communication will take place

◇ Specifying which lower-layer protocols will be used for transmission

Data Transfer and Dialog Control

Data transfer and dialog control involves

- ❖ The actual transfer of data

- ❖ Any acknowledgments that are needed

- ❖ Responses to requests that the sender or the receiver makes

Termination of the Connection

Once the session is complete, the connection is terminated. This allows other sessions to use the connection.

> **NOTE**
>
> At the Session layer of the OSI model, data is referred to as a packet.

Dialog Control

There are three types of dialog control at the Session layer. Dialog control services include:

- ❖ Simplex communication, which specifies that communication is one-way only

- ❖ Half-duplex communication, which specifies that communication can be two-way but only one channel can communicate at a time

- ❖ Full-duplex communication, which specifies that communication can be two-way simultaneously

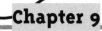

Using the Presentation Layer

The Presentation layer of the OSI model is responsible for

◇ Character code translation

◇ Data encryption

◇ Data compression and expansion

Character Code Translation

EBCDIC, or Extended Binary Coded Decimal Interchange Code
The 8-bit character set used in the IBM environment.

We humans understand symbolic characters; for example, "hello." Computers understand data as a series of ones and zeros. In order to communicate, there must be some translation. This process occurs at the Presentation layer of the OSI model through character code translation. Examples of character codes include

◇ ASCII

◇ **EBCDIC**

ASCII		Symbolic Character
10001000		h
01011000	Presentation Layer	e
00111001	←——————→	l
00111001		l
01101001		o

Data Encryption

Data encryption is the process of coding data so that it is protected from unauthorized access. Some of the methods used to encrypt data include:

- Transposing information within the data.
- Substituting one character for another. (Think of this as the secret code you used when you were a kid.)
- Mathematical calculations that the sender and the receiver determine to scramble the data. This is the most secure encryption method.

Data Compression and Expansion

Data compression occurs at the sender's end and compresses the data so that it can be sent more efficiently.

Data expansion occurs at the receiver's end when the data is returned to its original format.

NOTE

At the Presentation layer of the OSI model, data is referred to as a packet.

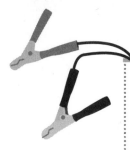

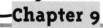

Using the Application Layer

The Application layer of the OSI model supports these services:

File services allow you to store, move, control access to, and retrieve files.

Print services allow you to send data to local or networked printers.

Message services allow you to transfer text, graphics, audio, and video over a network.

Application services allow you to process applications locally or through distributed processing.

Database services allow you to use the local computer to access a network server for database storage and retrieval functions.

> **NOTE**
>
> Applications like Word and Excel do not directly interface with the Application layer of the OSI model. However, the Application layer provides the user applications with underlying services, such as file and print services.

In addition, the Application layer of the OSI model advertises any services that are being offered and determines whether requests made by the client should be serviced locally or remotely.

Service Advertisement

Service advertisement means that the computer is offering network services. For example, the computer is able to share file and print resources. In NT, any computer running the server service automatically advertises services.

Service Processing

Service processing determines whether a request should be processed locally or remotely. Assume this situation:

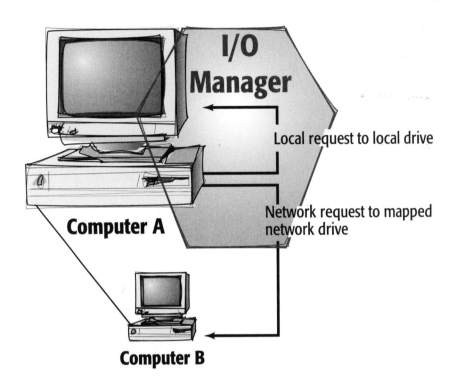

In this case, you have two computers: computer A and computer B. If computer A makes a request to its local drive, the I/O manager will direct the call to be handled locally. If the computer makes a network request—in this case, computer A has the F: drive mapped to computer B—the I/O manager will process the request and redirect it to the network.

NOTE

At the Application layer of the OSI model, data is referred to as a message or a packet.

Review Questions

1. List the two main advantages of the OSI model.

   _____

   _____

Questions 2–8 involve matching these layers to their descriptions:

- **A.** Application
- **B.** Presentation
- **C.** Session
- **D.** Transport
- **E.** Network
- **F.** Data-Link
- **G.** Physical

2. _____ The layer that is responsible for establishing, maintaining, and synchronizing the data connection

3. _____ The layer that is responsible for identifying the source and destination hardware addresses and organizing bits into frames

4. _____ The layer that is responsible for file and print services. It also determines whether a service request should be processed locally or routed to the network.

5. _____ The layer that is responsible for moving data over an internetwork

6. _____ The layer that is responsible for moving bits over physical media

7. _____ The layer that is responsible for formatting and translating data

8. _____ The layer that is responsible for reliable delivery. This layer manages connections, error control, and flow control.

9. What are the two sublayers of the Data-Link layer?

   _____

   _____

10. Which device routes packets between two network segments at the Network layer of the OSI model?

_____

11. What is the difference between connection-oriented services and connectionless services? Which is more reliable? Which is more efficient?

_____

12. What is the difference between a physical address and a network address?

_____

_____

13. List the seven layers of the OSI model from bottom to top.

_____

_____

_____

_____

_____

_____

_____

Acronyms to Know
- ❏ OSI
- ❏ ISO
- ❏ ISDN
- ❏ EPROM
- ❏ CRC
- ❏ ASCII
- ❏ EBCDIC

Chapter

10

Network Models:
Common Network
Architectures

When designing a network, you can choose from several network architectures. Some of the considerations that go into choosing a network architecture include the size of the network, the number of users you will support, and the network operating system you will use. This chapter provides an overview of these common network architectures:

 Peer-to-peer networks

 Client-server networks

 Domain model

 Directory services

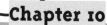

Considering Peer-to-Peer Networks

Peer-to-Peer Networks

Do not use dedicated network servers for authenticating users and providing secure access to network resources. In this model, clients share resources, and other clients have access to whatever has been shared.

Server

A computer on the network that provides network services.

Client

A computer on the network that requests network services.

Network

Two or more computers connected for the purpose of sharing resources such as file or print resources.

A true **peer-to-peer network** does not have a dedicated network **server** that authenticates users and shares network resources. Instead, by using a network **client**, a user sitting at a computer can share **network** resources while also accessing local resources (such as the hard drive) for running local applications.

Some peer-to-peer clients have the ability to locally authenticate users. For example, to access a Windows NT Workstation, a user would need guest access or a valid user account that was defined on the NT Workstation they were trying to access. Other peer clients, such as Windows 95 or Windows 98 clients, do not have user account databases. For these clients, a resource is simply shared or not shared with all network users.

Windows 95   Windows 98   NT Workstation

- **Clients can share resources**
- **Other clients can only access resources that have been shared**
- **No network server authenticates clients**

When Appropriate

Typically you use the peer-to-peer network model in very small networks where you need to share resources, but there is no central server or dedicated administrator.

Benefits

Here are some advantages to choosing a peer-to-peer network:

- ❖ For a small number of users, it is easy to set up.

- ❖ There is no need for dedicated server hardware.

- ❖ Peer-to-peer networking software typically is less expensive than the software that other networking models use.

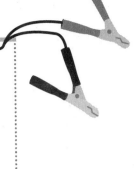

Drawbacks

There are also some disadvantages:

- ◆ This model does not work well if there is a large number of users.
- ◆ This model does not offer the security features of the other networking models.
- ◆ Because network resources are more scattered, backup is usually more of a problem.

Common OS Examples

Common examples of peer-to-peer networks include

- ◆ Windows NT Workstation
- ◆ Windows 95 and Windows 98
- ◆ Windows for Workgroups 3.11
- ◆ NetWare Lite

NOTE

In a network with a small number of computers—for example, a small business with three computers that wants to have limited file sharing and share a printer—the peer-to-peer network model is an economical choice.

Considering Client-Server Networks

A **client-server network** uses a server to authenticate users and provide network resources. This model was very common in the late 1980s and early 1990s. The benefit of this model is that it allows you to centralize the administration of network resources.

The problem with this model is that most network users need to access more than one server because of the way many organizations store data. In this case, the administrator must add the user's account to each network server that the user will access.

In the example below, users have access to the servers on which they have user accounts.

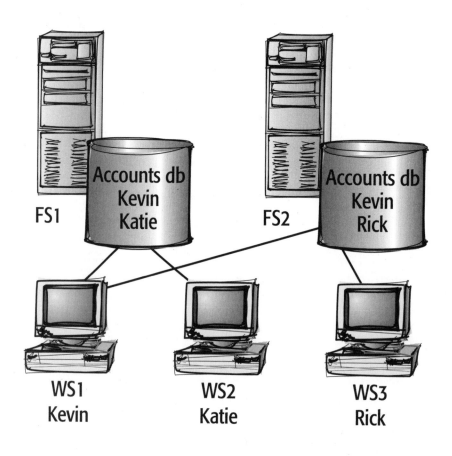

When Appropriate

The client-server architecture is a good choice if the network is fairly small, but you need centralization of account management and network resources.

Benefits

Client-server networks

- ◆ Allow you to centralize administration
- ◆ Provide centralization of resources for easier backups
- ◆ Provide network security through user account management and control of access to network resources

Drawbacks

However, the client-server model

- ◆ Normally needs a dedicated server
- ◆ Needs a more experienced administrator to install and manage the network than the peer-to-peer network model does
- ◆ Needs duplicate administration if users need to access more than one server

Common OS Examples

Common examples of client-server networks include

- ◆ NetWare 2.*x*
- ◆ NetWare 3.*x*

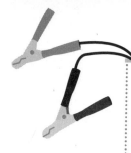

Considering the Domain Model

The **domain model** is used by NT 3.x and NT 4.x. The domain model allows you to logically group resources into a domain.

All domain account administration is written to a special server called a PDC, or **primary domain controller**. The domain accounts database is called the SAM, or Security Accounts Manager.

Copies of the domain database are stored on BDCs, or **backup domain controllers**. BDCs serve two primary functions. They offload logon authentication requests from the PDC, and they provide fault tolerance. If the PDC fails, the BDC can be promoted to PDC.

The main advantage of the domain model is that all users need only one user account to log on to the domain. Users can then access any resources within the domain that they have been granted access to.

This graphic shows a sample domain:

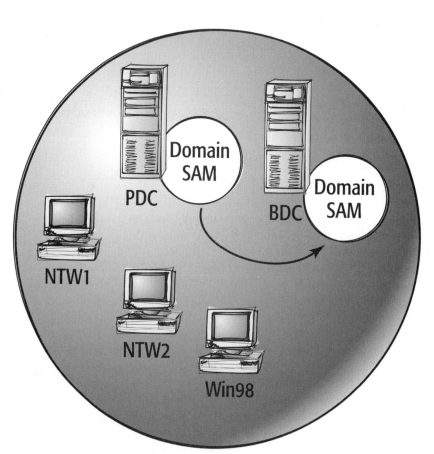

Domain Model

Logically groups computers, users, and groups into a domain. Users log on to the domain and have access to any resources within the domain to which their user account has permission.

Primary Domain Controller (PDC)

Is used in an NT domain. The PDC contains the read-write copy of the domain accounts administration database, called the Security Accounts Manager, or SAM.

Backup Domain Controllers (BDCs)

Are used in NT domains and get read-only copies of the PDC accounts database. BDCs serve two primary functions: They offload logon authentication requests from the PDC, and they provide fault tolerance. If the PDC fails, the BDC can be promoted to PDC.

When Appropriate

The domain model is very scalable (meaning it works well with small and large networks), and you can use it in small or large organizations.

Benefits

The domain model offers these benefits:

◆ Users need only one logon account, no matter how many servers the user needs to access.

◆ You can easily define and manage security.

◆ You can centralize account and resource management.

Drawbacks

There are also some drawbacks:

◆ This model needs an educated and experienced administrator to install and manage it.

◆ The domain model uses a flat structure for storing account information. You can have up to 40,000 accounts, but there is no way to hierarchically organize the users.

◆ Domain models do not scale as well in enterprise environments as directory services models do.

Common OS Examples

Common examples of domain model networks include

◆ NT 3.1, 3.5, and 3.51

◆ NT 4

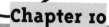

Considering Directory Services

In a **directory services network model**, a hierarchical database contains all of the network resources. Conceptually the database looks like an upside-down tree structure, which is similar to the DOS directory structure. When a user logs on to the network, they are actually logging on to the directory services database. The user can access any objects within the database that they have been given access to.

The directory services database consists of a hierarchical structure of container objects. You can think of container objects like a directory structure. This structure allows you to logically group your directory services objects. Objects are users, groups, servers, printers, and so on.

Below is an example of NetWare's directory services model.

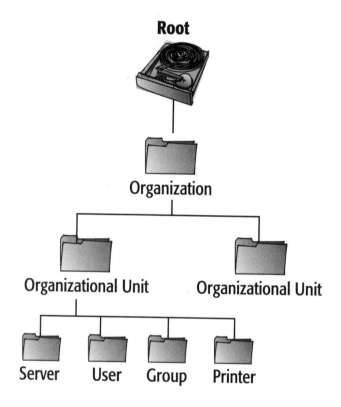

Directory Services Network Model

Uses a hierarchical database to logically organize the network resources. This model scales well to small, medium, or large enterprise networks.

When Appropriate

For medium-size to large networks, this model is the wave of the future. The two main network operating systems—NetWare 4.x and 5.x, and Windows 2000—use a directory services network architecture.

Benefits

Consider these advantages to using directory services:

- ◇ This model scales well to any size network.
- ◇ The administrator can logically group users and resources within the directory services tree.
- ◇ You can centralize or decentralize account and resource management as much as you wish. There are many options to granularity in administrative tasks.

Drawbacks

You should also consider these disadvantages:

- ◇ This model is the most difficult to design and manage.
- ◇ This model requires an educated and experienced network administrator to install and manage it.

Common OS Examples

Common examples of directory services networks include

- ◇ NetWare 4.x
- ◇ NetWare 5.x
- ◇ Windows 2000

Review Questions

Terms to Know
- ❏ Peer-to-Peer Network
- ❏ Server
- ❏ Client
- ❏ Network
- ❏ Client-Server Network
- ❏ Domain Model
- ❏ Directory Services Network Model

1. Define a peer-to-peer network model.

   _____

   _____

2. What is the role of a PDC?

   _____

3. What are the two primary functions of BDCs?

   _____

   _____

4. Which network model will Windows 2000 use?

   _____

5. True or false: The domain model is always the best network model to choose.

6. Which network model is the best choice if you have a small number of users and no dedicated server hardware?

   _____

7. What is the difference between a container and an object in the directory services model?

   _____

8. True or false: In a client-server model, if you have an account on one server, you can access resources on other servers even if you do not have a user account defined.

9. True or false: In a domain model network, you must add users and groups to the PDC and the BDCs.

10. Which network model provides the most scalability and is the best solution for large, enterprise networks?

Chapter
11

Connecting the Computers: Networking Hardware

Before you can even begin to install your networking software, you must have some type of hardware that connects
all of the computers. In this chapter, you will learn about network topologies and the two most common protocols for connecting network hardware: Ethernet and Token Ring.

The following topics are covered:

 Physical and logical topologies

 Star, bus, and ring topologies

 How Ethernet works

 Ethernet standards and hardware

 How Token Ring works

 Token Ring standards and hardware

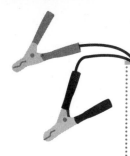

Understanding Topologies

A topology is defined as the layout of the network. Topologies can be physical or logical.

- ◆ A physical topology describes how the network looks physically or how the network is physically designed.
- ◆ A logical topology describes how data is transmitted through the network.

The concept of a topology is important, because each network card is designed to work with a specific topology. For example, if you know you want to use 10BASET Ethernet, you must use a physical star topology. Conversely, if your network cable is already installed and you want to use existing wiring, you must select your network cards based on what is preexisting.

Ideally, you can design your network from scratch. At this point, you can choose your topology, cabling, and network cards based on what best meets your needs.

This subsection will review the commonly defined topologies:

- ◆ Star topology
- ◆ Bus topology
- ◆ Ring topology

Star Topology

Physically, the star topology looks like a star. There is a central device called a **hub** to which all devices attach.

Logically, a star topology works by sending the data signal to all nodes at once. In a logical star topology, the hub works as a signal splitter, which means the signal is split and sent to all computers at the same time.

NOTE

The term *hub* is used generically to specify the central device in a star topology. In a 10BASET network, the hub is technically called a concentrator. In a Token Ring network, the hub is technically called a Multi-Station Access Unit, or MSAU.

Hub

The central device in a star topology. It connects several computers.

200

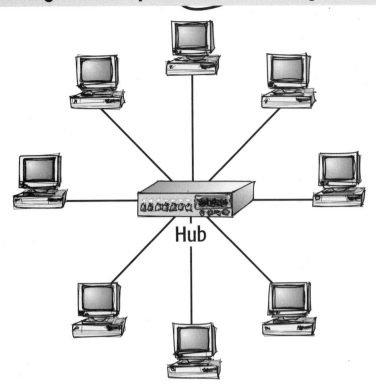

Hub

Benefits

The benefits of a star topology include the following:

- ❖ A star topology is more fault tolerant than other topologies, because a cable break does not bring down the entire segment.

- ❖ It is easy to reconfigure the network, or add nodes, because each node connects to the central hub independent of other nodes.

- ❖ It is easy to isolate cable failures, because each node connects independently to the central hub.

Drawbacks

The drawbacks of a star topology include the following:

- ❖ If the central hub fails, the network becomes unavailable.

- ❖ This topology uses more network cable than other network models.

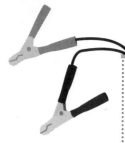

Bus Topology

A bus topology uses a physical linear segment to connect all network devices. Each end of the bus is terminated, and devices typically connect to the bus through T-connectors.

This topology logically works by broadcasting network packets bidirectionally on the network segment. Termination makes sure the signal is removed from the cable when it reaches either end.

Benefits

The benefits of a bus topology include the following:

◇ This is one of the least expensive topologies to install, because it uses less cable than the star topology and needs no hardware for a central device.

◇ It is an easy way to network a small number of computers.

Drawbacks

The drawbacks of a bus topology include the following:

◇ If there is a break in the cable, the entire network segment will fail.

◇ This topology can be difficult to troubleshoot.

◇ On a medium-size to large network, reconfiguration is more difficult.

NOTE

In the early days of networking, the bus topology was very popular. It uses less equipment than other topologies and is an inexpensive way to set up a network. Now Ethernet concentrators are very inexpensive. The cost, combined with the fault tolerance of the star, has now made 10BASET with the star topology the most popular Ethernet configuration.

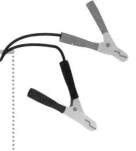

Ring Topology

The physical ring topology is circular in nature. This is similar to a bus, except in a ring the two ends are connected to form a ring. Other than **Fiber Distributed Data Interface (FDDI)**, no current networks use a physical ring topology, because a break in the ring makes the entire segment unavailable.

Logically, a ring topology works by passing the signal from one node to another in a logical ring. Token-passing schemes use the logical ring topology.

Fiber Distributed Data Interface (FDDI)
A network specification that defines a logical ring topology of fiber transmitting at 100Mbps. FDDI provides similar network connectivity as Ethernet and Token Ring, and functions at the same layers of the OSI model.

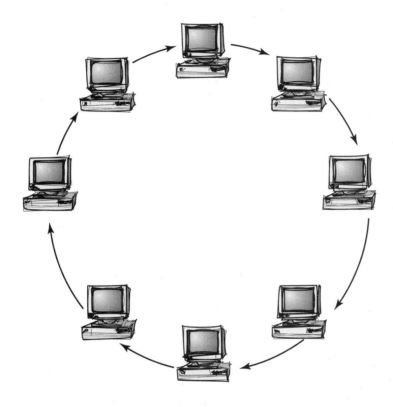

Benefits

A logical ring topology ensures access to the network without the risk of collisions, which can occur in logical star or bus topologies.

Drawbacks

The drawbacks of a ring topology include the following:

- ❖ If there is a break in the cable of a physical ring topology, the network becomes unavailable.
- ❖ Physical ring topologies are difficult to troubleshoot.
- ❖ Physical ring topologies are hard to reconfigure.

203

Understanding Ethernet

Ethernet is one of the oldest and most popular networking standards. Xerox first developed it in the 1970s. In the 1980s, Xerox, Intel, and Digital proposed formal Ethernet specifications. It has its own standard from the **Institute of Electrical and Electronic Engineers (IEEE)**, the IEEE 802.3 standard. The Ethernet protocol is at the Physical and Media Access Control (MAC) layers of the OSI model (see Chapter 9, *The Networking Model: OSI Overview*).

Ethernet works with a contention scheme (a way of accessing the network) called CSMA/CD, or Carrier Sense Multiple Access with Collision Detection.

CSMA/CD works by allowing any computer to transmit at any time, assuming the line is free. These steps take place:

1. When a station wants to send a packet, the station listens to see if any other nodes are transmitting packets over the network.

2. If the network is in use, the station defers.

3. If the network is not in use, the station sends its packet.

4. If two or more stations send packets at the same time because they both thought the line was free, a collision occurs.

5. If a collision occurs, both stations cease transmission and a jam pattern is sent to let all stations know that a collision has occurred.

6. At a random interval, both stations can retransmit their packets.

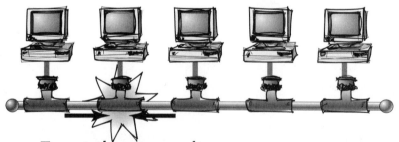

**Two stations transmit
at the same time—
a collision occurs**

Institute of Electrical and Electronic Engineers (IEEE)

Pronounced "I triple E," an organization that defines computing and telecommunications standards. The LAN standards defined by IEEE include the 802-workgroup specifications. The IEEE is an international standards organization.

Benefits

The benefits of Ethernet include the following:

- ◆ The protocol is fairly simple and does not have the overhead associated with Token Ring.

- ◆ As long as the network segment is not too busy, stations can transmit without any wait.

- ◆ Because Ethernet hardware is nonproprietary and involves less complicated hardware, Ethernet is less expensive than Token Ring hardware.

Drawbacks

The drawbacks of Ethernet include the following:

- ◆ As network traffic increases, so does the probability of network collisions, which degrade network performance.

- ◆ Because all stations have equal access, there is no way to establish higher priority for nodes such as servers.

Ethernet Rules

Ethernet is the most popular networking hardware. It is estimated to have about 70 percent of the network hardware market. It is fairly easy to install and uses inexpensive hardware compared with Token Ring and FDDI.

The most popular form of Ethernet is 10BASET. With 10BASET Ethernet, you connect to the network with an unshielded twisted-pair cable that looks like a large telephone connector. One end of the cable attaches to the network card and the other end connects to a central hub called a concentrator.

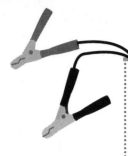

Ethernet Standards

Ethernet has two primary standards:

- ◆ 10Mbps Ethernet
- ◆ 100Mbps Ethernet

Traditionally people think of Ethernet as a 10Mbps standard. However, with the emerging standards that require networks to support voice, video, and other high-capacity bandwidth items, 100Mbps Ethernet is the wave of the future.

Ethernet has many standards in addition to speed. Depending on which Ethernet standard you choose, you will have flexibility in which physical topology and which cable type you use.

Ethernet can use these cable types:

- ◆ Thin coaxial cable (RG-58AU)
- ◆ Thick coaxial cable (RG-8 or RG-11)
- ◆ Unshielded twisted-pair cables (type depends on access speed needed)
- ◆ Fiber-optic cable

Ethernet Standard Naming Conventions

The IEEE has defined naming conventions for Ethernet standards. Here is what the standard defines:

- ◆ The first part of the name specifies the speed in megabits per second.
- ◆ The second part of the name specifies that the standard is using **baseband** (BASE) or **broadband** (BROAD) **signaling**.
- ◆ The last part of the name describes the type of cable being used, or an estimate of a maximum cable run for the standard.

For example, the 10BASET standard defines 10Mbps speed, using baseband signaling, over twisted-pair cabling.

Baseband Signaling
Uses the entire bandwidth of the signal to send a digital signal.

Broadband Signaling
Splits the signal into multiple channels to send an analog signal.

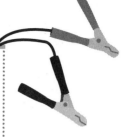

Connecting the Computers: Networking Hardware

This table summarizes the Ethernet standards.

Ethernet Standard	Speed in Mbps	Physical Topology	Cable Used
10BASE2	10	Bus	Thin coaxial cable RG-58AU (50-ohm cable)
10BASE5	10	Bus	Thick coaxial cable RG-8 or RG-11 (50-ohm cable)
10BASET	10	Star	Unshielded twisted-pair cable (Category 3 or better)
10BASEF	10	Star	Fiber-optic
100BASET	100	Star	Unshielded twisted-pair cable (Uses category 5 with all four pairs.)
100BASETX	100	Star	Unshielded twisted-pair cable (Uses a data-grade cable with only two pairs, specified by **ANSI.**)
100BASEFX	100	Star	Fiber-optic cable (Uses two strands of fiber as specified by ANSI.)

American National Standards Institute (ANSI)

An organization that seeks to develop standardization within the computing industry. ANSI is the American representative to the ISO, or International Standards Organization, which was covered in Chapter 9, *The Networking Model: OSI Overview.*

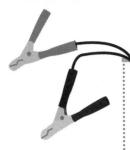

Ethernet Hardware

Depending on which Ethernet standard you choose, you can configure Ethernet as a physical bus or a physical star topology. This section will provide an example of each topology and the hardware needed to support each configuration.

Ethernet Bus Topology

In the 1980s, before 10BASET became standardized, the most popular way of configuring Ethernet was in a bus topology. You might still use the bus topology in very small networks, because it does not require a concentrator (the central hub device) as the star configuration does. However, because the cost of Ethernet hardware has dropped drastically over the last 10 years, this is often not a large concern.

The most popular configuration for the bus topology uses the 10BASE2 standard, or thin coaxial cable. In this configuration, you connect a T-connector to the network card. You attach the cables to either side of the T-connector to form a linear bus network. At the ends of the bus, you need 50-ohm terminators. You should ground one end.

Ethernet Star Topology

The Ethernet star topology is by far the most commonly implemented topology for Ethernet networks. This topology is easier to set up and configure. It also provides more fault tolerance than the bus topology, because a cable break does not cause the entire segment to go down.

In the star topology, you attach all of your devices to a central device called a hub, or concentrator. You can buy concentrators with whatever number of ports you require.

When determining the hardware that you will use, you should first decide whether you will need 10Mbps or 100Mbps networking capabilities. This factor determines which concentrator, Ethernet card, and cabling you will need. Once your hardware is in place, the star will look like this diagram:

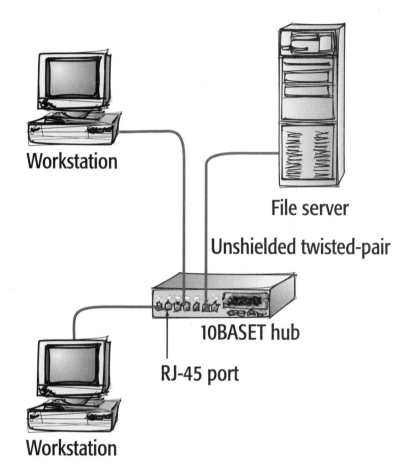

Workstation

File server

Unshielded twisted-pair

10BASET hub

RJ-45 port

Workstation

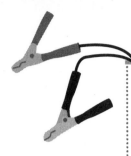

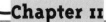
Understanding Token Ring

IBM originally developed Token Ring as a way to connect mainframe computers with each other. Since then, it has also become a popular network connectivity protocol. The IEEE 802.5 standard has also standardized it. Token Ring works with a token-passing scheme. Physically, Token Ring looks like a star, but logically, it passes data in a ring. Token Ring specifies two access speeds, 4Mbps and 16Mbps.

With Token Ring, you designate one node on the network as the active monitor. The active monitor is responsible for generating a special packet called a **token**, and it issues only one token for the entire ring. The only time a station can transmit data is when it accesses the token. Because each network only has one token, collisions never occur.

Token-passing schemes are called deterministic, because they produce predictable access, which allows you to set a priority on each computer. This capability is an advantage for large networks running mission-critical applications.

Logically, a Token Ring looks like this:

Token

A special packet that signifies that a user can transmit data to a Token Ring network.

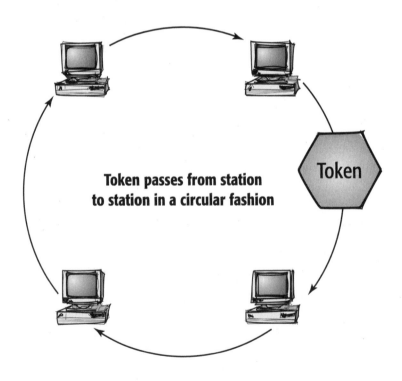

Token passes from station to station in a circular fashion

Token

Benefits

The benefits of Token Ring include the following:

- Token Ring eliminates the collisions associated with Ethernet.

- Token Ring provides connectivity to IBM mainframes and is compatible with **SNA** software.

- Token Ring offers predictable access and load management.

- You can assign priorities to computers to allow faster access to mission-critical computers, like network servers.

- In high-load networks, Token Ring produces better network throughput than Ethernet.

Systems Network Architecture (SNA)
Defined by IBM, it specifies how devices can interface with IBM software.

Drawbacks

The drawbacks of Token Ring include the following:

- Token Ring software and hardware are more complicated than Ethernet, which makes Token Ring more costly to implement.

- Token Ring needs more management than Ethernet, thus requiring a more experienced network manager.

NOTE

At this point, 4Mbps Token Ring is obsolete.

NOTE

Token Ring physically uses a star topology but logically passes data in a ring. This is sometimes referred to as a star-ring topology.

Token Ring Hardware

You can see common Token Ring hardware in this graphic:

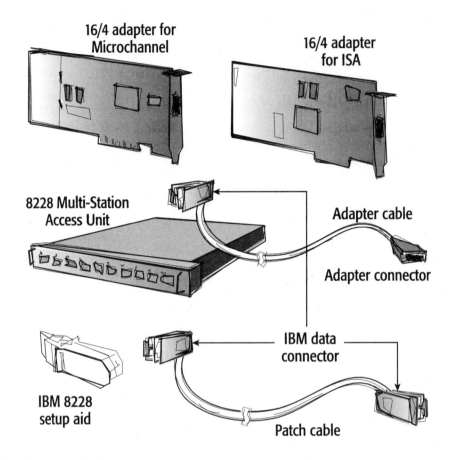

16/4 adapter for
Microchannel

16/4 adapter
for ISA

8228 Multi-Station
Access Unit

Adapter cable

Adapter connector

IBM 8228
setup aid

IBM data
connector

Patch cable

The hardware includes

◆ A network interface card. (You must configure all nodes in the ring for the same speed, either 4Mbps or 16Mbps.)

◆ A central device. In this case, the hub is an 8228 Multi-Station Access Unit (MSAU).

◆ If you are using an 8228 MSAU, a setup aid to initialize ports on the MSAU.

◆ Adapter cables to attach the network card to the MSAU.

◆ Patch cables to connect MSAUs or to act as an extension cable for extending the distance between an MSAU and an adapter cable.

Common Token Ring Configurations

In a very small network, you might need only a single Token Ring MSAU. In most cases, you will want to form a larger ring. The MSAU (or whichever Token Ring hub you choose) will have two ports that are identified as Ring In and Ring Out. The Ring In and Ring Out ports form a larger ring. The Token Ring stations attach to the data ports. You can see this in this graphic:

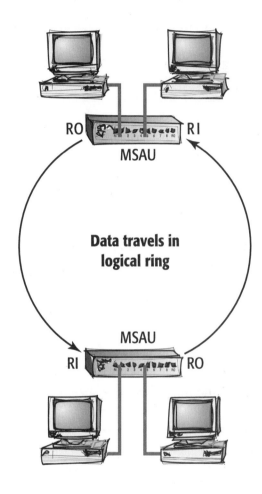

Review Questions

1. List the three common topologies:

_____

_____

_____

2. What is the difference between a physical topology and a logical topology?

_____

_____

3. What does CSMA/CD stand for?

_____

4. What are the two access speeds at which Ethernet transmits?

_____

5. What are the two access speeds at which Token Ring transmits?

_____

6. Which topology offers the most fault tolerance and is the easiest to reconfigure?

_____

7. True or false: You can use any topology with Ethernet or Token Ring.

8. Which cable does 10BASE2 Ethernet use?

    A. Thin coaxial cable

    B. Thick coaxial cable

    C. Unshielded twisted-pair cable

    D. Shielded twisted-pair cable

9. Which physical topology does 10BASET Ethernet use?

_____

10. Token Ring uses a logical _____ topology and a physical _____ topology.

11. True or false: Token Ring offers better throughput in busier networks than Ethernet does.

12. Which is more commonly implemented, Ethernet or Token Ring?

_____

13. Which IEEE standard defines Ethernet?

_____

14. Which IEEE standard defines Token Ring?

_____

Chapter
12

Moving Data over the Network: Networking Protocols

In Chapter 9, *The Networking Model: OSI Overview*, you learned about the OSI model. The two layers responsible for moving data over an internetwork are the Network and Transport layers of the OSI model.

The Network layer of the OSI model determines the best route that a packet should take when it needs to be delivered over an internetwork. The Transport layer is primarily responsible for reliable data delivery.

In this chapter, you will learn about the popular Network and Transport protocols that are used in modern computer networks. This chapter will include topics on:

 TCP/IP

 IPX/SPX

 NetBEUI

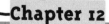

Using TCP/IP

One of the most popular networking protocols is TCP/IP, which stands for Transmission Control Protocol/Internet Protocol. TCP/IP was originally developed in the 1970s for the Department of Defense (DoD) as a way of connecting dissimilar networks. Since then, TCP/IP has become a **de facto** industry **standard**. It is important to note that while TCP and IP are the cornerstone protocols, TCP/IP is actually a collection of many protocols that are generically referred to as TCP/IP.

De Facto Standard
A standard that is widely accepted and implemented in the computer industry.

DHCP, or Dynamic Host Configuration Protocol
Automates the assignment of IP configuration information.

DNS, or Domain Name System
A system that resolves domain names to IP addresses using a domain name database for address resolution.

Benefits of TCP/IP

TCP/IP is commonly used as a transport protocol for these reasons:

◆ It is the most commonly used protocol and is supported by almost all network operating systems. It is the required protocol for Internet access.

◆ TCP/IP is scalable to large and small networks. In a large internetwork, TCP/IP is routable.

◆ The protocol is designed to be fault tolerant and is able to dynamically reroute packets if network links become unavailable (assuming alternate paths exist).

◆ Protocol companions like **DHCP** make TCP/IP easy to configure.

◆ **DNS** is used with TCP/IP to allow domain names to be reconciled with IP addresses.

Overview of TCP and IP

The two main protocols that make up the TCP/IP suite of protocols are TCP and IP. These protocols fall into the Transport and Network layers of the OSI model, respectively.

Transport	TCP UDP
Network	IP

OSI Model Layers

IP functions at the Network layer of the OSI model. The primary function of IP is to route packets over an internetwork. For example, assume that you have four subnets (independent network segments) connected through **routers**, and you want to send a packet from subnet A to subnet B. IP is responsible for routing the packet through the internetwork.

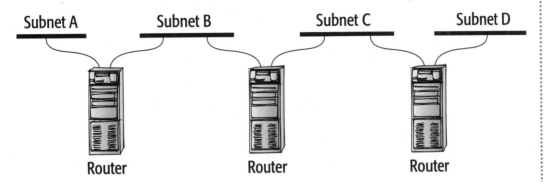

Subnet A Subnet B Subnet C Subnet D

Router Router Router

TCP functions at the Transport layer as defined in the OSI model. The primary function of TCP is to provide reliable data delivery. This is done by establishing a **fully duplexed**, **virtual circuit connection**. When you send data through TCP, you essentially have a handshake between the sender and the receiver, which is maintained throughout the entire transmission.

If you do not need the reliability of TCP, you can send packets through the Transport layer with a protocol called UDP, or User Datagram Protocol. UDP provides connectionless service and has considerably less overhead than TCP.

Routers
Network devices that connect two or more network segments. Routers can also route packets to and from the Internet.

Full Duplexing
Means that simultaneous two-way communication can take place.

Virtual Circuit
A logical connection between two devices. Both devices share a logical connection that transmits and receives data.

IP Addressing

A central concept of IP is addressing. Current IP configuration requires a four-field network address (a 32-bit address) for each network device. IP addresses must be unique for each network device that could potentially connect with another.

ISP, or Internet Service Provider
A third-party company that provides Internet services.

If you will connect to the Internet, you should get your IP addresses from Inter-NIC, which is the organization that coordinates all IP address assignment, or from an **ISP**. IP addresses commonly fall within three classes: Class A, Class B, and Class C. Depending on the size of the network, different class assignments are made.

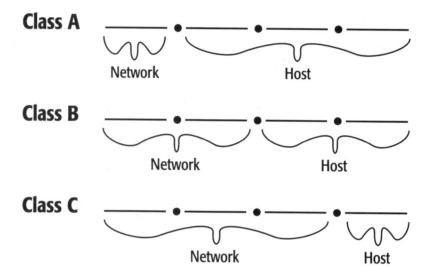

Network Class	Address Range of First Field	Number of Networks Available	Number of Host Nodes Supported
A	1–126	126	16,777,214
B	128–191	65,534	65,534
C	192–254	16,777,214	254

NOTE

The following addresses are reserved: 0 is not available, because it denotes that no routing is needed; 127 is a special loopback address used for diagnostic purposes; and 255 is used for broadcasts.

IP Configuration

When you configure a network device with TCP/IP, you typically need three pieces of information:

- ◆ IP address
- ◆ Subnet mask
- ◆ Default router

IP Address

As mentioned on the previous page, each network device needs a unique IP address. The system administrator, or someone who coordinates IP address assignment and configuration, should assign this address from the pool of addresses assigned by InterNIC or your ISP.

Subnet Mask

A subnet mask defines which part of the IP address is the network address and which is the host address. By defining subnet masks, you specify which network your node belongs to. With this information and the destination address for your data, TCP/IP can determine whether or not source and destination nodes are on the same network segment. If they are on different segments, routing will be needed.

Default Router

You need a default router configuration if you will route packets over an internetwork. The default router specifies the IP address of the router that will route packets across an internetwork.

NOTE

These are basic IP configuration options. Depending on the complexity of your IP network, you might also specify other configuration options, such as the DNS and **WINS** servers that will be used.

WINS, or Windows Internet Name Service

In NetBIOS networks, resolves NetBIOS names to IP addresses. NT requires NetBIOS network services.

Function of DHCP in an IP Network

Manual configuration of IP can potentially lead to misconfiguration and network errors. Luckily, there is a TCP/IP protocol that helps automate configuration. DHCP, or Dynamic Host Configuration Protocol, uses a DHCP server to automate IP configuration information.

You configure the DHCP server with the DHCP server service. The DHCP server contains a range of IP addresses called the scope that can be assigned to DHCP clients. The lease option for configuring the DHCP server specifies how long an IP address will be assigned to the DHCP client. As long as the client keeps using the IP address, it is allowed to keep it. If the address is not used within the lease period, it is returned to the DHCP server scope and is available for use by other DHCP clients.

DHCP uses this process to assign addresses:

broadcast requesting DHCP server →

offer to provide DHCP services ←

accepts DHCP server offer →

sends all IP configuration information and confirms lease ←

DHCP Client

DHCP Server

DHCP Servers in an NT Environment

In an NT environment, only NT Servers can act as DHCP servers. You install the DHCP service on the server under Control Panel ➤ Network ➤ Services.

Once you have installed the DHCP server, you must configure the scope and subnet mask that the DHCP clients will use. Through DHCP, you can also configure options such as the default gateway, WINS server, and DNS server.

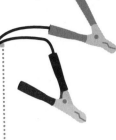

Function of DNS in an IP Network

The Domain Name System (DNS) is a database that allows IP addresses to be mapped to host names that people use to access network resources. To demonstrate the usefulness of DNS, take this quiz:

1. What is the **URL** to access Microsoft?

2. What is the IP address of Microsoft?

If you answered `microsoft.com` for question 1, you were right. Most people can answer this question; however, very few people can answer the second question. This is OK, though, because this is where DNS comes into play. DNS allows us to reference a name we can remember, and it translates that name into an IP address that we use to actually contact the host we wish to communicate with.

DNS uses domains to logically organize resources. DNS domains are different from Windows NT domains, and you should not confuse the two terms. Domains are logically grouped by type of function into a hierarchical structure. At the top of the structure is the root. Examples of domains include `.com` for business, `.edu` for education, and `.gov` for government. Domain names must be unique. InterNIC assigns and centrally manages them.

URL, or Uniform Resource Locator
Specifies the location of TCP/IP resources.

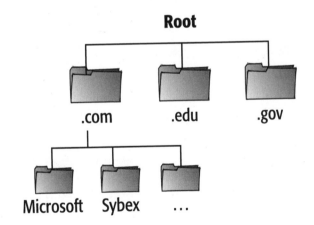

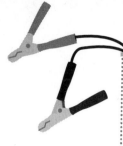

Using IPX/SPX

IPX/SPX stands for Internetwork Packet Exchange/Sequenced Packet Exchange and is a proprietary protocol that Novell **NetWare** uses. As with TCP/IP, IPX/SPX functions at the Network and Transport layers of the OSI model.

NetWare
A popular network operating system from Novell and a competitive product to NT.

Transport	IPX SPX
Network	IPX

OSI Model Layers

IPX

IPX works primarily at the Network layer of the OSI model. The main function of IPX is to route packets through an internetwork. If connection-oriented services are not needed, IPX is also used to send packets through the Transport layer of the OSI model.

SPX

SPX functions at the Transport layer of the OSI model. SPX provides connection-oriented, fully duplexed connections. For each packet that is sent, an acknowledgement is returned. In addition, SPX is responsible for segment development and segment sequencing.

NOTE

Because IPX/SPX is proprietary to Novell, it is not as commonly used as TCP/IP, which is a nonproprietary protocol. IPX/SPX is most commonly used in networks where NetWare connectivity is needed. The Microsoft version of IPX/SPX is called NWLink.

Using NetBEUI

NetBEUI stands for NetBIOS Extended User Interface. It was developed in the mid-1980s to connect workgroups running OS/2 and LAN Manager. You can use NetBEUI to connect Microsoft networks.

The following are NetBEUI advantages:

- ❖ It is easy to install.
- ❖ There are no configuration requirements.
- ❖ NetBEUI implements self-tuning capabilities.
- ❖ NetBEUI has less overhead than TCP/IP and IPX/SPX, thus it offers better performance.
- ❖ NetBEUI uses less memory than TCP/IP and IPX/SPX.

The disadvantages of NetBEUI include the following:

- ❖ NetBEUI is not routable, so you cannot use it in enterprise networks.
- ❖ NetBEUI is not as widely supported across network platforms as TCP/IP is.

TIP

On networks consisting of a single network segment, NetBEUI will provide the best performance, because of the low overhead associated with this protocol.

Review Questions

1. What are three common IP configuration requirements?

   _____

   _____

   _____

2. Which TCP/IP protocol allows you to automate IP configuration?

   _____

3. What proprietary protocol does Novell NetWare use?

   _____

4. What is the primary purpose of IP?

   _____

5. At which layer of the OSI model does IP function?

   _____

6. NetWare uses the _____ protocol to provide connection-oriented services at the Transport layer of the OSI model.

7. Which TCP/IP address class offers the largest combination of network addresses?

   _____

8. Which protocol offers the most efficient service?
   - **A.** TCP/IP
   - **B.** IPX/SPX
   - **C.** NetBEUI

9. Which protocol is most widely implemented?
   - **A.** TCP/IP
   - **B.** IPX/SPX
   - **C.** NetBEUI

10. True or false: NetBEUI is not a routable protocol.

11. What is the primary function of DNS?

_____

12. In TCP/IP configuration, what defines which part of the address is the network address and which part is the host address?

_____

13. True or false: IPX/SPX is a proprietary protocol.

14. What configuration does NetBEUI need?

_____

Acronyms to Know
❏ DHCP
❏ DNS
❏ TCP
❏ IP
❏ UDP
❏ ISP
❏ WINS
❏ URL
❏ IPX
❏ SPX

Chapter

13

Network Operating Systems: A Comparison

In the world of networking, you have many choices for a network operating system. Some factors to consider when choosing an operating system include price, functions, interoperability, the skill set required to manage the network, existing software, hardware and software compatibility, and personal preference. In this section, you will learn about some of the major network operating systems, which include

 Windows 95 and Windows 98

 NetWare

 Windows NT

Networking with Windows 95 and Windows 98

Windows 95 and Windows 98 are primarily designed to act as local operating systems. This topic is covered in Chapter 5, *Local Operating Systems: A Comparison.*

However, in addition to providing local support, these two operating systems include extensive network support. If the network consists exclusively of Windows 95 and Windows 98 computers, the network is a peer-to-peer type. If the network uses another operating system, the Windows computers function as workstations within the network. Either way, network support allows the Windows computer to use network resources or provide network resources through file and print sharing.

Configuration of Network Support

This section will focus on network configuration of a Windows 95 computer.

When you configure a Windows 95 or Windows 98 computer, you can specify whether or not to install the networking components. On a Windows 95 computer, you configure the computer for networking through Control Panel ➤ Network.

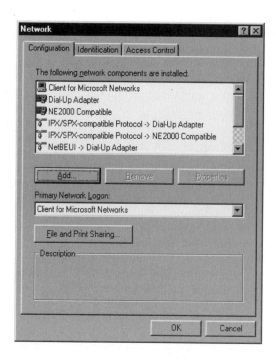

Within this Network applet, you can set many options, including

- ◆ Configuration of networking components
- ◆ Identification of the computer
- ◆ Access control of network resources
- ◆ Primary network logon
- ◆ File and print sharing

Configuration of Networking Components

To configure network components, you click the Add button within the Control Panel ≻ Network applet's Configuration tab.

From the Select Network Component Type dialog box, you can configure the options shown in this table.

Network Component	Description	Examples
Client	This option specifies which network client software to install. The software that processes network requests is sometimes called a redirector.	Client software that comes with Windows 95 includes support for Banyan, FTP Software, Microsoft, Novell, and Sunsoft clients.
Adapter	Adapters are hardware devices that connect the computer to the network. This is covered in more detail in Chapter 11, *Connecting the Computers: Networking Hardware.*	The list of supported adapters is quite extensive. Some manufactures that offer adapter drivers include 3Com, SMC, Novell, and Ungerman-Bass.
Protocol	Protocols transmit data over a network. Protocols are covered in greater detail in Chapter 12, *Moving Data Over the Network: Networking Protocols.*	There is support for protocols from different manufacturers. Common protocols include TCP/IP, IPX/SPX, and NetBEUI.
Service	Services support file and print sharing, automating system backup, and monitoring of network resources.	Examples include File and Print Sharing for Microsoft Networks and Hewlett-Packard JetAdmin, which manages network printers.

From the Configuration tab at Control Panel ➤ Network, you can also configure

- ❖ Primary network logon
- ❖ File and print sharing

The Primary Network Logon edit box specifies which network type you will log on to. When you specify this option, Windows 95 displays a screen at start-up that allows you to type in your username and password.

You use the File and Print Sharing button to share local file and print resources with other network users.

Identification of the Computer

The Identification tab allows you to configure the options shown in this screen.

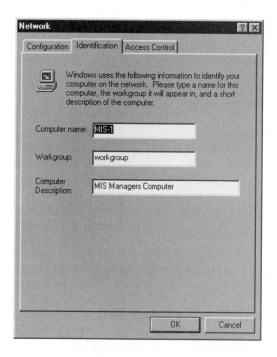

The Computer Name edit box identifies the computer on the network. This name must be unique to all other computers. The name can be up to 15 characters. It is also referred to as the computer's NetBIOS name.

The Workgroup edit box specifies which logical group your computer belongs to. This allows administrators to logically group computers.

The Computer Description edit box allows you to provide a description for informational purposes. For example, descriptions might be the department or user of the computer.

Access Control of Network Resources

The Access Control tab specifies the type of security to apply to the resources that the Windows 95 computer shares. The choices for access control are

◆ Share-level access control

◆ User-level access control

Share-level access control allows you to define a password for each shared file or print resource. Users have to supply the password when they access the network resource.

User-level access control allows you to assign access based on user or group assignment. Since Windows 95 does not maintain any user database, you must specify which user database to use. In the case of an NT domain, you use the NT domain database to specify which users and groups have access to the resource.

This graphic shows the Access Control dialog box.

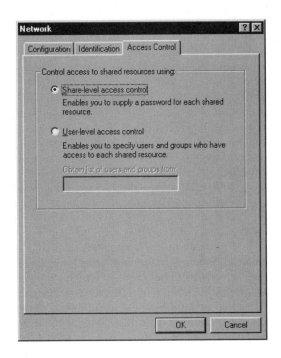

NOTE

By default, Windows 95 and Windows 98 share no local resources.

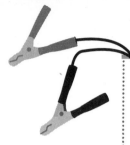

Networking with NetWare

From the mid-1980s until the mid-1990s, Novell dominated the network operating system market. Research shows that Novell still has the largest market share of existing network installations, but Microsoft has a larger share of new operating systems that are sold and installed. This section will provide an overview of three of Novell's network operating systems:

- ❖ NetWare 3.*x*
- ❖ NetWare 4.*x*
- ❖ NetWare 5

NetWare 3.*x*

NetWare 3.*x* is Novell's server operating system for small networks. It supports a client-server network model as defined in Chapter 10, *Network Models: Common Network Architectures.*

The way that NetWare 3.*x* works is that each server contains its own user accounts database, which is stored within three files called bindery files. These files store information about users and groups and the properties of users and groups. This information is local to each server and is not shared with any other servers on the network. If a user needs access to two NetWare 3.12 servers, two accounts must be created, one on each server.

When you install the server with the NetWare operating system and you run it, NetWare is the only operating system running on the server. This means that you can run no DOS or Windows commands from the server. This is called a dedicated server.

With NetWare servers, the only thing you do at the server is issue console commands (which are commands to configure or view configuration information about the server) and load NetWare Loadable Modules (NLMs). NLMs are modular components that allow you to add services. With NLMs, an administrator adds only the components they need. You can load and unload NLMs without having to restart the server.

NetWare clients load NetWare client software on their computers and log on to the NetWare server they specify using a username and password.

NetWare 4.x

NetWare 4 made a radical change in NetWare architecture by introducing the concept of Novell Directory Services (NDS). NDS uses the directory services network model, which is covered in Chapter 10.

NDS works by establishing a database of network objects. This database can be distributed and replicated throughout the network and is stored on network servers.

The other key network services that NetWare 4.x provides include security services, the ability to share network file and print resources, backup services, and a messaging service that you can use with compatible messaging applications to send e-mail and coordinate schedules.

The release of NetWare 4.11 (called IntraNetWare) added support for Web server, Web client, and IPX-to-IP translation software.

NetWare 5

NetWare 5 is Novell's most current networking software and adds or improves these features:

- ◆ Native IP support
- ◆ Multiprocessor support
- ◆ Better memory protection and use of virtual memory
- ◆ Domain name services support
- ◆ Distributed print services
- ◆ Public-key encryption services
- ◆ Support for Dynamic Host Configuration Protocol (DHCP)
- ◆ Improved backup support

Networking with Windows NT

Windows NT is Microsoft's network operating system. Windows NT 3.x and 4 use the domain network model, which is covered in Chapter 10.

This section will focus on the networking aspects of NT 4. The main configuration of NT takes place in the Control Panel ➢ Network applet.

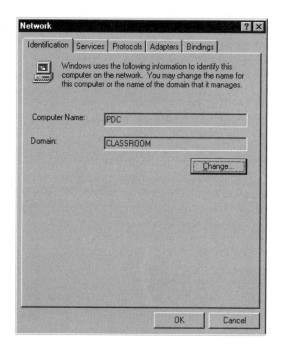

Through the Network applet, you can configure

- ◆ The computer's identification
- ◆ Which network services to use
- ◆ The network protocols to load
- ◆ Which network adapter card the computer has installed
- ◆ The bindings of the network card, protocols, and services

The following sections will cover these configuration options in more detail.

NOTE

NT is covered in greater detail in Chapter 14, *A Star Is Born: History of NT*, and in Chapter 15, *The NT Platforms: NT Workstation and NT Server*.

Identification Tab

On an NT Workstation or member server, the Identification tab of the Network applet specifies the computer name (the unique name that identifies the computer on the network) and the domain or workgroup that the computer belongs to. On an NT domain controller, you can specify only the computer name and domain.

Services Tab

A service is a task or operation provided through the operating system. Some services provide file and print sharing capabilities, while other services provide more specific tasks, like virus scanning or system backups.

Some of the network services NT uses include

- ❖ The Computer Browser service, which lists network resources
- ❖ The Server service, which provides network resources
- ❖ The Workstation service, which accesses network resources

You can see which network services are installed on your computer by accessing the Services tab of the Network applet. You use the Add and Remove buttons to add and remove network services. The Properties button allows you to configure the properties of each service. The Update button allows you to update services that have been modified or enhanced.

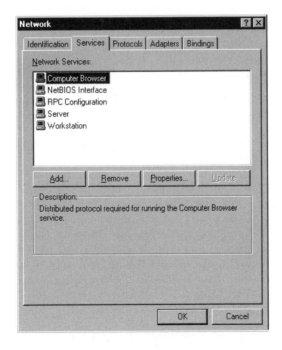

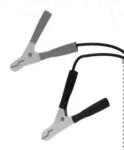

Protocols Tab

Through the Protocols tab, you can specify which network protocols your computer will use. Protocols are covered in more detail in Chapter 12.

When you initially install NT, you can choose to install these protocols:

- TCP/IP
- NWLink IPX/SPX
- NetBEUI

Once you have installed a protocol, you can configure it by clicking the protocol name and then clicking the Properties button. To add or remove protocols, use the Add and Remove buttons.

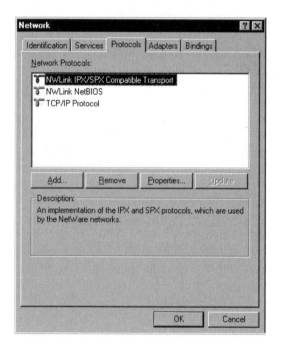

Adapters Tab

Use the Adapters tab to install and configure the drivers for your network adapter card. If you have no network card and still want to install NT networking, you can use the MS Loopback Adapter option.

TIP

To access Control Panel ➢ Network more quickly, you can right-click Network Neighborhood and choose Properties.

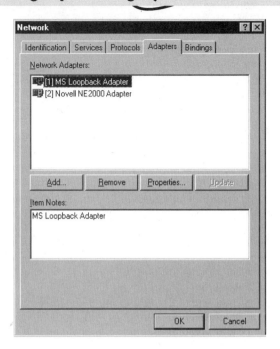

Bindings Tab

Bindings are the links between the network adapter card, the services that are loaded, and the network protocols that are used.

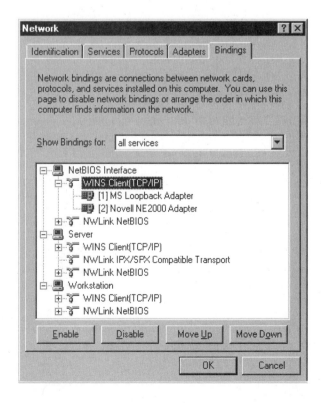

Review Questions

Terms to Know
- ❏ Windows 95
- ❏ Windows 98
- ❏ NetWare
- ❏ Windows NT

1. True or false: Windows 95 has the option of containing a user database that can authenticate user logon requests.

2. What is a network protocol used for?

   _____

3. What is a computer name used for in a Microsoft network?

   _____

4. What is the current version of NetWare?

   _____

5. What type of network model is used in a network that consists of only Windows 95 and Windows 98 computers?

   _____

6. What type of network model does NetWare 3.*x* use?

   _____

7. What type of network model does NetWare 4.*x* use?

   _____

8. What are the two levels of access control that you can apply on a Windows 95 computer?

   _____

   _____

9. List the three network protocols that you can install with an NT Server.

   _____

   _____

   _____

10. What does NLM stand for, and what is the purpose of an NLM?

_____

11. The _____ NT network service provides network services.

Acronyms to Know
❑ NLM

12. The _____ NT network service requests network services.

13. True or false: You can use a NetWare server as a desktop computer or as a server.

14. What are bindings?

_____

15. What does a network adapter do?

_____

Chapter 14

A Star Is Born:
History of NT

This chapter focuses on the origins of Windows NT. NT 3.1 was the first version to be released, in July 1993. NT 3.5 followed in September 1994. In July 1996, NT 4 was released. The next major version of NT to be released will move away from the NT name and will be called Windows 2000. This chapter will cover the different versions of NT and the differences between each version.

 Overview of NT origins

 NT 3.*x*

 NT 4

 Windows 2000

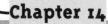

Understanding the Origins of NT

During the 1980s and early 1990s, Novell had the network operating system market cornered. Microsoft offered networking software through OS/2 (which was originally developed by IBM) and LAN Manager, but these operating systems never really caught on.

Microsoft decided to create a new operating system from the ground up. Designing a new operating system would eliminate the inherent limitations of legacy software.

In late 1988, Microsoft hired Dave Cutler, a veteran of minicomputer systems architecture, from Digital Equpment Corporation to design the new network operating system. This "New Technology" was to become Windows NT.

Before the programmers could get to work creating this new operating system, the design team had to come up with the software design goals that would define what the NT operating system should do.

The next few sections cover the design goals of NT.

Provide Flexibility in OS Code

The operating system code had to be written so that it could easily accommodate changes in marketplace requirements.

In this sense, NT is fairly modular and can add and delete components as current software and hardware standards dictate. It is also modular in the sense that you can configure each server or workstation to use only the services and drivers that each unique configuration needs. New services and drivers can be written as standards change, and they do not affect the core operating system.

Offer High Performance

A major design goal of NT was that it had to be a high-performance operating system. Each component of NT has been optimized to provide the highest performance.

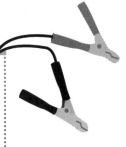

Be a Reliable OS

The operating system had to be able to handle errors in a reliable and fault-tolerant manner. This means that NT shields itself from most hardware and software errors so that the system will continue to operate.

NT manages memory through virtual memory. Virtual memory is the combination of physical RAM and the page file—a special file on the hard drive that acts like RAM. Whenever you launch an application (with the exception of Windows 16-bit applications), the application uses its own separate memory space. This technique keeps a failed application from affecting other applications or the operating system.

The NT File System (NTFS) is also designed so that it is able to recover from many different types of file errors.

POSIX
Stands for Portable Operating System Interface and is a standard interface for Unix implementations.

Use Portable Code

As hardware standards change, NT should have the capability of being ported from one processor type to another. For example, NT can run on an Intel processor or an Alpha processor.

Be Compatible with Existing Standards

NT should be compatible with existing standards. No network operating system can exist in a homogeneous environment. NT needs to be able to support heterogeneous networking environments. In addition, NT should be able to support existing applications written to run under other operating systems.

NT is compatible with existing network standards. For example, NT supports networking transport protocols such as TCP/IP, IPX/SPX, and NetBEUI (which are covered in Chapter 12, *Moving Data over the Network: Networking Protocols*). There is also support for interoperability with other networks, such as NetWare, SNA, Unix, and AppleTalk networks. These network operating systems are covered in Chapter 13, *Network Operating Systems: A Comparison*.

NT also supports applications by providing modular subsystems for DOS, OS/2, and **POSIX** applications. As new standards emerge, new subsystems can be developed. Each configuration loads only the necessary subsystems.

Understanding NT 3.x

The NT 3.x series featured three versions:

- ❖ NT 3.1
- ❖ NT 3.5
- ❖ NT 3.51

NT 3.1

The first released version of NT was NT Advanced Server 3.1 and NT Workstation 3.1. Microsoft named this version 3.1 to be consistent with Microsoft Windows 3.1, which was the current Windows software when NT was released.

The first version of NT focused on the design goals described on the previous pages. NT 3.x used the Windows 3.1 interface.

NT 3.5

NT 3.5 included bug fixes to 3.1 and added several features.

The name Advanced was dropped from Server, making the product NT Server 3.5 and NT Workstation 3.5.

The account lockout feature was added. Account lockout specifies that if a user's attempt to log on is unsuccessful, the user account will be locked. You can configure how many bad logons can be made before the account is locked.

The Network Monitoring Agent was added. The Network Monitoring Agent works with Systems Management Server (SMS). With the addition of the agent to an NT computer, SMS is able to analyze network packets being sent or received from the NT computer running the agent.

Performance Monitor (which monitors performance on your NT computer) had counters added for the **browser service**, **DHCP servers**, **WINS servers**, and **FTP server** service traffic, and for Network Monitor Statistics. These counters track performance of different items on your computer.

The Disk Administrator utility was enhanced so that you did not have to reboot after each configuration change.

Browser Service

In NT networks, broadcasts the availability of network services such as network shares or printers.

DHCP (Dynamic Host Configuration Protocol) Server

Automates the assignment of IP configurations.

WINS (Windows Internet Name Service) Server

Maps the NetBIOS names that NT uses to identify computers with an IP address.

FTP (File Transfer Protocol) Server

Transfers files between the FTP server and FTP clients. Most Web browsers use FTP client software to download and upload files to Internet servers running the FTP service.

You could use the Windows NT Diagnostic utility to view information on remote computers.

The RDISK utility was added so that you could create emergency repair disks, which store parts of your computer's configuration. You can use them to restore information in the event of system failure.

Control Panel was enhanced to add options for configuring your display, adding system environment variables, and creating a memory dump file if the computer crashed.

Long filename support was added, which allowed you to create filenames up to 255 characters long on a FAT partition. You could enable or disable this feature.

Additional printer support was added for print devices such as **plotters** and for PostScript font support. The LPR (Line Printer) and Digital Print Server Monitors were added. You use these monitors with Unix and Digital print devices.

NT 3.51

NT 3.51 included bug fixes to 3.5 and added several features:

- The **PowerPC** platform was supported.
- NTFS supported file compression.
- Support was added for Windows 95 common controls and Windows 95 Help.
- **RAS** security was improved.
- You could configure the MS-DOS prompt through Control Panel.

NOTE

All versions of NT 3.5x used the Windows 3.1 user interface. This made the operating system easier to use for people who already had experience with the Windows operating system. One of the first differences users noticed with NT 4 was that it used the Windows 95 user interface.

Plotter
A special type of print device that draws high-resolution diagrams, charts, graphs, and other layouts.

PowerPC
A type of microprocessor designed by Apple, Motorola, and IBM.

RAS (Remote Access Service)
Allows computers to access the network remotely; for example, through a phone, ISDN, or Internet connection.

Understanding NT 4

The most obvious change in NT 4 is that the operating system no longer uses the Windows 3.1 graphical interface. NT 4 uses the Windows 95 interface. While the interface has changed, administrators who are familiar with NT 3.51 notice that the utilities used in NT 4 are the same as in NT 3.5*x*.

NT Server 4 has two versions:

- ◆ NT Server 4 (standard)
- ◆ NT Server/E (Enterprise version) 4

NT Server 4

Several enhancements have been made in NT 4.

Better performance over NT 3.51 has been provided. On a single-processor computer, NT 4 runs up to 66 percent faster in file and print tests.

More drivers are supported during installation. Support is available for more than 1,000 computers beyond what NT 3.51 supported. This makes installation and setup much easier, because drivers are likely to be available through installation media.

Hardware profile support, which is typically used for laptops that have different configurations when docked or undocked, has been added.

Critical error messages have been rewritten to provide clearer information and possible solutions.

Administrative Wizards have been added to walk administrators through common tasks.

Task Manager has been improved to add features of Performance Monitor, which allows you to very easily and quickly view memory and resource use.

New services, such as Internet Information Server (IIS) and Index Server, can be added.

A new protocol has been added for Remote Access Service (RAS). Point-to-Point Tunneling Protocol (PPTP) allows you to route RAS connections through the Internet.

NT Server/E (NT Server Enterprise Version) 4

This version of NT Server adds greater support by including many features and services.

Clustering services are supported for two-server clusters. Cluster services (formerly known by the code name Wolfpack, now known as Microsoft Cluster Server, or MSCS) provide fault tolerance and load-balancing features. Clustering services are able to monitor server health and reliability, and recover applications and data in the event of system failure by using the second server in the cluster.

The user is licensed to run more than four **symmetric processors** without special OEM versions of NT Server. Windows Server/E can support up to eight Symmetric MultiProcessing (SMP) processors.

Better memory tuning exists for applications with high memory requirements. This version can also use up to 3GB of RAM per application as opposed to previous versions of NT, which support only 2GB of RAM per application.

NT Server/E also ships with these services: Service Pack 3, Internet Information Server (IIS) 3, Microsoft Transaction Server (MTS), Microsoft Message Queue Server (MSMQ), and FrontPage 97. These services support an enterprise network environment.

Symmetric Processor

When an NT computer has more than one processor, it uses symmetric processing to use all processors in order to improve performance.

NOTE

Microsoft periodically releases Service Packs for its operating system and BackOffice products. Service Packs typically contain fixes to known problems. NT Server Enterprise version requires that you install Service Pack 3 before you can install MSCS, MSMQ, MTS, FrontPage 97, or Internet Explorer 3.02.

WARNING

If you are currently running NT Server with Service Pack 2 or later and you wish to upgrade to NT Server Enterprise version, you should not use the WINNT32.EXE program. This upgrade method can cause severe problems for your server. Instead, you should use the WINNTUP.EXE program to upgrade to NT Server Enterprise version.

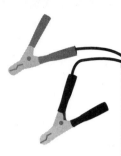

Understanding Windows 2000

Just when you have become familiar with the NT name, Microsoft announces that the next major operating system version will be named Windows 2000 instead of NT 5. Originally, NT 5 was supposed to ship in 1998 but has been delayed. Most industry experts expect it to ship in the first or second quarter of the year 2000.

Windows 2000 will have three platforms:

◆ NT Workstation 5 will be called Windows 2000 Professional.

◆ NT Server 5 will be called Windows 2000 Server.

◆ NT Server 5 Enterprise Edition will be called Windows 2000 Advanced Server.

All versions of Windows 2000 will include several major changes:

◆ A 64-bit operating system will support Intel's 64-bit Merced processor.

◆ Plug-and-Play capability will be included. This capability enables the operating system to recognize hardware additions or changes through a combination of hardware and software support, so that user intervention is not needed for hardware configuration changes.

◆ Microsoft Management Console (MMC) will be introduced. MMC is a common console that centrally manages all of the administrative tools. With MMC, administrators can customize the console they use.

◆ FAT32 disk partitions will be supported. FAT32 is a way of formatting your logical drives to store data more efficiently than FAT. This has been supported by Windows 95/98 but not by previous versions of NT.

◆ MIPS and PowerPC platforms will be phased out because of lack of demand.

Windows 2000 Professional

Windows 2000 Professional extends the functionality of NT Workstation 4 in many ways.

- ◆ It uses second-generation Plug-and-Play capabilities and power management.

- ◆ It offers a more Web-integrated GUI (graphical user interface) on the Desktop. This interface makes it easier for users to access Internet resources, and Internet browsing capabilities have been improved.

- ◆ It provides better reliability, security, and networking features over NT Workstation 4. It also offers much broader hardware and software support.

- ◆ Windows 2000 Professional has IntelliMirror Management capabilities, which offer administrators the ability to mirror a workstation's applications and data on a Windows 2000 Server. The advantage is, if a workstation fails, it can be quickly recovered from the mirror on the server.

- ◆ The product provides better support for roaming user profiles. A profile defines the user's Desktop. With roaming profiles, a user can get their own unique Desktop from any Windows 2000 computer on the network.

- ◆ A new Hardware Wizard makes adding commonly used hardware devices easier to install.

- ◆ New support for NTFS includes defragmentation support and the ability to limit how much disk space each user can take.

- ◆ This version allows users to upgrade from Windows 95 and 98, which was not an available option under NT Workstation 4.

- ◆ It provides better backup support, which includes the ability to back up to tape drives, external hard drives, recordable compact disks (CD-R), and Zip drives. Under NT Workstation 4, the backup utility supported only tape drive backup.

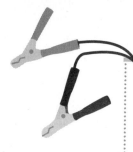

Windows 2000 Server

Windows 2000 Server offers many new features. Some of them are discussed in the following sections.

Active Directory

One of the main differences in Windows 2000 Server is that it moves away from the NT domain model and instead uses Active Directory. Active Directory uses a directory services network model.

With Active Directory, the network is represented as a hierarchical database. The database consists of containers and objects. A container stores objects. It is similar to a folder within the file structure. Objects represent network users, groups, or resources. Examples of resources include servers, network shares, printers, applications, and fax servers.

Distributed File System (DFS)

DFS is a service that allows administrators to create a virtual directory structure. The directory structure is logical in nature. What appears to be a single directory structure can be composed of folders from multiple servers. The DFS directory is assigned a logical name, and where data and applications are stored is transparent to the users.

The advantages of DFS are that it is easier for users to use and it makes backups easier for administrators, who can back up a single DFS structure as opposed to many separate network folders.

Kerberos Security

With the Kerberos security protocol, users have a secure single logon to the Active Directory. This allows users to access Active Directory resources (objects) to which they have been granted access permission.

Windows 2000 Advanced Server

These features have been added to Windows 2000 Advanced Server.

Microsoft Cluster Server

MSCS was first released with NT Server Enterprise version 4. MSCS offers three main advantages: availability, manageability, and scalability.

Availability means that if a server within the cluster fails, this condition will be detected, and another server within the cluster will start the services and applications that were running on the failed server. This is transparent to users, and the users experience only a small delay when accessing these resources.

Manageability allows network administrators to view the status of the clustered servers and manually balance the workload of shared resources within the cluster.

Scalability means that if applications have been written to be cluster aware, dynamic load balancing can be used to manage applications.

TCP/IP Load Balancing

TCP/IP load balancing works with MSCS by allowing Dynamic Host Configuration Protocol (DHCP) servers to participate within the cluster. DHCP automatically assigns IP configuration information. Without MSCS, DHCP servers are configured as independent servers and are not capable of sharing configuration information. With MSCS, you can balance TCP/IP configuration information while also providing the fault-tolerant capabilities of MSCS.

Review Questions

1. List the five major design goals of the NT operating system design:

   _____

   _____

   _____

   _____

   _____

2. Which three versions of software will replace NT 4?

   _____

   _____

   _____

3. Which version of NT first used the Windows 95 Desktop interface?

   _____

4. Which version of NT first supported long filenames?

   _____

5. Which version of NT first supported NTFS file compression?

   _____

6. What does MSCS stand for?

   _____

7. What is the first version of NT to support 64-bit processing?

   _____

Terms to Know
- ❏ Browser Service
- ❏ Plotter
- ❏ PowerPC
- ❏ Symmetric Processor
- ❏ Cluster Services
- ❏ Active Directory

8. What is the purpose of MMC?

_____

9. What is the first version of NT to support FAT32?

_____

10. What is the purpose of IntelliMirror?

_____

Chapter

15

The NT Platforms: NT Workstation and NT Server

One of the first decisions you make for your computer is what operating system you will use. Microsoft has many options to choose from. In this section you will learn about the different operating system platforms and the characteristics of each platform. These topics are covered:

 Features of NT Workstation

 Features of NT Server

 Comparison of Windows 95 and NT Workstation

 Comparison of NT Workstation and NT Server

 Types of NT Servers

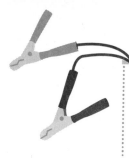

Understanding the Features of NT Workstation

NTFS

A file system used on NT computers that supports features such as local security.

OEM

Stands for Original Equipment Manufacturer and is the original manufacturer of equipment. In this case, a hardware vendor may make a server that is designed for NT Server and bundle a special version of NT that is optimized to take advantage of the hardware.

Alpha Processor

Typically offers better performance than Intel processors. NT is the main operating system that takes advantage of Alpha processors. Some versions of Unix also use Alpha processors.

NT Workstation is designed to be a powerful desktop operating system. The benefits of NT Workstation include the familiar Desktop Windows 95 uses, combined with better performance and security features, such as mandatory logon and local file security through **NTFS**.

NT Workstation includes a familiar Windows 95 interface, which makes the transition to NT Workstation easier for users.

NT Workstation is a much more stable platform than Windows 95 and crashes much less often.

With NT Workstation, you can support multiple processors, which you can use for multitasking performance. This technique offers the highest level of desktop performance. By default, NT Workstation can support two processors, but with **OEM** support, you can have up to 32 processors.

This operating system is hardware independent, and you can run it from an Intel or **Alpha processor** platform.

NT Workstation offers a comprehensive security model, which requires users to be authenticated through NT security before they can access the OS. In addition, with NT Workstation, you can create NTFS disk partitions, which allow you to define local security for your file system.

There is a tool called NT Explorer, which you can use to manage your file structure more easily.

NT Workstation comes with Internet Explorer, which provides a Web browser that is easy to use.

Peer Web Services (PWS) is bundled with the NT Workstation OS. PWS allows you to run your own mini–Web server, which you use to publish Web pages.

You get a tool called Task Manager, which you can use to manage tasks and applications. With Task Manager, you can start and stop applications. You can also see a quick overview of how your processor and memory are being used.

NT Workstation allows you to support one incoming remote access session. There is also a utility called Dial-Up Networking, which you can use to make outgoing remote connections.

Hardware profiles allow you to maintain multiple hardware configuration pro-files. For example, you might have two hardware configurations for your laptop that are dependent on whether or not the laptop is docked or undocked.

With NT Workstation, you can define system policies, which define which Desk-top environment is presented to users as they log on. For example, with system policies, you can define which Desktop options are presented and which options are not presented, like Network Neighborhood.

NT Workstation maintains and creates user profiles, which define the user's Desktop each time they log on. Desktops contain all of the user preferences, such as shortcuts and wallpaper selection. User profiles are customized per user, so if multiple users share the same computer, each user will still access their customized user profile.

NT Workstation 4 Technical Requirements

This table lists the technical requirements for NT Workstation.

Component	Minimum Requirement	Recommended Requirement
Processor	Intel 486DX/33	Intel Pentium or higher
Memory	12MB on Intel	16MB–32MB
Hard disk	110MB	Depends on what will be stored
Display	VGA	High-resolution VGA
Peripherals	Mouse, CD drive, or access to distribution files from network	Network adapter card if network access is required

NOTE

NT Workstation differs from NT Server primarily in how it is tuned. NT Work-station is tuned for user applications, and NT Server is tuned for server-based applications.

Understanding the Features of NT Server

NT Server is designed to be a powerful network server that can provide file, print, application, and domain controller functions. The benefits of NT Server include the familiar Desktop Windows 95 uses, combined with better performance and security features, such as mandatory logon and local file security through NTFS.

NT Server is a very stable platform and is optimized for file, print, and application services.

With NT Server, you can support multiple processors, which you can use for multitasking performance. This technique offers the highest level of server performance. NT Server can support four processors by default, but with OEM versions of NT, up to 32 processors can be supported.

This operating system is hardware independent, and you can run it from an Intel or Alpha processor platform.

NT Server offers a comprehensive security model, which requires users to be authenticated through NT security before they can access the OS. In addition, with NT Workstation, you can create NTFS disk partitions, which allow you to define local security for your file system.

There is a tool called NT Explorer, which you can use to manage your file structure more easily.

NT Server comes with Internet Explorer, which provides a Web browser that is easy to use.

Internet Information Server (IIS) is bundled with the NT Server OS. IIS allows you to run your own Web server and supports the **HTTP** and **FTP** protocols.

You get a tool called Task Manager, which you can use to manage tasks and applications. With Task Manager, you can start and stop applications. You can also see a quick overview of how your processor and memory are being used.

NT Server allows you to support 256 incoming remote access (**RAS**) sessions. There is also a utility called Dial-Up Networking, which you can use to make outgoing remote connections.

HTTP

Stands for Hypertext Transfer Protocol and provides access on the World Wide Web (WWW) to hypertext documents.

FTP

Stands for File Transfer Protocol and transfers files between two hosts.

RAS (Remote Access Service)

A service that allows remote computers to dial in to your network and act as network nodes.

Hardware profiles allow you to maintain multiple hardware configuration profiles. For example, you might have two hardware configurations for your laptop that are dependent on whether or not the laptop is docked or undocked.

With NT Server, you can define system policies, which define which Desktop environment is presented to users as they log on. For example, with system policies, you can define which Desktop options are presented and which options are not presented, like Network Neighborhood.

NT Server can maintain user profiles, which define the user's Desktop each time they log on. By storing profiles on servers, you can define roaming profiles, which allow users to access their profile from any NT computer attached to the network.

NT Server 4 Technical Requirements

This table defines the technical requirements for NT Server.

Component	Minimum Requirement	Recommended Requirement
Processor	Intel 486DX/33	Intel Pentium or higher
Memory	16MB on Intel	32MB or higher
Hard disk	110MB	Depends on what will be stored
Display	VGA	High-resolution VGA
Peripherals	Mouse, CD drive, or access to distribution files from network	Network adapter card if network access is required

NOTE

NT Server can support as many incoming connections as you need. The only thing you need is a license for each connection. NT Workstation will only accept up to 10 incoming connections.

Comparing Windows 95 and NT Workstation

This table compares Windows 95 to NT Workstation 4.

Comparison Feature	Windows 95	NT Workstation 4
Minimum hardware requirements	Intel 386 with 4MB of RAM (really needs 486 with at least 16MB of RAM).	Supports Intel, RISC, Alpha, and PowerPC. With Intel, requires 486DX/33 with 12MB of RAM (really needs Pentium or better with 16MB–32MB of RAM).
Existing application and device compatibility	Very high. Supports almost all DOS and Win16 applications. Hardware requirements are not as stringent.	Supports DOS and Win16 applications, but does not support applications that try to directly access the hardware. Hardware devices must be on Hardware Compatibility List (HCL) for Microsoft support to be offered.
Performance	Good performance for 32-bit applications, which can be preemptively multitasked.	Offers the highest performance, and all applications can be preemptively multitasked.
Reliability	Better than previous versions of Windows, but still prone to system crashes on occasion.	Very stable.
Plug-and-Play compatibility	Fully supported.	Not supported.
Security	No required logon or local file security.	High security through required logon, and NTFS folder and file-level security.

Comparing NT Workstation and NT Server

NT Workstation is designed and tuned to be a desktop operating system. It is tuned to run front-end desktop applications, like Microsoft Office applications—Word, Excel, Outlook, etc.

NT Server is designed and tuned to act as a network server. As a server, it is tuned for file and print services, application services, and domain controller functions. NT Server is tuned to run back-end applications, like Microsoft Back-Office. BackOffice includes applications like SMS (Systems Management Server), SQL Server (Structured Query Language), Exchange Server, and SNA Server (System Network Architecture).

Differences

NT Workstation can only support up to 10 incoming connections. NT Server can support unlimited incoming connections.

NT Workstation supports one RAS connection, while NT Server supports up to 256 RAS connections.

NT Workstation uses PWS as its Web server, while NT Server uses IIS, which is more functional and offers more services.

The standard version of NT Workstation supports up to two processors, while the standard version of NT Server supports up to four processors. OEM versions of NT Workstation and NT Server support up to 32 processors.

NT Workstation does not require as much RAM as NT Server requires.

NT Servers can run TCP/IP services like **DHCP server**, **WINS server**, and **DNS server**. NT Workstations can be clients, but not servers, for these services.

DHCP (Dynamic Host Configuration Protocol)
A TCP/IP service that dynamically allocates and assigns IP addresses.

WINS (Windows Internet Name Service)
A TCP/IP service that maps the computer names that Microsoft uses to IP addresses.

DNS (Domain Name System) Server
A TCP/IP service that maps domain names (not the same domain as NT, but domains as defined by InterNIC) to IP addresses.

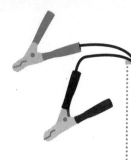

Considering the Types of NT Servers

Internetwork

Two or more network segments that are connected. Network segments can be connected through bridges, routers, and gateways.

NT Servers can play one of three roles:

◆ Primary domain controller (PDC)

◆ Backup domain controller (BDC)

◆ Member server

You select the type of server during installation. Server roles are an important part of domain management.

A domain is a logical collection of servers and client computers that share the same user and group accounts database. The accounts database is called the Security Accounts Manager (SAM). Each domain has a unique name from other domains that might be connected to the same network or **internetwork**.

Server Role Selection

It is important that you choose server roles carefully for these reasons:

◆ Once a PDC or BDC is installed into a domain, it cannot change to another domain without reinstallation.

◆ If a server is installed as a PDC or BDC, it cannot become a member server without reinstallation.

◆ Conversely, a server that is installed as a member server cannot become a PDC or BDC without reinstallation.

NOTE

Other computers besides servers can participate in the domain. For example, NT Workstations, Windows 95 and 98 computers, Windows 3.1 computers, DOS computers, OS/2 computers, Unix, and Macintosh computers can participate in an NT domain.

Primary Domain Controller

The PDC is the first server that is installed into the domain. The PDC contains the only read/write copy of the domain SAM. Changes that are made at the PDC are copied to the BDCs.

Each domain can have only one PDC.

Backup Domain Controller

BDCs store read-only copies of the SAM database. A BDC serves two main purposes:

- ◆ It offloads logon authentication from the PDC.
- ◆ It provides fault tolerance if the PDC fails and can be promoted to PDC.

In order to install a BDC into a domain, you must have the PDC for the domain up and running. When the BDC is installed, it will contact the PDC to find out the domain's SID, or security identification. The BDC will be configured to use the same SID. This is required for SAM synchronization to occur properly.

By default, the PDC will send SAM update changes to the BDCs every five minutes. NT comes with a utility called Server Manager, which can manually synchronize the SAM database.

For fault tolerance, each domain should have at least one BDC. The size and geographical scope of your domain determines the number and placement of BDCs.

Member Server

Member servers participate in the domain, but do not store a copy of the domain SAM. This allows servers such as file and print servers or application servers to provide optimal performance without the overhead of domain SAM synchronization and the processing of logon requests.

Member servers do not share the domain SID that the PDC and BDCs use, so they are able to switch domains without reinstallation.

NOTE

It is important to note that only the SAM database is synchronized between the PDC and the BDCs. There is no synchronization of folders, files, or data.

Review Questions

1. How many PDCs can a domain contain?

_____

2. What is the name of the accounts database that the domain controllers manage?

_____

3. True or false: A BDC can change from one domain to another without reinstallation.

4. True or false: A member server can change from one domain to another without reinstallation.

5. How many processors does a standard version of NT Workstation support?

_____

6. How many RAS connections does NT Server support?

_____

7. True or false: You can install the Windows 95 operating system on an Intel or Alpha computer platform.

8. What are the minimum CPU and memory that you can use to install NT Server?

_____

9. What is the list called that verifies whether or not NT Workstation or NT Server supports your hardware?

_____

10. What do PDC and BDC stand for?

_____

_____

11. True or false: A BDC can become a PDC without reinstallation.

12. True or false: A member server can become a PDC without reinstallation.

13. True or false: NT supports Plug-and-Play capabilities.

14. Which Microsoft software would you install on an NT Server so that it could support the HTTP and FTP services?

_____

15. Why would you install a server as a member server instead of a domain controller?

_____

16. True or false: For the best performance, you should install NT Server as your desktop operating system.

Chapter

16

Users and Groups: NT Account Management

One of the most fundamental tasks in NT system administration is the creation of user and group accounts. Each user should have their own user account that uniquely identifies them as a network user. You primarily use groups to simplify permission assignments. NT is different from other network operating systems in that it uses two types of groups, local and global groups.

In this chapter, you will learn about these NT account management tasks:

 Managing NT users

 Managing properties of NT users

 Administration of NT account policies

 How to manage NT local and global groups

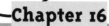

Managing NT Users

Each network user should have their own personal logon name and password that uniquely identifies their user account. In NT, only administrators or members of a group called Account Operators are able to create NT user accounts.

In an NT domain environment, you use User Manager for Domains to create users. In an NT workgroup environment, you use User Manager to create accounts. In this chapter, you should assume that you are configuring user accounts in a domain environment.

When you create users, you should observe these guidelines:

Security Accounts Manager (SAM)
The database NT uses to store user and group information.

- ◆ Each username must be unique within the **Security Accounts Manager (SAM)** database.

- ◆ A username can be as short as a single character or as long as 20 characters.

- ◆ Alphanumeric names are easier for users to remember.

- ◆ These characters cannot be part of the username:
  " / \ [ ] ; : | = , + * ? < >

You can access the dialog to create a user in User Manager for Domains by going to Start ≻ Programs ≻ Administrative Tools (Common) ≻ User Manager for Domains.

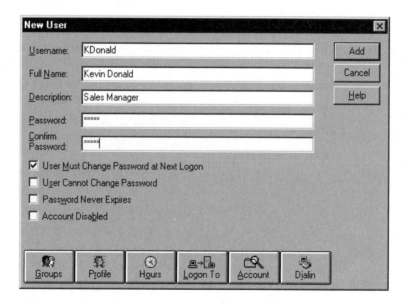

The New User dialog screen also allows you to configure the options shown in this table.

New User Option	Description
Full Name	Specifies the user's first and last name for informational purposes.
Description	Allows you to input descriptive information, such as title or location of user.
Password and Confirm Password	Allows you to assign the user's initial password. You also use this option to reset the password later on without having to provide the previous password. After you fill in this screen, it will always display 14 asterisks so that the length of the password is not disclosed.
User Must Change Password at Next Logon	Specifies that the user must change the password the next time they log on. This forces the user to discard the password that the network administrator assigned and select a personal password.
User Cannot Change Password	This option prevents the user from changing the password that the administrator assigned. You define this option for the guest account or a single-user account that multiple users share.
Password Never Expires	Specifies that if you define a maximum age through User Policies, this user's account is exempt and will not expire. You set this option on service accounts.
Account Disabled	Allows you to disable an account that is no longer in use so that it does not pose a security risk. At a later date, you can still reactivate this account, as opposed to deleted accounts, which you can never reinstate.

NOTE

Usernames in NT are not case sensitive, but passwords are case sensitive.

Defining Properties of User Accounts

When you create an NT user account, you can define the user properties of the account. User properties define

- ❖ Which groups the user belongs to

- ❖ Profile information, including whether or not the user will use a logon script, a roaming profile, and/or a home folder

- ❖ The logon hours that are allowed for the user account

- ❖ The NetBIOS computer names from which the user is allowed to log on

- ❖ Account options, such as whether or not the account has a predetermined expiration date

- ❖ Whether or not the user account has Remote Access Server dial-in permissions

Groups

The Groups user property dialog box displays which groups the user account is a member of and allows you to add or remove the user account from groups.

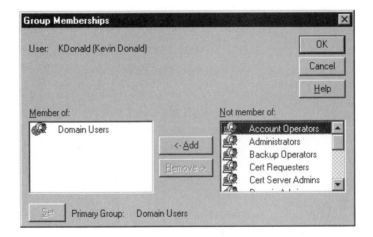

Profile

The Profile user property dialog box defines

- ◇ Whether or not the user is using a roaming profile
- ◇ Whether or not the user is using a logon script
- ◇ Whether or not the user is using a home folder and, if so, whether the home folder is local or on a network share

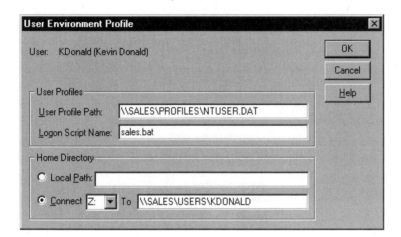

This table describes each option.

User Profile Property	Description
User Profile Path	A profile is the look and configuration of each user's desktop. By default, profiles are stored on the NT computer where a user has logged on and made changes. This option allows you to specify the network location of a user profile so that the user gets their profile from any network computer. This is called a roaming profile.
Logon Script Name	A logon script is a `.bat`, `.com`, or `.exe` file that executes whenever a user logs on to the network.
Home Directory	Allows you to specify the home folder that will be mapped when the user logs on to the network. You can specify that the home folder be on a local drive or on a network share. Many network administrators specify network locations, because this simplifies data backup.

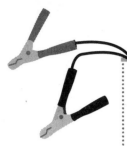

Hours

The Hours user property dialog box specifies the hours that allow or disallow the user to log on to the network. By default, users can log on to the network 24 hours a day, but you could limit this for purposes of backup or security.

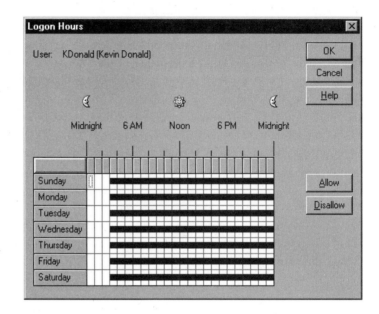

Log On To

By default, users can log on to the network from any networked computer. The Log On To user property dialog box limits which computers a specific user is able to log on from. You set this limit mainly for security purposes.

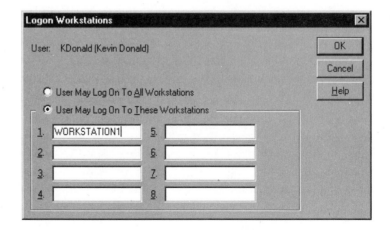

Account

The Account user property dialog box defines whether or not the account has a predetermined expiration date. By default, user accounts do not expire. You might use this option in an academic environment to cause student accounts to expire on the last day of the semester.

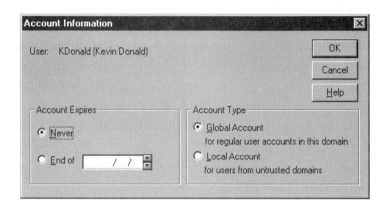

Dialin

The Dialin user account property dialog box specifies whether or not the user account has permission to dial in to a Remote Access Server. By default, users are not granted this permission. If you allow dial-in access, you can specify whether or not callback security is required.

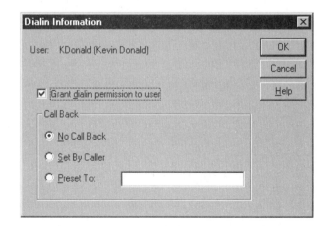

Administering NT Account Policies

NT account policies specify password and account lockout restrictions on a domain-wide basis. To access this dialog box from User Manager for Domains, select Policies Account.

NOTE

With the exception of account policies, you do all other user configuration on a per-user basis. For example, you cannot set time restrictions or station restrictions as an account policy, nor can you configure this as a group property.

This table defines the account policies.

Account Policy	Description
Maximum Password Age	Defines the maximum number of days that you can keep your password. By default, this is 42 days.
Minimum Password Age	Specifies how many days you have to keep your password before you can change it. By default, you can change your password immediately after it has been changed.
Minimum Password Length	Specifies the minimum number of characters required for each user's password. By default, no passwords are required, but you can specify minimum password lengths from one to 14 characters.
Password Uniqueness	Defines the number of passwords that the system will remember, so that the user has to use unique passwords. For example, if you set this number to 10 and the current user password was "bunny", 10 unique passwords would have to occur after "bunny" before you could use this password again. By default, no password history is retained.
No account lockout or Account lockout	Specifies whether or not you want to enable account lockout. Account lockout prevents unauthorized users from accessing your system by limiting the number of unsuccessful logon attempts that can be made within x minutes. By default, account lockout is not enabled.
Lockout after	Determines the number of unsuccessful attempts that the user can make before the user account is locked out.
Reset count after	Specifies how long the system will remember that the user has made a failed logon attempt.
Lockout duration	Defines the number of minutes that an account will remain locked if account lockout is triggered. You can also specify that only an administrator can unlock accounts that have been locked.

Managing NT Groups

A group is an NT account that you use for logically organizing users who need similar rights. The main function of a group is that it allows you to apply permissions to the group rather than assigning permissions to individual users. This makes NT security management easier and more consistent.

Within a workgroup environment, NT uses only local groups. In an NT domain environment, global groups are also used.

The main functions of the groups are the following:

◆ Global groups logically organize users who need similar rights.

◆ Local groups are granted access to resources; for example, a network share.

Here is an example of how groups work within the NT domain environment, assuming that a group of accounting users need to access a share called \\ACCT\data:

1. At the primary domain controller (PDC) for the domain, you would create a global group and add all of the users who will need to access the accounting information. In this case, you would create a global group called ACCOUNTING and add all of the accounting users.

2. At the NT computers that contain resources that users will need to access, you create local groups. You would assign the local group the permission that it would need to access the resources. For example, assume you have a member server called ACCT with a share called \\ACCT\data that you wanted your users to access. You would create a local group called DATA USERS and assign it Change permission to the share.

3. Finally, you would add the global group to the local group.

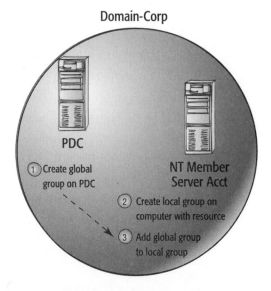

Users and Groups: NT Account Management

With this method of account management, you logically organize users in a central location and manage resources in a more decentralized fashion. This allows you to share network resources on computers other than NT domain controllers.

Here is a more complex example of how group interaction works. Assume that you have three users who make up the sales department: Larry, Curly, and Moe. These users need to access these resources with these access permissions:

- The SALES NT member server `Sales Data` share with Change permission
- The CURLY NT workstation with the `Curly Data` share with Read permission
- The APPS NT member server with the `Apps` share with Read permission

In this case, you would take these actions:

1. On the PDC for the domain, you would create a global group called SALES and add Larry, Curly, and Moe to the global group.
2. At each of the resource computers, you would create local groups that were assigned access permissions to the resources that the SALES group needed permission to access.
3. You would then add the global group to each local group.

Now, if Curly leaves the group and is replaced by Rick, you would remove Curly from the global group SALES and add Rick, giving him access to all of the resources that the global group SALES has permission to access.

Local Groups

Local groups have these characteristics:

◆ You can create local groups on any NT computer.

◆ Local groups remain local to the SAM database on the computer where they were created.

◆ The main function of a local group is to allow a mechanism for assigning permissions to NT resources that are not located on NT domain controllers.

◆ Local groups can contain user accounts from the local SAM database, user accounts from the domain SAM database, user accounts from trusted domain SAM databases, global groups from within the domain, and global groups from trusted domains. You can define trust relationships that allow users from one domain to access resources in another domain.

These local groups are created by default on NT domain controllers:

Default Group	Purpose
Account Operators	Can administer NT user and group accounts.
Administrators	Have full control over administration of domain controllers within the domain. Includes all administrative task permissions.
Backup Operators	Are given full access to back up and restore the domain controller's file structure even if they do not have folder and file access permissions.
Guests	Have limited guest access permissions.
Print Operators	Possess the ability to manage printers within the domain.
Replicator	Is a special account used to manage a service called Directory Replication.
Server Operators	Can manipulate NT servers, but are not able to manage user and group accounts.
Users	Are the regular domain users.

Global Groups

Global groups have these characteristics:

- You use global groups to logically organize users who need similar rights.
- Global groups exist only on NT domain controllers.
- Global groups can only contain users from within their domain SAM database.

These global groups are created by default on NT domain controllers:

Default Group	Purpose
Domain Admins	Allow members to have administrative rights to all NT computers within the domain.
Domain Guests	Allow you to logically organize all users who should have limited guest access.
Domain Users	Automatically organize all users who are created within the domain SAM database with the exception of the Guest account.

NOTE

You use the default local groups to grant some type of access permission. You use the default global groups only to logically organize users who need similar rights.

NOTE

You can easily identify default local groups because they are mostly named _____ Operators. You can identify default global groups because they are all named Domain _____.

Review Questions

1. What is the maximum length of an NT username?

   _____

2. Which utility do you use to create users in an NT domain environment?

   _____

3. Which new user option do you use to force a user to change their administrator-assigned password the first time they log on?

   _____

4. What is the difference between disabling a user account and deleting a user account?

   _____

5. True or false: A profile determines which desktop a user will use.

6. True or false: You can specify which group a user belongs to as a property of the user account.

7. True or false: NT account names and passwords are case sensitive.

8. Which user property dialog box specifies that the user should use a logon script?

   _____

9. What default hours are defined that specify when users can log on to an NT domain?

   _____

10. What is the primary purpose of account lockout?

   _____

11. Which account policy specifies how many unique user passwords must be used before a user can recycle an old password?

_____

12. Which group type do you use to logically organize users in NT?

_____

13. Which group type do you use to assign permissions to resources in NT?

_____

14. What default local group manages NT user and group accounts but cannot fully manipulate NT servers?

_____

15. What default global group logically organizes all NT users that are created within the domain?

_____

16. What users or groups can be contained within a global group?

_____

17. What permissions are assigned to the Backup Operators group?

_____

Chapter

17

NT Resources: File and Print Management

Before there were networks, people shared data through "sneakernet," which meant moving files by using floppies and leg power. Now, with networking, sneakernet is becoming obsolete. With networking, you can share files and folders through the network. In this chapter, you will learn how to share folders and apply network security to the shared folders.

Another powerful feature of NT is the ability to secure resources by using NTFS security. NTFS is a file system accessible only through the NT operating system.

The last resource that will be covered in this chapter is the management of NT printers. You can use printers locally or share them through the network. Just as you can apply permissions to folders, you also can apply security to printers. This chapter will cover these topics:

 Sharing folders

 Shared folder security

 NTFS partitions

 Print resources

 Assigning permissions to resources

Sharing Folders

If more than one user needs access to the same data, the easiest way to provide access is by creating a network share. In NT you can share folders on a local drive that network users can then access. By applying security to the folders, you can control how users access the folders. For example, assume you have a folder called DATA on the Sales server. You might assign members of the Sales group full access to the share, assign members of the Accountants group read access to the share, and not allow any other users any access to the share.

Local users can see which folders are shared on their computer through My Computer or NT Explorer, because a hand underneath the folder indicates shared folders.

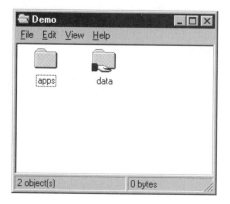

Once a folder is shared, network users access the share through the Network Neighborhood utility (assuming the user has permission).

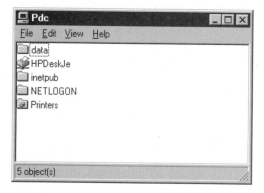

In order to share a folder in NT, you must be logged in to the computer as a member of one of these groups:

- ❖ Administrators
- ❖ Server Operators (on an NT PDC or BDC)
- ❖ Power Users (on an NT Workstation on an NT member server)

You can create network shares from My Computer, NT Explorer, or through Server Manager (this utility only comes with NT PDC and BDCs). To create a network share, you click on the file you want to share and access Properties ➤ Sharing. At this point, you will see this dialog box:

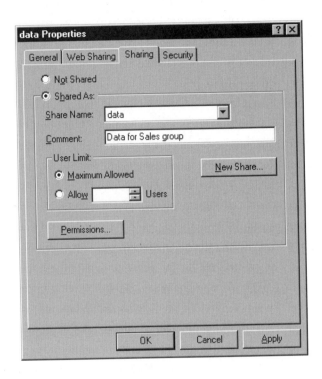

This table defines the Sharing tab options.

Option	Description
Not Shared or Shared As	Indicates whether or not the folder will be available for network access. You must select one of these radio buttons.
Share Name	Specifies the name to be displayed through Network Neighborhood that the users will see when they access the share. This name can be up to 32 characters.
Comment	Allows you to provide a description of the folder. Users will see this description through Network Neighborhood.
User Limit	Specifies how many concurrent users can access the share. In NT Workstation, the maximum number is 10. In NT Server, the number is unlimited.
Permissions	Assigns which permissions users and groups have when accessing the folder over a network share.

Applying Shared Folder Security

When a folder is shared, you have the option of applying share permissions to the folder for users and/or groups. Share permissions include:

- Full Control
- Change
- Read
- No Access

This table defines these access permissions.

Share Permission	Description
Full Control	With Full Control permission, a user can read and change files within the folder. In addition, a user can change the share permissions for other users and groups and take ownership of files on NTFS partitions.
Change	This permission allows a user to read files, add files and subfolders, edit the data within existing files, delete files and subfolders, and edit file attributes of files within the shared folder.
Read	The Read permission allows a user to display files, read the contents of a file, execute program files, copy files to other folders, and display file attributes.
No Access	This permission is very restrictive. With No Access, you can connect to the shared folder, but you are denied any access to the folder, and the folder contents will not be displayed.

NOTE

The default permission for shared folders is that the group Everyone has Full Control permission.

Handling User and Group Permission Interaction

You can apply share permissions to users and groups. When a user attempts to access a shared resource, the operating system must determine what access the user should have. When users log on to an NT Workstation or an NT domain, an access token is created for the user that specifies the user's unique user identification and any groups that the user belongs to. This information verifies if the user has share access permissions to the share that they are attempting to access.

If the user has access permissions applied through user and group permissions, or if the user belongs to multiple groups that have access permissions assigned, the user's effective permission will be the most permissive permission that has been assigned. The exception to this rule is if the user has No Access permission through user or group assignment. If No Access has been assigned, the user has No Access even if they have other, more permissive permissions through other assignments.

For example, assume that you have two users, Kate and Magda. Kate is a member of the groups Sales and Execs, and Magda is a member of the groups Sales and Temps. These permissions have been assigned:

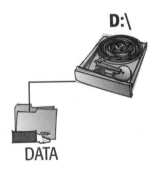

D:

DATA

Share Permissions

Temps – No Access
Sales – Change
Execs – Full Access

In this case,

- Kate has Full Access permission, because it is most permissive.
- Magda has No Access, because she is a member of a group with No Access permission.

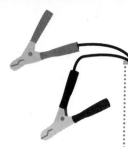

Applying Share Permissions

In order to apply share permissions, you take these steps:

1. From NT Explorer right-click the folder that is or will be shared.

2. Click the Sharing option.

3. From the Sharing dialog box, select the Permissions button.

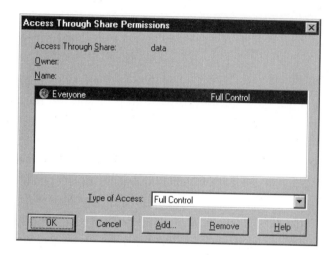

4. If you do not want to leave group Everyone with Full Control permission, highlight this group and click the Remove button.

5. To add new share permission assignments, select the Add button.

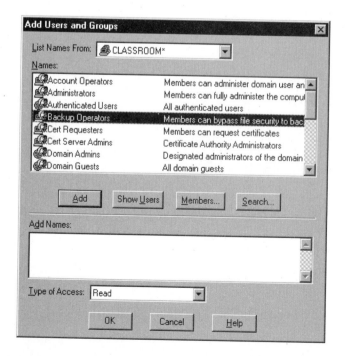

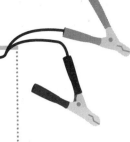

6. You can add groups by highlighting the group. Once the group is highlighted, at the bottom of the dialog box select the type of access to assign to the user and click the OK button. To add user assignments, first select the Show Users button, then complete the same steps that you used to assign the group permission.

TEST IT OUT

1. Start by creating two users on which you can test share permissions. Make sure you are logged on as Administrator, and go to Start ➢ Programs ➢ Administrative Tools (Common) ➢ User Manager (for NT Workstation, or User Manager for Domains for NT domain controller servers) ➢ User ➢ New User. At this point, create a user named Kate and a user named Magda. Make sure to uncheck the User Must Change Password at Next Logon box.

2. Next, create a folder that the users will share. From Start ➢ Programs ➢ Windows NT Explorer ➢ File ➢ New ➢ Folder, name your new folder SHAREME.

3. To share the folder, single-click the SHAREME folder. Click File ➢ Properties ➢ Sharing tab. Click the Shared As radio button. The folder is now shared. If you go back to Windows NT Explorer, you will notice that the folder has a hand underneath it, which indicates that the folder is shared.

4. From the Sharing dialog box, click the Permissions button. Remove group Everyone from the permissions list by clicking Everyone and clicking the Remove button.

5. To add users and groups to the shared permission list, click the Add button from the Access Through Share Permissions dialog box. Click the Show Users button, and add Kate with Full Control permission. Click OK, and repeat the same steps to add the local group Administrators with Full Control permission and Magda with Read permission.

6. You can test share permissions by logging on as Magda and accessing the share through Network Neighborhood. If you try to create a file, you should be denied access, because Magda only has Read permission to the share. It is important that you use Network Neighborhood for this test, because this accesses the resource as a share. If you use Explorer or My Computer, you access the resource locally, and no share permissions are applied. Log on as Kate, and repeat the test.

Selecting a File System

After you create your disk partitions, you must format them with a file system that NT can use. NT supports three file systems:

◇ FAT (File Allocation Table).

◇ NTFS (NT File System).

◇ CDFS (Compact Disc File System). This file system is used by CDs and is read-only.

When you format your disk partition, you use FAT or NTFS.

This table describes some of the major differences between FAT and NTFS.

FAT	NTFS
Operating systems such as DOS, OS/2, Windows 3.x, Windows 95, Windows 98, and Windows NT support FAT. If you require dual-boot capability to another operating system, you must use FAT.	NT is the only operating system that can access an NTFS partition. If your computer uses only NT, this partition type will be accessible.
FAT offers no local security. This means that if multiple users share the same computer, all data stored on the FAT partition is available to all users.	One of the main advantages of NTFS is that you can specify local security. Because logon is mandatory, you can specify what rights users and groups have to NTFS folders and files.
No file compression is available through NT.	File compression is supported.
No support is available for Macintosh files.	You can store and share Macintosh files on NTFS partitions.
You can convert FAT to NTFS at any time.	The only way you can go from NTFS back to FAT is to reformat your partition. This means that you will lose all data, and you must restore it from backup.

Understanding the Basics of NTFS

NTFS is a file system that only the NT operating system can use. You can format a disk partition to use NTFS through the NT installation or with the Disk Administrator utility. To convert an existing FAT disk partition to NTFS, you use the CONVERT command line utility as seen here:

```
CONVERT [drive letter]: /fs:NTFS
```

For example, if you want to convert the C:\ drive, you use this syntax:

```
CONVERT C: /fs:NTFS
```

The main advantage of the NTFS file system is that you can apply local security, which is also referred to as local permissions. For example, assume that you have two users, Terry and Ron, who share the same computer. Each user has a folder at the root of C:\ called TERRY and RON respectively. With NTFS permissions, you can specify that only user Terry has permission to the TERRY folder and only user Ron has permission to the RON folder. This is only possible with NTFS and cannot be defined on FAT partitions.

When you format a partition as NTFS, permissions are applied in two ways:

♦ To any user who accesses the computer locally, meaning they are logged on to the computer where the resource is located

♦ To any user who accesses an NTFS folder that has been shared over the network

NOTE

NTFS permissions are different from share permissions in that you can apply them to folders and files.

WARNING

As with shared folders, the default NTFS permission is that group Everyone has Full Control.

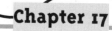

Assigning NTFS Permissions

NTFS permissions allow more granularity in permission assignment than share permissions. This table defines NTFS permissions.

NTFS Permission	Description
No Access	Means that you have no rights to the folder. No Access is an overriding right. This means that even if you have access permissions through other user or group assignments, the No Access right will be applied.
List	Allows you to view folder and filenames but not to display the contents of files. With List, you can change to a subfolder within a folder.
Read	Is similar to List. However, with Read you can view the contents of a file, execute program files, and copy files from a folder.
Add	Lets you add folders and files to the folder.
Add and Read	Combines the permissions of Add and Read.
Change	Allows you to combine the permissions of List, Read, and Add. In addition, you can manipulate the data within a file or folder and delete files and folders.
Full Control	Combines the List, Read, Add, and Change permissions. In addition, you can manipulate NTFS permissions and take ownership of folders and files.
Special Directory Access	Lets you customize the access that a user or group has to a folder. With Special Directory Access, you can choose from these permissions: Read, Write, Execute, Delete, Change Permissions, and Take Ownership.
Special File Access	Allows you to customize the rights a user or group has to a file. With Special File Access, you can choose from Read, Write, Execute, Delete, Change Permissions, and Take Ownership.

Using NTFS Effective Permissions

You apply NTFS permissions in a similar fashion to share permissions. One difference is that you apply share permissions to folders, and you apply NTFS permissions to folders and files.

NTFS is similar to share permissions in the sense that if a user belongs to multiple groups that have been granted access to the same resource, the highest access permission is applied. The exception to this rule is if the No Access right has been granted. If a user has been given No Access through any user assignment or through a group membership, they have No Access to the specified resource.

If a user has a different set of permissions for a folder and the files within the folder, the file permissions are applied.

For example, assume this directory structure:

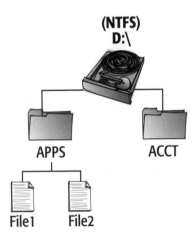

These assignments have been made:

Resource	Assignment	Permission
D:\APPS	Everyone	Read
D:\APPS\FILE2	Everyone	Change
D:\ACCT	Temps	No Access
	Accountants	Change
	Managers	Full Control

These assignments mean

- ❖ When accessing the D:\APPS folder, all users have Read permissions to the files in the folder except for FILE2, which has been explicitly assigned a different permission.
- ❖ If a user belonged to Temps and Accountants, they would still have No Access to D:\ACCT, because No Access overwrites any other permission assignments.

Implementing NTFS Permissions

In order to implement NTFS permissions, you must first format the disk partition as NTFS. If you have an existing partition, you use the CONVERT command to save existing data.

To access the Directory Permissions dialog box, which you use to assign NTFS security, complete these steps:

1. From NT Explorer, single-click the folder you want to apply permissions on.
2. Click the secondary mouse button to access Properties.
3. Select the Security tab to see the Directory Permissions dialog box.

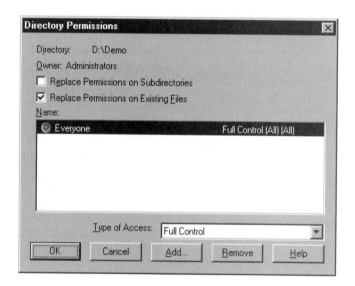

This dialog box contains the components shown in this table.

Directory Permissions Option	Description
Directory	Displays the name of the directory that is being accessed.
Owner	Shows the user who created the folder or who has taken ownership of the folder.
Replace Permissions on Subdirectories	Specifies whether or not subdirectories will inherit the permissions that you define on the parent folder. By default, this box is not checked.
Replace Permissions on Existing Files	Specifies whether or not files contained within the folder will inherit the permissions of the parent folder. By default, this box is checked.

4. You will notice that the group Everyone has Full Control permission by default. To remove this assignment, highlight Everyone and click the Remove button.

5. To make a new assignment, click the Add button to see the Add Users and Groups dialog box.

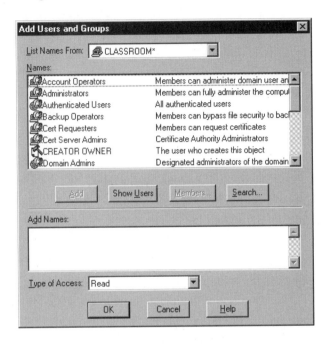

6. For each group you want to assign permissions to, highlight the group in the Names box and click the Add button. At the bottom of the dialog box, select the type of access you want to assign and click the OK button. Repeat these steps for each additional group assignment.

7. You make user assignments in a similar fashion, but in the Add Users and Groups dialog box, you must click the Show Users button to see the user list. At this point, user NTFS permission assignments are similar to group permission assignments.

NOTE

You may notice that you cannot assign Special Directory Access or Special File Access permissions through the Add Users and Groups dialog box. You can make these assignments by modifying the permission assignments from the Directory Permissions dialog box.

NOTE

To manipulate NTFS permissions, you must be logged on as a user with Full Control permission, Special Access Change permission, or Special Access Take Ownership permission to the folder whose permissions you will manipulate.

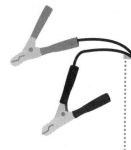

Understanding Share and NTFS Permission Interaction

Assume that you have a folder that has NTFS permissions and share permissions applied. Share permissions and NTFS permissions work together.

⬦ If a resource is accessed locally, NTFS permissions will be applied.

⬦ If a resource is accessed over the network, the more restrictive of either the NTFS permissions or the share permissions will be applied.

Consider this example:

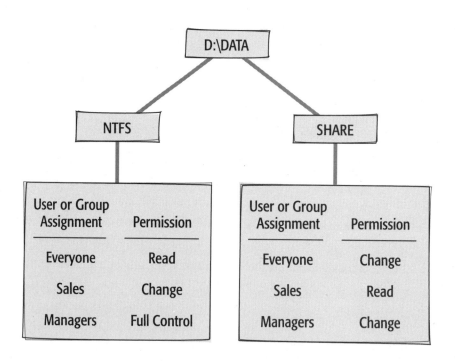

Scenario 1: Lars is a member of the Sales group and wants to access the DATA folder. If he accesses the folder locally, he will have only NTFS security applied and will have Change access. If Lars accesses the DATA folder over a network share, the system will look at his NTFS access, which is Change, and his share permission, which is Read. Since Read is more restrictive, this is the permission that will be applied over the share.

Scenario 2: Peter is a member of the Everyone group and the Managers group and wants to access the DATA folder. If he accesses the folder locally, he will have only NTFS security applied and will have Full Control access. If Peter accesses the DATA folder over a network share, the system will look at his NTFS access, which is Full Control, and his share permission, which is Change. Since Change is more restrictive, this permission will be applied over the share.

Understanding Flow of Resource Access

Flow of resource access is what happens when a user tries to access any NT object. The object can be a share, an NTFS object, or a network printer. By understanding resource access, you can more effectively troubleshoot access problems.

When a user logs on to an NT workgroup or domain, an access token is created. The access token is created only at logon. The access token identifies the user and any groups that the user belongs to. If the user is added to a group after they have already logged on, the user has to log off and log on again in order for the access token to be updated.

When the user attempts to access a resource, NT checks the Access Control List (ACL), which identifies the users and groups that can access the resource. The ACL is part of the object and determines if the user has permission to access the resource from a user or group permission assignment.

If the user is on the ACL, the system checks the Access Control Entries (ACE) to see which permissions the user should be granted based on user and group assignments. The No Access permission is always at the top of the ACE. If the user has No Access listed in the ACE, NT will not even check for other permission assignments.

TIP

A common error in access assignment is for a user to access a resource that they have been given permissions to through a new user group assignment. Users do not realize that they have to log off and log back on again for the group assignment to be updated in the user's access token. Whenever you make new group assignments, you should advise users to log off and log on again.

Understanding Network Printing Basics

In addition to file access, printer access is another common resource that users share over a network. To understand how network printing works, you should first contrast network printing with local printing. With local printing, you attach a physical printer to your computer (usually through your parallel port) and install the software that oomes with the printer. This is usually very straightforward.

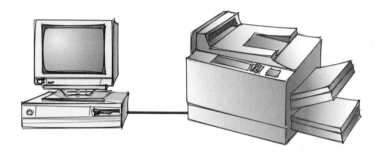

In a large computing environment, this can be an expensive way to manage printing, because each computer requires its own printer.

The next evolutionary step in shared printing was to allow multiple computers to access a single printer through some kind of device like a switch box. With an A/B/C switch box, three users can share a printer. One user is assigned port A, the second user is assigned port B, and the third user gets port C. In order to print, a user must walk over to the switch box and turn the dial to their port. This is not an efficient way to manage printing for a large number of users.

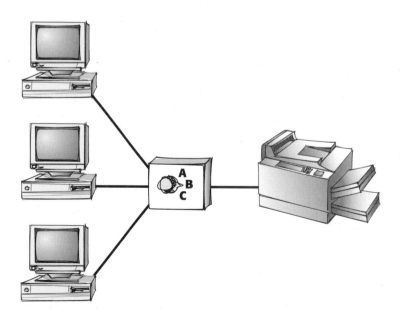

Network printing works in a different fashion. In this case, a special computer is designated as a print server. The print server runs a service called a print spooler that stores print jobs in a queue until they can be printed.

An analogy for network printing is that the print spooler is like the air traffic controller of printing. The spooler processes all jobs and determines when print jobs are printed. The print queue is like the take-off taxi and is a place where print jobs can hang out before they are actually printed. The print queue is a special directory on the print server, so you need to make sure that your print server has enough disk space to accommodate all of the print jobs that potentially could be submitted at any one time. Once a print job has completed, it is deleted from the print queue.

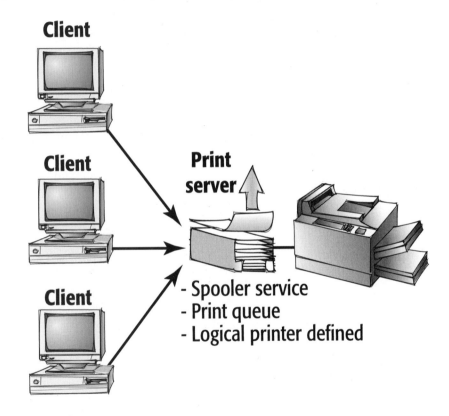

- Spooler service
- Print queue
- Logical printer defined

Here are some important terms that you should know for NT printing:

Printer refers to the logical printer that is defined in the NT printer configuration, as opposed to the print device, which is the physical printer.

Print device is the actual physical printer or hardware device to which you print.

Print server is the computer on which the printer has been defined. Print jobs are sent to print servers before they are sent to the print device.

Print spooler is the service responsible for managing incoming print jobs and passing the print jobs to the print device.

Print queues are special directories that reside on print servers and store print jobs until they are sent to the print device.

Creating a Printer

In order to create a printer, you must be logged on as an Administrator, Server Operator, or Print Operator. The NT Workstation and Server software provides a Printer Wizard to help facilitate the creation of printers. To access the Printer Wizard, you go to Start ➢ Settings ➢ Printers. Once you are in the Printers folder, you double-click the Add Printer icon.

This table describes the printer configuration options.

Configuration Option	Description
My Computer or Network Print Server	Specifies whether you will create a new printer (My Computer) or connect to an existing network printer (Network Print Server).
Port	Specifies whether the print device will be connected to a local computer port (a parallel or serial port) or the printer has a network card and will be directly attached to the network.
Printer Manufacturer and Model	Defines the printer so that the correct printer driver will be installed.
Printer Name	Allows you define a name that will be used for the printer.
Shared or Not Shared	Specifies whether the print device will be configured as a local printer or a network printer.
Select Operating Systems That Will Print to This Printer	If your printer will be accessed by other versions of NT or Windows 95 computers, you can install print drivers for these platforms on your print server through this option.
Print Test Page	Prints a sample page so that you can verify that you properly installed and configured the printer.

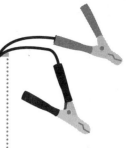

Configuring Printer Properties

Once you have created a printer, you can change the settings of the printer through printer properties. To access printer properties, you highlight the printer you want to manipulate and click Printers ➢ Properties.

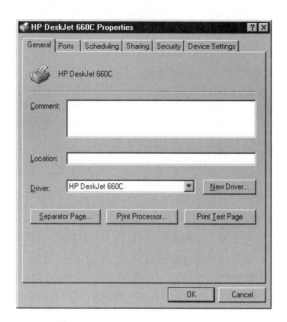

This table shows the options you can configure.

Configuration Option	Description
General	Specifies the general properties of the printer and includes comment information, location information, the driver that the printer will use, whether or not a **separator page** will be used, and the **print processor** that will be used. It also gives you the option of printing a test page.
Ports	Configures the port that the printer is attached to. Ports can be local ports or network ports.
Scheduling	Configures many options. You can specify which hours the printer is available, set the priority of the printer, specify whether or not jobs must be completely spooled before they are printed, and bypass network printing and print directly to the printer.
Sharing	Configures the printer as a local printer or a network printer.
Security	Configures the printer's permissions.
Device Settings	Allows you to configure print properties that are unique to your printer (based on the print driver you select). Device settings include options such as form assignments to paper trays and font cartridges used by the printer.

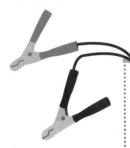

Establishing Print Security

In NT a printer is an object, like a share or an NTFS folder. Because they are objects, you can assign permissions to printers as you do to shares. For example, if you have an expensive printer that is intended for the marketing department, you can share the printer as a network printer but allow only the Marketing group to have Print permission.

This table defines the print permissions.

Print Permission	Description
Full Control	Allows you to create, manage, and delete printers.
Manage Documents	Allows you to manage documents that are submitted to the printer. With this permission, you can pause, restart, resume, and delete print jobs.
Print	Allows you to submit print jobs to a network printer.
No Access	Denies any access to the network printer.

To manipulate printer permissions, you highlight the printer and go to Printer ≻ Properties ≻ Security Tab ≻ Permissions. You will see this dialog box:

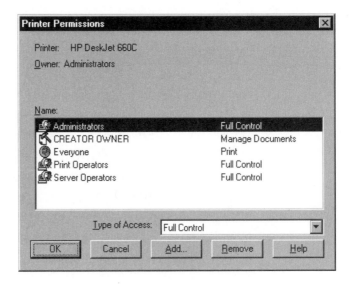

NOTE

When a printer is created, the default assignment is that group Everyone gets Print permission.

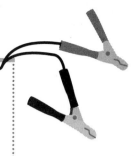

Sending Jobs to Network Printers

The two common ways you submit print jobs are

⬦ To choose the application's print option from within an application

⬦ To drag and drop the file that will be printed to the Printer icon

Auditing

In addition to managing file and print resources with shares and security assignments, you can manage resources with auditing.

You can audit NTFS resources and print resources. Auditing allows you to see how resources are accessed. For example, with NTFS resources you can audit which users access a particular file or folder. You can audit the success or failure of accesses such as Read, Write, Execute, or Delete. With print resources, you can audit which users are using a particular printer and how many pages each user is printing.

You should use auditing with caution, because it creates quite a bit of overhead. Auditing uses a good deal of processing time, and the auditing files can become very large.

By default, no auditing is enabled. If you enable auditing, you can view the results through Event Viewer ➤ Security.

Review Questions

1. Which groups can share folders on NT computers?

   _____

   _____

   _____

2. What is the default permission assigned when a folder is shared?

   _____

3. Sam is a member of the Sales and Managers groups. These share permissions have been assigned to the \\SALES\DATA share:

Sales	Change
Managers	Full Control
Peons	No Access

   What permission will Sam have when he accesses this share?

   _____

4. Dianne is a member of the Sales, Peons, and Managers groups. These share permissions have been assigned to the \\SALES\DATA share:

Sales	Change
Managers	Full Control
Peons	No Access

   What permission will Dianne have when she accesses this share?

   _____

5. True or false: You can apply local permissions to a FAT partition.

6. Which command do you use to change a FAT partition to NTFS while preserving existing folders and files?

   _____

7. True or false: When you apply NTFS permissions to a folder, they are applied to the folder's subfolders by default.

8. What minimum NTFS permission would you assign to a user who needed to create, edit, and delete files within a folder?

_____

9. If a user's combined share permissions to a resource are Change and their combined NTFS permissions to the resource are Read, what access will the user have to the resource when it is accessed over the share?

_____

10. If a user's combined share permissions to a resource are Change and their combined NTFS permissions to the resource are Full Control, what access will the user have to the resource when it is accessed locally?

_____

11. What is the purpose of the print spooler?

_____

12. Which default permissions are assigned when a printer is created?

_____

13. True or false: An NT print server can provide print drivers for Windows 95 and Windows NT clients.

14. True or false: In NT terminology, a printer is the physical print device.

Appendix A

Answers to Review Questions

Chapter 1

1. Intel 8088

2. The 8-bit 8088 provided a more cost-effective product for IBM to release, replacing the true 16-bit 8086 processor.

3. The number of operations that are processed in one second

4. Erasable Programmable Read-Only Memory

5. Real mode accesses memory in a linear format, whereas protected mode can allocate memory to a specific task.

6. Clock cycles represent the internal speed of a computer or processor expressed in megahertz. The faster the clock speed, the faster the computer performs a specific operation.

7. Virtual Real Mode allows DOS programs to run within the Windows operating system.

8. PROM stands for Programmable Read-Only Memory and is a special type of chip that is manufactured without any configuration. Manufacturers can then "burn in," or program, the chip to contain whatever configuration is needed.

9. Clock doubling refers to the mechanism that allows the internal system clock to run at twice the normal rate of speed.

10. 3.1 million

11. Asymmetrical multiprocessing uses a separate processor to run the operating system and a second processor to run the application threads. Symmetrical multiprocessing shares the tasks equally among the processors.

12. A numeric processor is a secondary processor that speeds operations by taking over some of the main processor's work. It typically performs mathematical calculations, freeing the processor to tend to other tasks.

13. The Pentium II contains onboard cache within its cartridge to increase performance, whereas the PII Celeron has no onboard cache.

14. The Alpha processor

15. RAM is dynamic, meaning that its contents constantly change. Permanent information, such as the BIOS, is stored in ROM.

Chapter 2

1. IDE
   SCSI

2. False. IDE drives can use either the controller that is integrated with most motherboards or a simple paddleboard, which facilitates the connection but is not considered an adapter.

3. 40

4. 50

5. SCSI

6. A physical drive is the physical drive itself; for example, drive 0 or drive 1 in a two-drive configuration. A logical drive is based on how you partition your physical drive and is assigned a logical drive letter; for example, C:\.

7. A volume set is two or more partitions that have been combined into a single logical drive.

8. Disk mirroring (including duplexing)

   Disk striping with a parity stripe

   Disk striping with a parity drive

9. Disk mirroring uses a single controller and two drives to mirror data. Disk duplexing uses two controllers and two drives to mirror data.

10. False. You can regenerate a stripe set only if a single drive fails. If two or more drives fail, you must restore data from the most recent backup.

11. True

12. Online storage is available without any user intervention. Offline storage requires the user to access the data from media that is not immediately accessible.

13. 640MB

14. 1.44MB

15. True

Chapter 3

1. Serial communication is the process of transmitting and processing data one bit at a time.

2. Data that is transmitted serially is transmitted 1 bit at a time; parallel data is transmitted 8 bits (1 byte) at a time.

3. False. Refresh rate signifies the number of times the beam of electrons shot from the electron gun redraws the screen.

4. Extended Graphics Array (XGA) adapter with more memory installed

5. Serial

    Bus

    PS/2

6. False. Digital data represents discreet voltage values. One value is represented at a given moment in time.

7. A modem uses a standard telephone line to dial out to another modem or Internet provider. A cable modem uses the CATV network and maintains an active connection to the Internet.

8. True

9. False. Motherboards are manufactured to support more than one bus type to accommodate various add-in components.

10. Printers are networked to provide many users with access to a single print device to save money by sharing the resource.

Chapter 4

1. You use a DIP switch or jumper to accomplish the physical configuration of a hardware device.

2. Interrupts

    Base memory

    I/O memory

    DMA

3. An interrupt allows a hardware device to interrupt the microprocessor to request attention. When the request is satisfied, the microprocessor is free to carry out its responsibilities.

4. IRQ 5

5. False. Not all devices need a reserved area of memory in which to operate.

6. 1F0–1F8

7. DMA allows a device to transfer data directly to RAM without involving the processor.

8. DMA channel 2

9. Software drivers are special programs that tell the computer how to communicate with and control a hardware device.

10. False. There is no such thing as the Software Driver Association. Drivers are written for specific operating systems.

11. False. Each device must have its own IRQ.

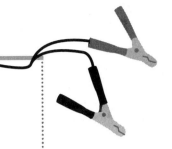

12. Direct Memory Access

13. Input/Output

14. Interrupt request

Chapter 5

1. Disk Operating System

2. Graphical User Interface

3. Windows for Workgroups 3.11

4. False

5. False. OS/2 is proprietary to IBM.

6. Windows NT Workstation

7. Windows 95

8. DOS 6.22

9. Windows 98

10. X Windows

11. USL System V UNIX
BSD Unix

12. Linux

13. False

14. POSIX

Chapter 6

1. FORMAT

2. SYS

3. All of these options are valid answers:
Create DOS partitions or logical drives
Set the active partition
Delete partitions or logical drives
Display partition information
Change the current fixed drive

4. FORMAT /Q

5. FORMAT /S

6. COMMAND.COM
   IO.SYS
   MSDOS.SYS

7. CD\

8. DEL C:\TEST\TEST.DOC

9. To copy whatever is written on the screen to a text file

10. B

11. False. You use the TYPE command.

12. REN

13. You use ? to represent a single character, while * can represent any number of characters.

14. With COPY, you maintain a copy of the file in both the source and destination directories. With MOVE, you maintain a copy only in the destination directory.

15. ATTRIB TEST.DOC +H

Chapter 7

1. The Recycle Bin

2. The Internet

3. My Computer

4. The Taskbar

5. The Start button

6. Documents

7. Settings

8. Help

9. Shut down the computer
   Restart the computer
   Restart the computer in MS-DOS mode
   Close all programs and log on as a different user

10. True

11. They allow you to create a pointer that you can use to quickly and easily access another object.

12. A Wizard is a program that steps you through the installation of a particular item.

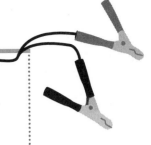

13. Windows Explorer explores the local computer and network, and Internet Explorer explores the Internet.

14. The right mouse button

Chapter 8

1. Spreadsheets

2. Internet browsers

3. Word processors

4. E-mail

5. Desktop publishing

6. Netscape Navigator
Microsoft Internet Explorer

7. Uniform Resource Locator

8. A file is a collection of records.
A record is a complete set of fields.
A field is a single piece of information within a record.

9. False. SQL is a common query language associated with databases.

10. Hypertext Markup Language. HTML is a standard for documents that are accessed through the Internet.

11. FTP (File Transfer Protocol)

12. File infector virus
Boot sector virus
Master boot record virus
Multipartite virus

13. What You See Is What You Get. The WYSIWYG technique displays information on the screen the same way that it is presented in the final document.

Chapter 9

1. It makes networking easier to understand.
It makes it easier to replace modular components as technology changes.

2. C

3. F

4. A

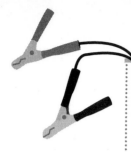

5. E

6. G

7. B

8. D

9. Logical Link Control (LLC)

    Media Access Control (MAC)

10. Router

11. Connection-oriented services establish a connection between the sender and the receiver and are more reliable. Connectionless services send data without establishing a connection and are more efficient.

12. A physical address is identified at the Data-Link layer of the OSI model and is hard coded on the network interface card. A network address is associated with the Network layer of the OSI model and is a logical address that the network administrator assigns.

13. Physical

    Data-Link

    Network

    Transport

    Session

    Presentation

    Application

Chapter 10

1. Peer-to-peer networks do not use dedicated network servers for authenticating users and providing secure access to network resources. In this model, clients share resources, and other clients have access to whatever has been shared.

2. The role of the primary domain controller, or PDC, is to store the domain accounts database, called the Security Accounts Manager, or SAM. The PDC also sends updates of the SAM database to any BDCs within the domain.

3. BDCs offload logon authentication from the PDC. They also provide fault tolerance if the PDC is offline.

4. Directory services

5. False. Each network model has its own strengths and drawbacks. No one network model meets the needs of every network.

6. Peer-to-peer network

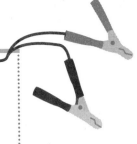

7. The container allows you to logically group your resources, and an object is something that you would use, such as a user account, server, or printer.

8. False. In a client-server model, you need an account on each server on which you want to access resources.

9. False. You add users only to the PDC. They are automatically updated to the BDCs.

10. The directory services network model

Chapter 11

1. Star

   Bus

   Ring

2. A physical topology is the way that the network is physically defined and cabled, and a logical topology is the way that the data is transferred through the network.

3. Carrier Sense Multiple Access with Collision Detection

4. 10Mbps and 100Mbps

5. 4Mbps and 16Mbps

6. The star topology

7. False. The standard you choose defines the topology. For example, Token Ring cannot use a physical or logical bus topology.

8. A

9. The star topology

10. Ring, star

11. True

12. Ethernet

13. IEEE 802.3

14. IEEE 802.5

Chapter 12

1. IP address

   Subnet mask

   Default router

2. DHCP

3. IPX/SPX

4. Routing packets through a TCP/IP internetwork

5. Network layer

6. SPX

7. Class C networks

8. C

9. A

10. True

11. DNS maps domain names to IP addresses, which makes accessing resources easier for people.

12. The subnet mask

13. True

14. It needs no configuration.

Chapter 13

1. False

2. Protocols are used to transmit data over a network.

3. It is a name up to 15 characters long that uniquely identifies the computer.

4. NetWare 5

5. Peer-to-peer

6. Client-server

7. Directory services

8. Share-level access control
   User-level access control

9. TCP/IP
   NWLink IPX/SPX
   NetBEUI

10. NetWare Loadable Module. An NLM loads and unloads server and network services dynamically.

11. Server

12. Workstation

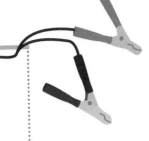

13. False

14. Binding are the links between the network adapter card, the services that are loaded, and the network protocols that are used.

15. A network adapter connects the computer to the network.

Chapter 14

1. Provide flexibility in OS code.
   Be a reliable OS.
   Offer high performance.
   Use portable code.
   Be compatible with existing standards.

2. Windows 2000 Professional
   Windows 2000 Server
   Windows 2000 Advanced Server

3. NT 4

4. NT 3.5

5. NT 3.51

6. Microsoft Cluster Server

7. Windows 2000

8. MMC, or Microsoft Management Console, provides a common interface and utility for all administrative tasks. The administrator can customize this utility.

9. Windows 2000

10. It is a service that mirrors a workstation's applications and data to a Windows 2000 server. If the workstation fails, you can use the mirror to more quickly and easily restore the workstation.

Chapter 15

1. Each domain requires only one PDC, and only one PDC is allowed.

2. Domain Security Accounts Manager (SAM)

3. False. The BDC shares the same domain SID as the PDC, which is used for synchronization. The only way to change this configuration is to reinstall the BDC.

4. True. Member servers do not include the domain SAM and are not configured with a domain SID, so they can change domains.

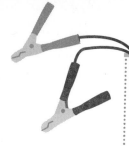

5. Two

6. 256

7. False. The Windows 95 operating system is supported only on the Intel platform.

8. A 486DX/33 with 16MB of RAM

9. Hardware Compatibility List (HCL)

10. Primary domain controller

    Backup domain controller

11. True

12. False

13. False. Windows 95 and 98 support this feature, and future implementations of NT are supposed to support it.

14. Internet Information Server (IIS)

15. If you wanted the server to be a file or print server or an application server that did not have the performance overhead of managing domain logon authentication and domain SAM synchronization.

16. False

Chapter 16

1. 20 characters

2. User Manager for Domains

3. User Must Change Password at Next Logon

4. A disabled account can be reenabled. Once a user account is deleted, it can never be accessed again.

5. True

6. True

7. False. NT account names are not case sensitive. NT passwords are case sensitive.

8. Profile

9. By default, users can log on 24 hours a day.

10. To prevent unauthorized users from guessing account names and passwords. After a specified number of bad passwords, accounts are locked with account lockout.

11. Password uniqueness

12. Global groups

13. Local groups

14. Account Operators

15. Domain Users

16. Global groups can only contain users from within the domain SAM database.

17. Backup Operators have permissions to back up and restore the file system.

Chapter 17

1. Administrators
   Server Operators (on NT domain controllers)
   Power Users (on NT member servers and NT workstations)

2. Everyone has Full Control.

3. Full Control

4. No Access

5. False. You can apply local permissions only to NTFS partitions.

6. CONVERT

7. False. Permissions are applied to the files within the folder by default but not to the subfolders.

8. Change

9. Read, because it is the most restrictive permission of the share and NTFS permissions assigned.

10. Full Control. If a resource is accessed locally, only NTFS permissions are applied.

11. The print spooler is the service responsible for managing incoming print jobs and passing the print jobs to the print device.

12. Everyone has Print permission.

13. True

14. False. The physical printer is referred to as a print device. Printer refers to a logical software printer defined through NT.

Appendix

B

Glossary

Numbers

10BASE2 An Ethernet standard that defines 10Mbps Ethernet using thin coaxial cable in a linear bus topology.

10BASET An Ethernet standard that defines 100Mbps Ethernet using unshielded twisted-pair cabling in a star topology.

A

Active Partition The partition on a hard drive that is read at computer start-up. This partition should have the operating system files that are needed to boot the operating system.

Alpha Processor A type of computer processor that typically offers better performance than Intel processors. NT is the main operating system that takes advantage of Alpha processors. Some versions of Unix also use Alpha processors.

American National Standards Institute An organization that seeks to develop standardization within the computing industry. ANSI is the American representative to the ISO, or International Standards Organization.

American Standard Code for Information Interchange A 7-bit coding scheme that translates symbolic characters into the ones and zeros that are stored as data on a computer. Extended ASCII uses an 8-bit coding scheme.

ANSI See American National Standards Institute.

Application Layer The layer of the OSI model responsible for supporting file and print services. It also manages whether requests are processed locally or remotely.

ASCII See American Standard Code for Information Interchange.

Asynchronous Communication Begins transmission of each character with a start bit and ends transmission of each character with a stop bit. This method of communication is not as efficient as synchronous communication but is less expensive, because no clocking hardware is needed.

AUTOEXEC.BAT A special DOS file whose main function is as a batch file that runs every time you start your computer.

B

Backups Copy all of your data to a secondary storage option. If your primary storage option becomes unavailable, you can use backups to restore the operating system, application, and data files.

Backup Domain Controllers   Are used in NT domains and get read-only copies of the PDC accounts database. BDCs serve two primary functions. They offload logon authentication requests from the PDC, and they provide fault tolerance. If the PDC fails, the BDC can be promoted to PDC.

Baseband Signaling   A signaling scheme that uses the entire bandwidth of the signal to send a digital signal.

Base Memory   The reserved area in memory where devices can store data so that the processor can directly access the data. Some devices need this allocated memory range located in the system RAM. The area is typically located in the upper area of RAM called the Upper Memory Area (UMA).

Basic Input/Output System   A special collection of services that are included on a ROM chip. The services enable the operating system, hardware, and software used with the computer.

BDC   See Backup Domain Controllers.

BIOS   See Basic Input Output System.

Bit   A binary digit. The digit is the smallest unit of information and represents either an off state (zero) or an on state (one).

Boot Partition   The partition on a hard drive that contains the operating system files.

Bridge   Works at the Data-Link layer of the OSI model and connects two or more network segments. A bridge determines how to pass network packets based on the hardware address of the packet.

Broadband Signaling   A signaling scheme that splits the signal into multiple channels to send an analog signal.

Browser Service   In NT networks, broadcasts the availability of network services such as network shares or printers.

Bus Topology   Uses a physical linear segment to connect all network devices. Each end of the bus is terminated, and devices typically connect to the bus through T-connectors.

Byte   A single binary character, or 8 bits.

C

Cable Modem   Allows high-speed access to the Internet over cable TV (CATV) lines. The cable modem needs two connections: one to the cable outlet and the other to the computer. Cable modems are more economical than ISDN, and you do not need to install an additional phone line. There is no need to dial; it is always active.

Carrier Sense Multiple Access with Collision Detection   A contention scheme used by Ethernet. CSMA/CD allows any node to access the network, assuming no transmissions are taking place. If two nodes transmit at the same time, a collision is detected, and both nodes must retransmit.

CD   See Compact Disc.

Central Processing Unit   The microprocessor that is the brain of the computer. It uses logic to perform mathematical operations that are used in the manipulation of data.

CISC   See Complex Instruction Set Computing.

Client   The computer on the network that requests network services.

Client-Server Networks   Use a dedicated server to centralize user and group account management. Users log on to servers where they have user accounts and access resources on the server to which their user account has permission.

Clock Cycles   The internal speed of a computer or processor expressed in megahertz (MHz). The faster the clock speed, the faster the computer performs a specific operation.

Clock Signal   Controls the rate at which synchronous data is transmitted.

Compact Disc   An optical disk that stores data. Most CDs can be written to one time but can be read many times.

Complex Instruction Set Computing   The most common type of processor produced. CISC is composed of a full complement of instructions used by the processor. Intel processors are currently based on this standard.

Concentrator   A network device that connects several computers. The terms concentrator and hub are often used interchangeably. Normally, hub is a more generic term, and concentrator is associated with 10BASET Ethernet networks.

CONFIG.SYS   A special DOS file that configures system hardware and sets the computer's environment parameters.

CPU   See Central Processing Unit.

CRC   See Cyclic Redundancy Check.

CSMA/CD   See Carrier Sense Multiple Access with Collision Detection.

Cyclic Redundancy Check   A form of error detection that performs a mathematical calculation on data at the sender's end and the receiver's end to ensure that the data is received reliably.

D

Databases   Collections of data organized so that users can easily add, edit, or access data. Databases can be created for personal use on a desktop computer or can exist as distributed databases throughout a network.

Data-Link Layer   The layer of the OSI model that includes information about the source and destination hardware addresses of the communicating devices. It also specifies lower-layer flow control and error control.

Data Path   Represents the largest number of instructions that can be transported into the processor chip during one operation.

Dedicated Server   A special computer that acts only as a server and does not perform any other tasks.

De Facto Standards   Standards that are widely accepted and implemented in the computer industry.

Defragmentation   The process of reorganizing your files on a disk so that they are arranged contiguously. This process better uses disk space.

Desktop Publishing   Software that produces high-quality page designs. This popular application integrates word processing and graphics programs.

DHCP   See Dynamic Host Configuration Protocol.

Differential Backup   A backup of all files with the archive bit set. The archive bit is not cleared when you complete the backup. If you have to restore data, you need only your last full backup and your last differential tape.

DIP Switch   Stands for Dual In-line Package switch. It contains parallel rows of contacts that can configure computer components and peripheral devices.

Direct Memory Access   The method of directly transferring data from a device, such as a storage device, to memory without involving the processor.

Directory Services Network Model   Uses a hierarchical database to logically organize the network resources. This model scales well to small, medium, or large enterprise networks.

Disk Controllers   Manage floppy and hard disks. Disk controllers can be a separate piece of hardware, or they can be integrated with the hard drive.

Disk Duplexing   A mirrored set with two disk controllers and two hard drives.

Disk Mirroring   A mirrored set with one disk controller and two hard drives.

Disk Operating System   An operating system developed by Microsoft. DOS predominately uses command lines to manage the operating system.

Disk Partitioning   The process of creating logical disks from a physical disk. You can then format the logical disks and use them to store data.

Disk Stripe Set   A disk drive configuration that combines several logical partitions of the same size into a single logical disk. Stripe sets stripe data evenly over the entire set.

DMA   See Direct Memory Access.

DNS   See Domain Name System.

Domain Model   Used in NT networks to logically group computers, users, and groups into a domain. Users log on to the domain and have access to any resources within the domain to which their user account has permission.

Domain Name System   A system that resolves domain names to IP addresses using a domain name database for address resolution.

DOS   See Disk Operating System.

Dot Pitch   Measures the distance in millimeters between two dots of the same color on the monitor.

DRAM   See Dynamic RAM.

Dual Booting   Having two or more operating systems on your computer. At system start-up, you can select which operating system you will boot.

Dynamic Host Configuration Protocol   Automates the assignment of IP configuration information.

Dynamic RAM   A type of memory that uses capacitors and transistors to store electrical charges representing memory states. The capacitors that make up this type of memory need to be refreshed every millisecond and are unreachable by the processor during that time.

E

EBCDIC   See Extended Binary Coded Decimal Interchange Code.

ECP   See Extended Capabilities Port.

EEPROM   See Electrically Erasable Programmable ROM.

Electrically Erasable Programmable ROM   Typically maintains the BIOS code, which you can update through a disk that the BIOS manufacturer supplies.

Electron Gun   The device that shoots electrically charged particles called electrons toward the back of the monitor screen.

E-mail   Short for electronic mail. E-mail is probably the most commonly used application. At its heart, e-mail is basically text messages transmitted and stored over communication networks. It has evolved to be able to send varied media images, such as pictures, audio files, and video files.

Emulator   A device that imitates computer operation through a combination of hardware and software that allows programs to run on otherwise incompatible systems.

Enhanced Parallel Port   The standard developed for parallel communication by Intel, Xircom and Zenith Data Systems to allow for data transfer rates of more than 2MBps. It supports bidirectional operation of attached devices and an addressing scheme.

EPP   See Enhanced Parallel Port.

EPROM   See Erasable Programmable Read-Only Memory.

Erasable Programmable Read-Only Memory   A chip that maintains its contents without the use of electrical power. The stored contents of an EPROM chip are erased and reprogrammed by removing the protective cover and using special equipment to reprogram the chip.

Ethernet   A networking protocol that works at the Physical and Data-Link layers of the OSI model. Ethernet works by using a shared media architecture called CSMA/CD.

Extended Binary Coded Decimal Interchange Code   The 8-bit character set used in the IBM environment.

Extended Capabilities Port   The standard developed for parallel communication by Hewlett-Packard and Microsoft to allow for data transfer rates of more than 2MBps. In addition to the high data transfer rates, it allows for bidirectional operation.

Extended Partition   A type of DOS partition created within logical partitions. You can have multiple extended partitions within a single logical partition.

F

FAT   See File Allocation Table.

FDDI   See Fiber Distributed Data Interface.

Fiber Distributed Data Interface   A network specification that defines a logical ring topology of fiber transmitting at 100Mbps. FDDI provides similar network connectivity as Ethernet and Token Ring, and functions at the same layers of the OSI model.

File Allocation Table   A type of file system that stores files and folders and keeps track of where files are stored on the disk. DOS made this file system widely available. Most operating systems support the FAT file system.

File Transfer Protocol   A protocol that transfers files between an FTP server and FTP clients. Most Web browsers use FTP client software to download and upload files to Internet servers running the FTP service.

Floppy Disk   A removable plastic disk that stores small amounts of data. This is a popular media because of its low cost and wide availability.

Formatting   The process of initializing a floppy disk or logical drive and preparing it so that you can store data on it.

Frame   A term for a data packet at the Data-Link layer of the OSI model.

Freeware   Software that you can use without payment.

FTP   See File Transfer Protocol.

Full Duplexing   Means that simultaneous two-way communication can take place.

G

Gateway   Works at the Application, Presentation, Session, and Network layers of the OSI model. A gateway connects two or more networks, even those of dissimilar network operating systems, such as Windows NT and Novell NetWare.

Graphical User Interface   A graphically based interface that presents information in a user-friendly manner. Windows and Macintosh operating systems both use GUI (pronounced "gooey") interfaces.

GUI   See Graphical User Interface.

H

Half Duplexing   Means that two-way communication can take place, but only one device can communicate at a time.

Hard Drives   Store data. They consist of a series of magnetically coated disks. Data is stored on the disks as ones and zeros. A positive charge indicates a one, and the absence of a charge indicates a zero.

Home Directory   A special folder that is assigned to a user where personal files can be stored.

HTTP   See Hypertext Transfer Protocol.

Hub   The central device in a star topology. It connects computers.

Hypertext Transfer Protocol   Provides access on the World Wide Web (WWW) to hypertext documents.

I

IDE   See Integrated Drive Electronics.

IEEE   See Institute of Electrical and Electronic Engineers.

Incremental Backup   A backup of only the files that have the archive bit set. After the incremental backup is complete, the archive bit is cleared. If you have to restore data, you must use your last full backup and each incremental backup that you have done.

Input/Output Channel   The channel between the computer and a peripheral device. If you have more channels for data transfer, you have better performance.

Institute of Electrical and Electronic Engineers   Usually referred to as IEEE and pronounced "I triple E." The IEEE is an organization that defines computing and telecommunications standards. The LAN standards defined by IEEE include the 802-workgroup specifications. The IEEE is an international standards organization.

Integrated Drive Electronics   A drive technology that integrates the drive and controller into a single piece of hardware. IDE drives are an inexpensive data storage solution.

Integrated Services Digital Network   A communication standard that uses a digital transmission channel, as opposed to regular phone service, which uses an analog transmission channel.

Internal Cache RAM   Internal high-speed memory included on a memory chip.

International Standards Organization   An international standards organization dedicated to defining global communication and informational exchange standards. ANSI is the American representative to the ISO.

Internet   The world-wide public network consisting of millions of nodes.

Internet Browsers   The media through which users navigate the Internet World Wide Web (WWW).

Internet Service Provider   A third-party company that provides Internet services.

Internetwork   Two or more network segments that are connected. Network segments can be connected through bridges, routers, and gateways.

Internetwork Packet Exchange/Sequenced Packet Exchange   A network communication protocol that is proprietary to Novell and is used primarily in NetWare networks.

Interrupt Request   The method a device uses for informing the microprocessor (CPU) that the device needs attention. Through this method of interruption, the microprocessor can function without needing to poll each device to see if it needs service.

I/O Channel   See Input/Output Channel.

I/O Memory   A memory address, called an I/O address, for a device. The address acts like a mailbox for the processor to send instructions to the device. The I/O address is also commonly called the port address.

IPX/SPX   See Internetwork Packet Exchange/Sequenced Packet Exchange.

IRQ   See Interrupt Request.

ISDN   See Integrated Services Digital Network.

ISO   See International Standards Organization.

ISP   See Internet Service Provider.

J

Jumper   A cable or wire that establishes or completes a circuit. It can also be defined as a shorting block to connect adjacent pins that are exposed on an expansion card.

K

Keyboard   The most common type of input device. The keyboard takes in information in the form of letters and numbers. The letters and numbers are translated into instructions that the computer must perform. The computer translates literally what you enter, so any typing mistakes result in an error.

L

Linux A popular version of Unix, because it is offered as shareware and freeware. Many of the utilities distributed with Linux are also freeware or shareware. This makes Linux an attractive offer for people who want a powerful desktop operating system at little or no cost.

LLC See Logical Link Control.

Logical Drives Are based on how you partition your physical drive. A logical drive is assigned a logical drive letter; for example, C:\.

Logical Link Control A sublayer of the OSI model Data-Link layer. The LLC sublayer contains information about service access points, which identify the higher-level protocol that will be used at the Network layer. Along with the MAC sublayer, the LLC sublayer provides physical access to the hardware to the upper-layer protocols.

Logical Partition Part of the hard drive that is allocated as a logical drive.

Logon Script A special script or batch file that is executed each time a user logs on to a computer or network.

M

MAC See Media Access Control.

Media Access Control A sublayer of the OSI model Data-Link layer. The MAC sublayer contains information about the physical address of the network adapter and, along with the LLC sublayer, provides physical access to the hardware to the upper-layer OSI protocols.

Megahertz One million cycles per second. The internal clock speed of a microprocessor is expressed in megahertz (MHz).

Member Server A special type of server in the NT environment that does not contain a copy of the domain user accounts database.

MHz See Megahertz.

Mirrored Set A disk drive configuration that contains a primary partition and a secondary partition. Anytime data is written to the first partition, it is automatically written to the second partition. You use a mirrored set for fault tolerance.

MMX See Multimedia Extension.

Modem Stands for modulation-demodulation. A modem converts digital data, modulated, into an analog signal so that it can be transmitted over a regular telephone line. At the other end, the signal is demodulated from an analog signal back to digital data.

Monitor   The most common type of output device. The monitor allows the human eye to interact with the computer. Without a monitor, the computer's output capabilities would be very limited.

Mouse   A common type of input device. You use the mouse for navigating, selecting, or drawing in the user environment. The mouse movements are translated into computer instructions by motion and button selection.

Multimedia Extension   A processor technology that dramatically improves the response time of games and multimedia-based applications. The technology was introduced through the MMX-equipped line of Intel Pentium chips. MMX processors contain additional instruction code sets that increase the processing speed of audio, video, and graphical data by up to 60 percent, compared with traditional processors.

Multiprocessor Computer   A computer that uses more than one processor installed in a single computer. Computers that contain more than one processor can scale to meet the needs of more demanding application programs.

N

NetBEUI   A simple network protocol developed by IBM. NetBEUI is faster than TCP/IP and IPX/SPX, but it is a nonroutable protocol.

NetBIOS   A layer of network software that provides low-layer network services.

NetWare   A popular network operating system from Novell and a competitive product to NT.

Network   Two or more computers connected for the purpose of sharing resources, such as file or print resources.

Network Drive   A mapping to a network path that appears to the user as a drive letter. You access it the same way you access a local drive.

Network Layer   The layer of the OSI model responsible for moving packets over an internetwork so that they can be routed to the correct network segment.

New Technology File System   A file system used on NT computers that supports features such as local security.

NTFS   See New Technology File System.

Numeric Coprocessor   A secondary processor that speeds operations by taking over some of the main processor's work. It typically performs mathematical calculations, freeing the processor to tend to other tasks.

O

OEM   See Original Equipment Manufacturer.

Offline Storage   A storage method in which data is not immediately available without user intervention. You use offline storage for large amounts of infrequently accessed data or to store computer backups.

Online Data Storage   A storage method in which data is readily available at high speed. You do not need to do anything special to access online storage.

Open Systems Interconnection Model   A theoretical model that defines how networks work from the ground up. The OSI model defines seven layers and the function of the data flow within each layer.

Original Equipment Manufacturer   The original manufacturer of equipment. For example, a hardware vendor may make a server that is designed for NT Server and bundle a special version of NT that is optimized to take advantage of the hardware.

OSI Model   See Open Systems Interconnection Model.

P

Parallel Communication   The process of transmitting and processing data 1 byte (8 bits) at a time.

Parity   In the context of a stripe set, a series of mathematical calculations based on the data stored. If a disk fails, the stored parity information can be used to rebuild the data.

PC Card   A device to enhance the capabilities of a computer. Adding a card to your computer allows you to customize it for your needs. Without this feature, the computer would not be as modular and would not allow you to add devices chosen to meet your specific needs.

PDC   See Primary Domain Controller.

Peer-to-Peer Networks   Do not use dedicated network servers for authenticating users and providing secure access to network resources. In this network model, clients share resources, and other clients have access to whatever has been shared.

Physical Hard Drives   The physical drives; for example, drive 0 or drive 1 in a two-drive configuration.

Physical Layer   The layer of the OSI model responsible for the transmission of data over a physical medium.

Plotter   A special type of print device that draws high-resolution diagrams, charts, graphs, and other layouts.

Plug-and-Play   A technology that automatically configures hardware devices for you.

Portable Operating System Interface   A standard interface for Unix implementations.

POSIX   See Portable Operating System Interface.

PowerPC   A type of microprocessor designed by Apple, Motorola, and IBM.

Presentation Layer   The layer of the OSI model responsible for formatting and translating data.

Primary Domain Controller   Used in an NT domain, the PDC contains the read/write copy of the domain accounts administration database, called the Security Accounts Manager, or SAM.

Primary Partition   The first logical partition you create on a hard drive.

Print Device   In NT terminology, the actual physical printer or hardware device to which you will print.

Print Processor   Processes a print job into language that the printer understands so that the job is formatted as the application specified.

Print Queue   In a print environment, a special directory that resides on print servers and stores print jobs until they are sent to the print device.

Print Server   In a print environment, the computer on which the printer has been defined. Print jobs are sent to print servers before they are sent to the print device.

Print Spooler   In NT terminology, the service responsible for managing incoming print jobs and passing the print jobs to the print device.

Programmable Read-Only Memory   A special type of chip that is manufactured without any configuration. Manufacturers can then "burn in," or program, the PROM chip to contain whatever configuration is needed.

PROM   See Programmable Read-Only Memory.

Protocol   A specification that defines a set of rules or procedures that different hardware or software use for communication.

R

RAID   See Redundant Array of Inexpensive Disks.

RAM   See Random Access Memory.

Random Access Memory   The main, or system, memory that runs the operating system and application programs. It is a temporary type of memory that the computer uses as a work area. This type of memory is dynamic, meaning that it is constantly being changed because of the activity of the processor. When you shut down the computer, all information in RAM is lost.

RAS   See Remote Access Service.

Read-Only Memory   A special type of memory in which data is written onto a chip during manufacturing. Information stored to ROM is permanent and thus cannot be changed. ROM stores the BIOS, the set of instructions a computer uses during the first stages of initialization.

Reduced Instruction Set Computing   A reduced set of instructions used by a processor. PowerPC and Alpha processors are manufactured using this standard. RISC allows a microprocessor to operate at higher speeds.

Redundant Array of Inexpensive Disks   A method of using a series of hard disks as an array of drives. Some implementations of RAID improve performance. Other implementations provide fault tolerance and improve performance.

Refresh Rate   The number of times the beam of electrons shot from the electron gun redraws the screen in one second.

Remote Access Service   Allows computers to access the network remotely; for example, through a phone, ISDN, or Internet connection.

Repeater   A device that works at the Physical layer of the OSI model. A repeater connects two or more network segments. It does not do anything with the data except repeat it. A repeater is similar to a high-tech extension cord.

Ring Topology   A physical topology that is circular. It is similar to a bus topology, except the two ends are connected to form a ring.

RISC   See Reduced Instruction Set Computing.

ROM   See Read-Only Memory.

Routers   Network devices that connect two or more network segments. Routers work at the Network layer of the OSI model and pass packets based on network address. Routers can also route packets to and from the Internet.

RS-232C   An interface standard for use between data communications equipment (DCE) and data terminal equipment (DTE).

S

SAM   See Security Accounts Manager.

SCSI   See Small Computer System Interface

Security Accounts Manager   In NT, the database that stores user and group information.

Separator Page   In a print environment, a special page that identifies a print job by owner and name.

Serial Communication   The process of transmitting and processing data 1 bit at a time.

Server   The computer on the network that provides network services.

Session Layer   The layer of the OSI model responsible for managing communication sessions between service requesters and service providers. This layer manages communications by establishing, synchronizing, and maintaining the connection between sender and receiver.

Shareware   Software that is generally available for trial use. If you like the software, you should pay a small licensing fee.

Silicon-On-Insulator   The microchip manufacturing innovation that IBM invented. SOI is based on the ability to enhance silicon technology for improved performance through a new generation of chips manufactured using this technology.

Single-Edge Cartridge   An advanced packaging scheme that the Intel Pentium II uses. The SEC processor is encased in a cartridge module with a single edge that plugs into a 242-pin slot on the system board, much as an expansion card plugs into the system board.

Small Computer System Interface   An interface that connects SCSI devices to the computer. This interface uses high-speed parallel technology to connect devices that include hard disks, CD-ROM players, tape backup devices, and other hardware peripherals.

SNA   See Systems Network Architecture.

Software Drivers   Special programs that tell the computer's operating system how to communicate with and control a hardware device. Each device has a driver that allows it to communicate with the computer. The driver is written to operate only within a certain operating system. For instance, a Windows 3.1x driver will not work for that device if Windows NT is installed.

Spreadsheet   An application that keeps track of data and performs mathematical calculations based on data organized within rows and columns. Spreadsheets appear as a series of cells, which are the boxes at the intersection of a row and a column.

SRAM   See Static RAM.

Star Topology   A network that is laid out so that all devices connect to a central device called a hub. In this sense, the physical network layout looks like a star.

Start Bit   The bit that synchronizes the clock on the computer receiving the data being sent. In asynchronous data transmission, the start bit is a space.

Static RAM   A type of computer memory that retains the information within it as long as power is supplied, allowing it to refresh. SRAM chips can store only about one-fourth the information a dynamic RAM chip can store. The typical application for SRAM is in cache memory.

Stop Bit   The bit that identifies the end of the character being transmitted so that the character is clearly recognized.

Stripe Set with Parity Drive   A disk drive configuration that is similar to a stripe set with a parity stripe, except that the parity information is stored on a single drive as opposed to being striped.

Stripe Set with Parity Stripe   A disk drive configuration that is similar to a stripe set, but it contains a parity stripe across all drives. This gives you the benefits of a stripe set while also offering fault tolerance.

Synchronous Communication   Transmits data by synchronizing the data signal between the sender and receiver and sending data as a continuous stream. This is the most efficient way of sending large amounts of data, but it requires expensive equipment between the sender and the receiver.

Systems Network Architecture   Defined by IBM, specifies how devices can interface with IBM software.

T

Tape   A magnetic media that you commonly use for backup. It is a slow media for accessing data, but its large capacity and low cost make it ideal for backup.

TCP/IP   See Transmission Control Protocol/Internet Protocol.

Telecommuter   Someone who remotely connects to their office to work from home or a remote location.

Termination   Used at both ends of a bus to specify the beginning and end of a data bus and to keep data signals from bouncing back on the data chain once they reach the end.

Token   A special packet that signifies that a user can transmit data to a Token Ring network.

Token Ring   A networking protocol that is specified at the Physical and Data-Link layers of the OSI model. Token Ring uses a token-passing scheme to transmit data within a logical ring topology.

Topology   The layout of the network. Topologies can be physical or logical. A physical topology describes how the network looks physically or how the network is physically designed. A logical topology describes how data is transmitted through the network.

Transmission Control Protocol/Internet Protocol   A networking protocol that supports computer communications. Most networks support TCP/IP, and it is needed for Internet access.

Transport Layer   The layer of the OSI model usually associated with reliable end-to-end connections. This layer is responsible for managing connections, error control, and flow control between sender and receiver.

U

UMA   See Upper Memory Area.

Uniform Resource Locator   Specifies the location of TCP/IP resources.

Unix   A popular operating system that is 32-bit, multiuser, and multitasking.

Upper Memory Area   The area of memory between 640KB and 1MB in an IBM-compatible computer. This area of memory was originally reserved for system and video use.

URL   See Uniform Resource Locator.

V

VAX   The Virtual Address eXtension technology built by Digital Equipment Corporation to run the VMS platform computers.

Video Display Adapter   The adapter inside your computer that connects to the monitor.

Virtual Circuit   A logical connection between two devices. Both devices share a logical connection that transmits and receives data.

Virus   Software that affects the way your computer works without your permission or knowledge. Viruses do not exist naturally and are written by programmers with specific agendas. Viruses have two main characteristics. The first is that they spread without user knowledge from one file to another through a technique called self-propagation. The second characteristic is that the virus has some action that it performs, which is called the payload. The payload may be something fairly harmless, such as displaying a message, or it might be more malicious, such as erasing your entire hard drive.

Virus Scanner   A special application that scans your computer for the presence of computer viruses. Most virus scanners also can remove viruses.

Volume Set   A disk drive configuration that extends the size of a partition beyond a single physical drive.

W

Windows Internet Name Service   In NetBIOS networks, resolves NetBIOS names to IP addresses. NT requires NetBIOS network services.

WINS   See Windows Internet Name Service.

Word Processor   A fully featured application that creates, edits, and prints documents.

World Wide Web   The name of the network of links consisting of hypertext documents.

WWW   See World Wide Web.

WYSIWYG   Stands for What You See Is What You Get and is a view within an application that lets you see the final document while you are creating or editing the document.

Appendix

C

Common
Acronyms

Acronym	Meaning
ANSI	American National Standards Institute
API	Application Programming Interface
ARPA	Advanced Research Projects Agency
ARPANET	Advanced Research Projects Agency Network
ASCII	American Standard Code for Information Interchange
BIOS	Basic Input/Output System
BNC	British Naval Connector
bps	Bits Per Second
Bps	Bytes Per Second
CCITT	Consultative Committee for International Telephony and Telegraphy
CD	Change Directory
CD	Compact Disc
CDFS	Compact Disc File System
CD-R	Compact Disc-Recordable
CD-ROM	Compact Disc Read-Only Memory
CMOS	Complementary Metal-Oxide Semiconductor
CNE	Certified NetWare Engineer
CPU	Central Processing Unit
CRC	Cyclic Redundancy Check
CSMA/CD	Carrier Sense Multiple Access/Collision Detection
DHCP	Dynamic Host Configuration Protocol
DNS	Domain Name System
DoD	Department of Defense
DOS	Disk Operating System
EBCDIC	Extended Binary Coded Decimal Interchange Code
EEPROM	Electrically Erasable Programmable Read-Only Memory
EPROM	Erasable Programmable Read-Only Memory
FAT	File Allocation Table
FDDI	Fiber Distributed Data Interface
FS	File Server

Acronym	Meaning
GB	Gigabyte
Gbps	Gigabits Per Second
GBps	Gigabytes Per Second
GUI	Graphical User Interface
HPFS	High Performance File System
IC	Integrated Circuit
IDE	Integrated Drive Electronics
IEEE	Institute of Electrical and Electronic Engineers
I/O	Input/Output
IP	Internet Protocol
IPX	Internetwork Packet Exchange
IPX/SPX	Internetwork Packet Exchange/Sequenced Packet Exchange
IRQ	Interrupt Request
ISDN	Integrated Services Digital Network
ISO	International Standards Organization
ISP	Internet Service Provider
Kb	Kilobit
KB	Kilobyte
Kbps	Kilobits Per Second
KBps	Kilobytes Per Second
LAN	Local Area Network
LLC	Logical Link Control
MAC	Media Access Control
MAN	Metropolitan Area Network
Mb	Megabit
MB	Megabyte
Mbps	Megabits Per Second
MBps	Megabytes Per Second
MCP	Microsoft Certified Professional
MCPS	Microsoft Certified Product Specialist
MCSE	Microsoft Certified Systems Engineer
MCT	Microsoft Certified Trainer

Acronym	Meaning
MD	Make Directory
MHz	Megahertz
MIDI	Musical Instrument Digital Interface
MODEM	Modulator/Demodulator
MSAU	Multi-Station Access Unit
MS-DOS	Microsoft Disk Operating System
NetBEUI	NetBIOS Extended User Interface
NetBIOS	Network Basic Input/Output System
NIC	Network Interface Card
NOS	Network Operating System
NT	New Technology
NTFS	New Technology File System
OEM	Original Equipment Manufacturer
OS	Operating System
OS/2	Operating System/2
OSI	Open Systems Interconnection
PC	Personal Computer
PCMCIA	Personal Computer Memory Card International Association
POSIX	Portable Operating System Interface Extension
PROM	Programmable Read-Only Memory
PSTN	Public Switched Telephone Network
RAID	Redundant Array of Inexpensive Disks
RD	Remove Directory
RFC	Request For Comments
RIP	Router Information Protocol
RJ	Registered Jack
SMP	Symmetric Multiprocessing
SNMP	Simple Network Management Protocol
SPX	Sequenced Packet Exchange
SQL	Structured Query Language
Tb	Terabit
TB	Terabyte

Common Acronyms

Acronym	Meaning
Tbps	Terabits Per Second
TBps	Terabytes Per Second
TCP	Transmission Control Protocol
TCP/IP	Transmission Control Protocol/Internet Protocol
THz	Terahertz
TR	Token Ring
URL	Uniform Resource Locator
USL	Unix Systems Laboratory
WAN	Wide Area Network
WINS	Windows Internet Name Service
WORM	Write Once, Read Many
WYSIWYG	What You See Is What You Get

Recommended Reading

You can find more detail on the topics covered in this book from these references:

Custer, Helen. *Inside Windows NT*. Redmond, Wash: Microsoft Press, 1993.

Feibel, Werner. *The Network Press Encyclopedia of Networking*. San Francisco: Sybex, 1996.

Groth, David. *A+: Core Module Study Guide*. San Francisco: Sybex, 1998.

Groth, David. *A+: Windows/DOS Study Guide*. San Francisco: Sybex, 1998.

Minasi, Mark. *The Complete PC Upgrade & Maintenance Guide*. 9th ed. San Francisco: Sybex, 1998.

Minasi, Mark. *Mastering Windows NT Server 4*. 6th ed. San Francisco: Sybex, 1999.

Mueller, Scott. *Upgrading and Repairing PCs*. 10th ed. Indianapolis: Que, 1998.

Rocsh, Winn. *The Winn L. Rosch Hardware Bible*. 3rd ed. Indianapolis: Sams Publishing, 1994.

Index

Note to the Reader: Throughout this index *italicized* page numbers refer to figures and **boldfaced** page numbers refer to significant discussions of the topic.

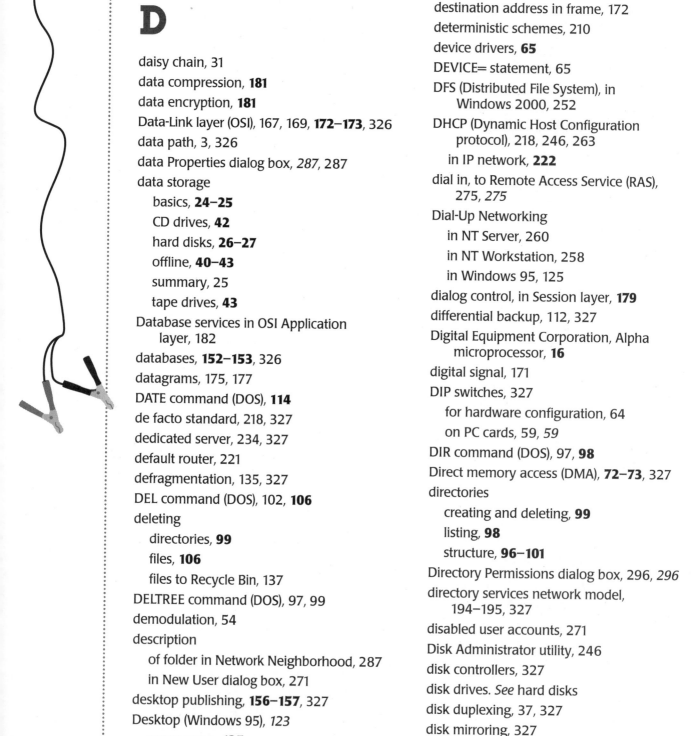

D

E

F

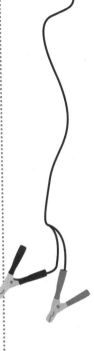

T

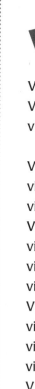

V

W